双语名著无障碍阅读丛书

经典集锦

人鼠之间

Of Mice and Men

[美国] 约翰·斯坦贝克 著

潘华凌 译

中国出版集团
中译出版社

图书在版编目(CIP)数据

人鼠之间：英汉对照/(美)约翰·斯坦贝克(John Steinbeck)著；潘华凌译.—北京：中译出版社，2019.1（2022.5重印）

（双语名著无障碍阅读丛书）

ISBN 978-7-5001-5584-3

I. ①人… II. ①约… ②潘… III. ①英语－汉语－对照读物 ②中篇小说－美国－现代 IV. ①H319.4: I

中国版本图书馆CIP数据核字(2018)第269690号

出版发行 / 中译出版社
地　　址 / 北京市西城区车公庄大街甲4号物华大厦6层
电　　话 / (010) 68359827；68359303（发行部）；53601537（编辑部）
邮　　编 / 100044
传　　真 / (010) 68357870
电子邮箱 / book@ctph.com.cn
网　　址 / http://www.ctph.com.cn

责任编辑 / 范祥镇

封面设计 / 潘　峰
排　　版 / 北京竹页文化传媒有限公司
印　　刷 / 北京玺诚印务有限公司
经　　销 / 新华书店

规　　格 / 710毫米×1000毫米　1/16
印　　张 / 12
字　　数 / 189千字
版　　次 / 2019年1月第一版
印　　次 / 2022年5月第三次

ISBN 978-7-5001-5584-3　　定价：29.00元

版权所有　侵权必究

中译出版社

出版前言

多年以来，中译出版社有限公司（原中国对外翻译出版有限公司）凭借国内一流的翻译和出版实力及资源，精心策划、出版了大批双语读物，在海内外读者中和业界内产生了良好、深远的影响，形成了自己鲜明的出版特色。

二十世纪八九十年代出版的英汉（汉英）对照"一百丛书"，声名远扬，成为一套最权威、最有特色且又实用的双语读物，影响了一代又一代英语学习者和中华传统文化研究者、爱好者；还有"英若诚名剧译丛""中华传统文化精粹丛书""美丽英文书系"，这些优秀的双语读物，有的畅销，有的常销不衰反复再版，有的被选为大学英语阅读教材，受到广大读者的喜爱，获得了良好的社会效益和经济效益。

"双语名著无障碍阅读丛书"是中译专门为中学生和英语学习者精心打造的又一品牌，是一个新的双语读物系列，具有以下特点：

选题创新——该系列图书是国内第一套为中小学生量身打造的双语名著读物，所选篇目均为教育部颁布的语文新课标必读书目，或为中学生以及同等文化水平的社会读者喜闻乐见的世界名著，重新编译为英汉（汉英）对照的双语读本。这些书既给青少年读者提供了成长过程中不可或缺的精神食粮，又让他们领略到原著的精髓和魅力，对他们更好地学习英文大有裨益；同时，丛书中入选的《论语》《茶馆》《家》等汉英对照读物，亦是热爱中国传统文化的中外读者所共知的经典名篇，能使读者充分享受阅读经典的无限乐趣。

无障碍阅读——中学生阅读世界文学名著的原著会遇到很多生词和文化难点。针对这一情况，我们给每一本读物原文中的较难词汇和不易理解之处都加上了注释，在内文的版式设计上也采取英汉（或汉英）对照方式，扫清了学生阅读时的障碍。

优良品质——中译双语读物多年来在读者中享有良好口碑，这得益于作者和出版者对于图书质量的不懈追求。"双语名著无障碍阅读丛书"继承了中译双语读物的优良传统——精选的篇目、优秀的译文、方便实用的注解，秉承着对每一个读者负责的精神，竭力打造精品图书。

愿这套丛书成为广大读者的良师益友，愿读者在英语学习和传统文化学习两方面都取得新的突破。

John Steinbeck

A few miles south of Soledad, the Salinas River drops **in**[1] close to the hillside bank and runs deep and green. The water is warm too, for it has **slipped**[2] twinkling over the yellow sands in the sunlight before reaching the narrow pool. On one side of the river the golden foothill slopes curve up to the strong and rocky Gabilan mountains, but on the valley side the water is lined with trees— willows fresh and green with every spring, carrying in their lower leaf **junctures**[3] the **debris**[4] of the winter's flooding; and **sycamores**[5] with **mottled**[6], white, **recumbent**[7] **limbs**[8] and branches that **arch**[9] over the pool. On the sandy bank under the trees the leaves lie deep and so **crisp**[10] that a lizard makes a great **skittering**[11] if he runs among them. Rabbits come out of the **brush**[12] to sit on the sand in the evening, and the **damp**[13] **flats**[14] are covered with the night tracks of **'coons**[15], and with the **spread**[16] **pads**[17] of dogs from the **ranches**[18], and with the **split-wedge**[19] tracks of deer that come to drink in the dark.

There is a path through the willows and among the sycamores, a path **beaten**[20] hard by boys coming down from the ranches to swim in the deep pool, and beaten hard by **tramps**[21] who come **wearily**[22] down from the highway in the evening to **jungle-up**[23] near water. In front of the low horizontal limb of a giant sycamore there is an ash pile made by many fires; the limb is worn smooth by men who have sat on it.

Evening of a hot day started the little wind to moving among the leaves. The shade climbed up the hills toward the top. On the sand banks the rabbits sat

① in [in] *ad.* 朝里，向（或至）某地，向某一方向
② slip [slip] *v.* 滑行
③ juncture ['dʒʌŋ(k)tʃə] *n.* 接合点，交接处
④ debris ['deibri:] *n.* 碎片，残骸
⑤ sycamore ['sikəmɔ:] *n.*【植】悬铃木（指树或其木材）
⑥ mottled ['mɔtld] *a.* 杂色的，斑驳的
⑦ recumbent [ri'kʌmb(ə)nt] *a.*【植】横卧的，平卧的
⑧ limb [lim] *n.*【植】大枝，主枝
⑨ arch [ɑ:tʃ] *v.* 拱起，成弓形
⑩ crisp [krisp] *a.* 脆的，易碎的
⑪ skittering ['skitəriŋ] *n.* 轻捷跳动声，嗖嗖声
⑫ brush [brʌʃ] *n.*【美】居民稀少的丛林地带
⑬ damp [dæmp] *a.* 潮湿的
⑭ flat [flæt] *n.* 浅滩
⑮ 'coon [ku:n] *n.*【动】浣熊（racoon 的缩略）
⑯ spread [spred] *a.* 展开的
⑰ pad [pæd] *n.*（动物的）脚印
⑱ ranch [rɑ:n(t)ʃ] *n.* 大牧场，农场
⑲ split-wedge（中间）裂开的楔形（的）
⑳ beaten ['bi:t(ə)n] *a.*（路）被踏成的，走出来的，人们常走的
㉑ tramp [træmp] *n.* 流浪者
㉒ wearily ['wεərili] *ad.* 疲劳地，疲倦地，消沉地，精神不振地
㉓ jungle-up 在游民露营地食宿，扎营露宿

　　索莱达[1]以南数英里处，萨利纳斯河[2]紧靠着山边的河岸缓慢流淌，形成一湾幽深的碧水。河水还很温暖，因为先前流淌之处阳光照耀，波光粼粼的河水流过黄沙，然后才注入这湾狭窄的静水中。河流的一侧，金黄色的山丘坡地逶迤着向上延伸，直达巍峨多岩的加比兰山脉。但在河流谷地一侧，水边生长着树木——有杨柳树，每逢春天，杨柳便抽芽吐翠，低端的枝丫上挂满了冬季洪水泛滥时留下的残枝败叶；有悬铃木树，树的枝丫表皮斑驳，呈白色，低斜着，呈弧形伸向水面。树下沙质土的河岸表面，落叶积了厚厚一层，干燥易碎，假如一条蜥蜴在其中穿梭爬行，定会发出嗖嗖的声响。傍晚时分，野兔会从灌木丛中蹿出来，蹲坐在沙地上。潮湿的浅滩上会布满浣熊夜间行走的足迹，来自农场成群的狗留下爪印，还有趁黑前来饮水的野鹿留下的裂口楔形蹄印。

　　杨柳树丛和悬铃木树丛中有一条小路。小路的表面被踩踏得硬邦邦的，因为农场的孩子们到静水中游泳时会顺着小路走，傍晚时分从公路上没精打采地下来的流浪者们到水边扎营露宿时也会顺着小路走。有棵巨大的悬铃木树上长着一根低矮的横枝，横枝前面有一堆灰烬，那是许许多多次篝火后累积起来的。树枝的表面则因为人们坐在上面而被摩擦得溜光。

　　一天傍晚，天气灼热，微风吹拂在树叶之间。夕阳让树丛投下的阴影顺着山丘向上爬，直达山顶。野兔蹲

---

1 加利福尼亚州的一座海滨城市，在旧金山以南。
2 萨利纳斯河地处美国加利福尼亚州西部。

Of Mice and Men

as quietly as little gray sculptured stones. And then from the direction of the state highway came the sound of footsteps on crisp sycamore leaves. The rabbits hurried noiselessly for cover. A **stilted**① **heron**② **labored**③ up into the air and **pounded**④ down river. For a moment the place was lifeless, and then two men **emerged**⑤ from the path and came into the opening by the green pool.

They had walked in single file down the path, and even in the open one stayed behind the other. Both were dressed in **denim**⑥ trousers and in denim coats with **brass**⑦ buttons. Both wore black, shapeless hats and both carried tight blanket rolls **slung**⑧ over their shoulders. The first man was small and quick, dark of face, with restless eyes and sharp, strong features. Every part of him was **defined**⑨: small, strong hands, slender arms, a thin and bony nose. Behind him walked his opposite, a huge man, shapeless of face, with large, pale eyes, and wide, sloping shoulders; and he walked heavily, dragging his feet a little, the way a bear drags his paws. His arms did not swing at his sides, but hung loosely.

The first man stopped short in the clearing, and the follower nearly ran over him. He took off his hat and wiped the **sweat-band**⑩ with his **forefinger**⑪ and **snapped**⑫ the **moisture**⑬ off. His huge companion dropped his blankets and **flung**⑭ himself down and drank from the surface of the green pool; drank with long **gulps**⑮, **snorting**⑯ into the water like a horse. The small man stepped nervously beside him.

"Lennie!" he said sharply. "Lennie, for God' sakes don't drink so much." Lennie continued to snort into the pool. The small man leaned over and shook him by the shoulder. "Lennie. You **gonna**⑰ be sick like you was last night."

Lennie **dipped**⑱ his whole head under, hat and all, and then he sat up on the bank and his hat dripped down on his blue coat and ran down his back. "That's good," he said. "You drink some, George. You take a good big drink." He smiled happily.

George **unslung**⑲ his **bindle**⑳ and dropped it gently on the bank. "I **ain't**㉑

① stilted ['stiltid] *a.* 踩高跷的，如踩高跷的
② heron ['her(ə)n] *n.*【鸟】鹭
③ labor ['leibə] *v.* 费力地前进
④ pound [paund] *v.* 连续重击，猛击
⑤ emerge [i'mə:dʒ] *v.* 出现
⑥ denim ['denim] *n.* 粗斜棉布，劳动布（经纱蓝或褐色，纬纱白色）
⑦ brass [brɑ:s] *a.* 黄铜制的，含黄铜的
⑧ slung [slʌŋ] *v.*（sling 的过去式和过去分词）吊挂，悬挂
⑨ define [di'fain] *v.* 画出……的线条，描出……的外形
⑩ sweat-band（用皮革或其他料制的）帽子（防）汗带
⑪ forefinger ['fɔ:fiŋɡə] *n.* 食指
⑫ snap [snæp] *v.* 使迅速地行动，急速做出
⑬ moisture ['mɔistʃə] *n.* 水分
⑭ flung [flʌŋ] *v.*（fling 的过去式和过去分词）使扑，使投身
⑮ gulp [ɡʌlp] *n.* 吞咽，一大口
⑯ snort [snɔ:t] *v.* 喷鼻息，鼓鼻
⑰ gonna ['ɡɔnə] *abbr.*〈口〉=going to
⑱ dip [dip] *v.* 浸，蘸
⑲ unslung [ʌn'slʌŋ] *v.*（unsling 的过去式和过去分词）从悬挂处取下，把……从背上取下
⑳ bindle ['bindl] *n.*〈美俚〉（尤指流浪汉肩挑的）铺盖卷
㉑ ain't [eint] *abbr.*〈口〉=am not

　　坐在沙质土的河岸边，悄没声儿的，犹如一群灰色的小石雕像一般。随后，州公路的方向传来踩踏在干燥易碎的悬铃木树叶上的脚步声。野兔迅速悄无声息地散开藏匿了起来。一只长脚鹭铆足了劲儿腾空飞起，猛烈地拍着翅膀飞向河的下游。一时间，此地了无生息。然后，两个男子从小路上走了出来，来到了碧水畔的空地上。

　　两个男子一前一后地向小路尽头走来，即便到了空旷地上时也还是如此。两个人都穿着粗斜棉布裤子和粗斜棉布外套，外套上配着黄铜色的纽扣。两个人都戴着变了形的黑色帽子。两个人的肩头都扛着捆得紧紧的铺盖卷。走在前面的那个身材矮小，动作敏捷，面部黝黑，眼睛左顾右盼，目光敏锐，五官棱角分明。他身上的每一个部位都特征鲜明：双手瘦小而强健，双臂精瘦，鼻梁瘦削而骨感。走在他身后的人却与他截然相反：身材魁梧，五官棱角不分明，长着一双浅色的大眼睛，一副倾斜着的宽肩膀。他走起路来步履沉重，略微拖着脚，好像熊拖着爪子走似的。他的两条胳膊并不在身侧摆动，而是松松地垂着。

　　突然，走在前面的男子在空旷地上停住了脚步，跟随在他身后的那位差点儿把他撞倒。他取下头上的帽子，用食指抹了一把帽子里的防汗带，随即甩了一把指头上的汗水。他那位身材魁梧的同伴放下铺盖卷，俯下身子，就着碧水的水面喝了起来，一大口接着一大口，鼻息喷进水里，犹如骡马鼓鼻饮水一般。小个子神色紧张，急忙走到他身边。

　　"伦尼！"他厉声说，"伦尼，看在上帝的分上，不要喝这么多啊。"伦尼依旧呼哧呼哧地往水面喷着。小个子俯下身子，揪住他的肩膀摇晃起来。"伦尼，你这样会像昨晚一样不舒服的。"

　　伦尼把他的整个脑袋浸到了水里，连帽子都没摘。然后，他起身坐到岸边，帽子上的水滴到了蓝色外套上，顺着后背往下流。"这样感觉挺爽，"他说，"你喝点儿水吧，乔治。你好好喝一顿。"他开心地笑了。

　　乔治卸下肩膀上的铺盖卷，轻轻地放在岸边。"我

sure it's good water," he said. "Looks **kinda**① **scummy**②."

Lennie **dabbled**③ his big paw in the water and **wiggled**④ his fingers so the water arose in little splashes; rings widened across the pool to the other side and came back again. Lennie watched them go. "Look, George. Look what I done."

George knelt beside the pool and drank from his hand with quick **scoops**⑤. "Tastes all right," he admitted. "Don't really seem to be running, though. You never **oughta**⑥ drink water when it **ain't**⑦ running, Lennie," he said hopelessly. "You'd drink out of a **gutter**⑧ if you was thirsty." He threw a scoop of water into his face and rubbed it about with his hand, under his chin and around the back of his neck. Then he replaced his hat, pushed himself back from the river, drew up his knees and embraced them. Lennie, who had been watching, imitated George exactly. He pushed himself back, drew up his knees, embraced them, looked over to George to see whether he had it just right. He pulled his hat down a little more over his eyes, the way George's hat was.

George stared **morosely**⑨ at the water. The **rims**⑩ of his eyes were red with sun glare. He said angrily, "We could just as well of rode clear to the ranch if that bastard bus driver knew what he was **talkin'**⑪ about. 'Jes'⑫ a little stretch down the highway,' he says. 'Jes' a little stretch.' God damn near four miles, that's what it was! Didn't **wanta**⑬ stop at the ranch gate, that's what. Too God damn lazy to **pull up**⑭. Wonder he isn't too damn good to stop in Soledad at all. Kicks us out and says 'Jes' a little stretch down the road.' I bet it was *more* than four miles. Damn hot day."

Lennie looked timidly over to him. "George?"

"Yeah, what **ya**⑮ want?"

"Where we goin', George?"

The little man **jerked**⑯ down the **brim**⑰ of his hat and **scowled**⑱ over at Lennie. "So you forgot that **awready**⑲, did you? I **gotta**⑳ tell you again, do I? Jesus Christ, you're a crazy bastard!"

"I forgot," Lennie said softly. "I tried not to forget. Honest to God I did, George."

① kinda ['kaində] 有点儿，有几分，相当，可以这么说（= kind of）
② scummy ['skʌmi] a. 浮渣（或浮垢、浮藻、铁渣等）的，似浮渣（或浮垢等）的，盖满浮渣（或浮垢等）的
③ dabble ['dæb(ə)l] v. 把（手、脚等）浸入水中
④ wiggle ['wig(ə)l] v. 使……扭动，使摆动
⑤ scoop [sku:p] n. 舀
⑥ oughta ['ɔːtə] abbr.〈口〉应当，应该（= ought to）
⑦ ain't [eint] abbr.〈粗〉= is not
⑧ gutter ['gʌtə] n.（道路的）排水边沟
⑨ morosely [mə'rəsli] ad. 阴郁地，脾气不好地
⑩ rim [rim] n. 边，边缘
⑪ talkin'= talking，非正式口语中 -ing 有时也作 'in
⑫ jes'= just
⑬ wanta = want to
⑭ pull up（人把车等）开到某处停下
⑮ ya [jə; jæ] pron.〈口〉（非规范）= you
⑯ jerk [dʒɜːk] v. 使猝然一动
⑰ brim [brim] n. 帽檐
⑱ scowl [skaul] v. 皱眉，作怒容，沉下脸，绷着脸
⑲ awready = already
⑳ gotta ['gɔtə] abbr.〈口〉= (have) got to

不能肯定这水是否干净，"他说，"看上去有浮渣呢。"

伦尼把一只大手放进水里，动了动手指，溅起一阵水花，一个个环形波纹四散开来，蔓延到静水的对岸，但又随即折返。伦尼不错眼珠地注视着这动静。"看吧，乔治，看我把水搅动了。"

乔治跪在静水畔，一只手快速舀了几捧水喝了下去。"味道挺正的，"他认可道，"不过，河水看起来并没有真正流动啊。不流动的水，千万不要喝啊，伦尼。"他不抱希望地说，"但你要是口渴了，恐怕连阴沟里面的水都会喝呢。"他捧了一手水泼在自己脸上，从脸到下巴再到后颈通通抹了几把。然后他重新戴上帽子，撑起身子，从水边离开，双臂抱膝坐下。伦尼一直注视着乔治，模仿对方的一举一动。他也收回了自己的身子，双臂抱住膝盖，目光溜向乔治，看看自己是否做得标准。他把帽檐往下拉了一点点，以便遮盖住眼睛，因为乔治的帽子也是这样戴着的。

乔治心情阴郁地盯着水面。他眼睛四周被炽热的太阳晒得通红。他满腔愤怒地说："要不是那个笨蛋司机胡说八道，我们便乘车直达农场了。'顺着公路走一小段路，'他说，'就一小段路。'结果呢，都将近他妈的四英里了。他就是不想在农场门口停车，就是这么回事呢。该死的，偷懒不愿意停车。他妈的能够在索莱达停车，已经算是了不得啦，就那么把我们踢下车，还说'顺着公路走一小段儿就到了'。我敢打赌，四英里都不止呢。真他妈的大热天啊。"

伦尼怯生生地朝他看了一眼。"乔治？"

"嗯，干什么？"

"我们这是要去哪儿呢，乔治？"

小个子猛地把帽檐往下一扯，绷着脸看向伦尼。"你已经忘记了，对吧？我还得告诉你一遍，对吧？天哪，你真是个笨蛋疯子啊！"

"我忘记了，"伦尼轻声说，"我是想努力记着这事儿来着的。向上帝保证，我是这样想的，乔治。"

"O.K—O.K. I'll tell ya again. I **ain't**[①] got nothing to do. **Might jus' as well**[②] **spen'**[③] all my time tellin' you things and then you forget **'em**[④], and I tell you again."

"Tried and tried," said Lennie, "but it didn't do no good. I remember about the rabbits, George."

"**The hell with**[⑤] the rabbits. That's all you ever can remember is them rabbits. O.K.! Now you listen and this time you got to remember so we don't get in no trouble. You remember settin' in that **gutter**[⑥] on Howard Street and watchin' that blackboard?"

Lennie's face **broke**[⑦] into a delighted smile. "Why sure, George. I remember that . . . but . . . what'd we do then? I remember some girls come by and you says . . . you says . . ."

"The hell with what I says. You remember about us goin' in to Murray and Ready's, and they give us work cards and bus tickets?"

"Oh, sure, George. I remember that now." His hands went quickly into his side coat pockets. He said gently, "George . . . I ain't got mine. I **musta**[⑧] lost it." He looked down at the ground in despair.

"You never had none, you crazy bastard. I got both of 'em here. Think I'd let you carry your own work card?"

Lennie **grinned**[⑨] with **relief**[⑩]. "I . . . I thought I put it in my side pocket." His hand went into the pocket again.

George looked sharply at him. "What'd you take **outa**[⑪] that pocket?"

"Ain't a thing in my pocket," Lennie said cleverly.

"I know there ain't. You got it in your hand. What you got in your hand — hidin' it?"

"I ain't got nothin', George. Honest."

"Come on, give it here."

① ain't [eint] abbr.〈口〉= have not

② might just as well 倒不如，（满）可以

③ spen'= spend

④ 'em [əm] pron.〈口〉= them

⑤ the hell with〈口〉让……见鬼去吧

⑥ gutter ['gʌtə] n.〈口〉贫民窟，贫困地区

⑦ broke [brəuk] v.（break 的过去式）突然出现

⑧ musta = must have（-a [ə] suf.〈口〉代替助动词 have）

⑨ grin [grin] v. 咧嘴而笑，露齿而笑

⑩ relief [ri'li:f] n.（痛苦、忧虑等消除后感到的）轻松，宽心，宽慰

⑪ outa=out of

"好啦——好啦。我就再告诉你一遍吧。我反正闲着没有事情干。正好可以把时间全部耗费在告诉你事情上，等你又忘记了，我再来告诉你一遍。"

"我尽力了，"伦尼说，"但毫无效果。我倒是记得那些兔子呢，乔治。"

"让那些兔子见鬼去。你唯一能记住的也就是兔子。行了！你现在可要听好啦，这次你可一定要记住，这样我们才不会惹上麻烦。你还记得我们坐在霍华德街那个贫民窟里，盯着黑板[1]瞧吧？"

伦尼的脸上露出了欣然的微笑。"当然记得啦，乔治，我记得的……不过……我们之后干了什么来着？我记得有些女人过来了，而你说……你说……"

"见鬼，提我说的干什么。我们进了默里－雷迪公司，那儿的人给了我们工作卡和公共汽车票，这你还记得吗？"

"噢，确实是呢，乔治。我现在想起来啦。"他急忙把双手插入衣服的两侧口袋里。他小声地说："乔治……我的工作卡不见了。我一定是弄丢了。"他神情绝望，垂眼看着地面。

"你压根儿就没有拿到过呢，你这个笨蛋疯子。我们两个人的都在我这儿呢。你以为我会让你拿着你自己的工作卡吗？"

伦尼如释重负，咧开嘴笑了。"我……我还以为我把工作卡放到侧兜里了呢。"他又把一只手插入了侧兜。

乔治看着他，目光敏锐。"你那个口袋里装着什么呢？"

"口袋里什么也没有呀。"伦尼避重就轻地答道。

"我知道那里面什么也没有。东西你正攥在手里呢。你手里捏着什么——藏着不让我看？"

"我没有捏着什么东西呀，乔治，真的没有。"

"得了吧，拿出来。"

---

1 中介机构会在办公室前的黑板上张贴招工信息。

Lennie held his closed hand away from George's direction. "It's **on'y**① a mouse, George."

"A mouse? A **live**② mouse?"

"Uh-uh. Jus' a dead mouse, George. I didn't kill it. Honest! I found it. I found it dead."

"Give it here!" said George.

"Aw, leave me have it, George."

"*Give it here!*"

Lennie's closed hand slowly **obeyed**③. George took the mouse and threw it across the pool to the other side, among the brush. "What you want of a dead mouse, **anyways**④?"

"I could **pet**⑤ it with my thumb while we walked along," said Lennie.

"Well, you **ain't**⑥ petting no mice while you walk with me. You remember where we're goin' now?"

Lennie looked **startled**⑦ and then in embarrassment hid his face against his knees. "I forgot again."

"Jesus Christ," George said **resignedly**⑧. "Well—look, we're gonna work on a ranch like the one we come from up north."

"Up north?"

"In Weed."

"Oh, sure. I remember. In Weed."

"That ranch we're goin' to is right down there about a quarter mile. We're gonna go in **an'**⑨ see the boss. Now, look—I'll give him the work tickets, but you ain't gonna say a word. You jus' stand there and don't say nothing. If he finds out what a crazy bastard you are, we won't get no job, but if he sees ya work before he hears ya talk, we're **set**⑩. Ya got that?"

"Sure, George. Sure I got it."

"O.K. Now when we go in to see the boss, what you gonna do?"

"I . . . I . . ." Lennie thought. His face grew tight with thought. "I . . . ain't

① on'y = only

② live [laiv] *a.* 活的，有生命的

③ obey [ə(u)'bei] *v.* 服从，顺从，听从

④ anyways ['eniweiz] *n.*〈美口〉〈美方〉不管怎么样，无论如何

⑤ pet [pet] *v.* 抚摸，轻按

⑥ ain't [eint] *abbr.*〈粗〉= are not

⑦ startled ['stɑ:tld] *a.* 受惊吓的，吃惊的

⑧ resignedly [ri'zainidli] *ad.* 听从地，顺从地

⑨ an' [强 æn, 弱 ən, n] *conj.*〈口〉和，与

⑩ set [set] *a.* 作好准备的

伦尼把那只握紧的手藏到了身后。"只是一只老鼠啊，乔治。"

"一只老鼠？一只活老鼠吗？"

"不对，不对，只是一只死老鼠，乔治。不是我弄死的，真的不是！是我发现的，我发现时它就是死的。"

"拿出来！"乔治说。

"哎呀，让我拿着呗，乔治。"

"快拿出来！"

伦尼遵从了，紧握着的手慢慢张开。乔治抓起老鼠，一把扔到静水对岸的灌木丛中去了。"我倒是要问一声，你要一只死老鼠干什么来着？"

"我们一路走，我可以一路用大拇指摸着玩。"伦尼说。

"好啦，你和我一块儿走时，可不要摸老鼠玩。你现在记得我们这是要去哪儿了吗？"

伦尼看上去被吓了一跳，然后尴尬地把脸伏在膝上。"我又忘记了。"

"天哪，"乔治无可奈何地说，"行了——听好啦，我们要去农场上干活儿，那农场跟我们从北方来的那座是一样的。"

"北方？"

"在威德呢。"

"噢，确实是呢。我记起来了，在威德。"

"我们要去的那座农场就在南边呢，还有几百米。我们要进农场去，去见场主。嗯，听好啦——我来给他工作卡，但你一声也别吭。你只要站在一旁就行，什么话都不要说。他要是发现你是个笨蛋疯子，我们就没有活儿干啦，但他要是在你开口之前看见你干活儿的样子，那我们就有门儿了。你听清楚了没有？"

"听清楚了，乔治，听清楚了呢。"

"好吧。那你说说看，我们到了农场见到场主后，你该怎么办呢？"

"我……我……"伦尼思索着，想得脸都绷紧了，

• 011 •

gonna say nothin'. Jus' gonna **stan'**① there."

"Good boy. That's **swell**②. You say that over two, three times so you sure won't forget it."

Lennie **droned**③ to himself softly, "I ain't gonna say nothin' . . . I ain't gonna say nothin' . . . I ain't gonna say nothin'."

"O.K.," said George. "An' you ain't gonna do no bad things like you done in Weed, neither."

Lennie looked puzzled. "Like I done in Weed?"

"Oh, so ya forgot that too, did ya? Well, I ain't gonna remind ya, fear ya do it again."

A light of understanding broke on Lennie's face. "They run us outa Weed," he **exploded**④ triumphantly.

"Run us out, hell," said George disgustedly. "We run. They was lookin' for us, but they didn't catch us."

Lennie giggled happily. "I didn't forget that, you bet."

George lay back on the sand and crossed his hands under his head, and Lennie imitated him, raising his head to see whether he was doing it right. "God, you're a lot of trouble," said George. "I could get along so easy and so nice if I didn't have you **on** my **tail**⑤. I could live so easy and maybe have a girl."

For a moment Lennie lay quiet, and then he said hopefully, "We gonna work on a ranch, George."

"**Awright**⑥. You got that. But we're gonna sleep here because I got a reason."

The day was going fast now. Only the tops of the Gabilan mountains **flamed**⑦ with the light of the sun that had gone from the valley. A water snake slipped along on the pool, its head held up like a little **periscope**⑧. The **reeds**⑨ jerked slightly in the current. Far off toward the highway a man shouted something, and another man shouted back. The sycamore limbs **rustled**⑩ under a little wind that died immediately.

"George—why ain't we goin' on to the ranch and get some supper? They

① stan'= stand
② swell [swel] a.〈美口〉[用以表示赞许] 极好的，第一流的，了不起的
③ drone [drəun] v. 低沉单调地说

④ explode [ik'spləud; ek-] v. 爆发，突发，迸发

⑤ on sb's tail 尾随

⑥ awright = all right

⑦ flame [fleim] v. 发光，闪耀
⑧ periscope ['periskəup] n. 潜望镜
⑨ reed [ri:d] n.【植】芦苇，[总称] 芦丛
⑩ rustle ['rʌs(ə)l] v.（如枯叶、绸衣、纸张等相擦时）沙沙作响，发出窸窣声

"我……用不着吭一声，站在一旁就行。"

"好孩子啊。太棒啦。你再把这话说上个两三遍，说到你保准再也忘不了了。"

伦尼轻声轻气对着自己咕哝起来："我用不着吭一声……我用不着吭一声……我用不着吭一声。"

"好啦，"乔治说，"还有你也不能像在威德那样干坏事。"

伦尼一脸困惑。"像我在威德那样干坏事？"

"噢，你连这个也忘记了，对吧？得啦，我可不会提醒你，免得你再干一回。"

伦尼脸上忽然显出一丝了悟。"那儿的人把我们赶出了威德。"他大声说着，一副得意扬扬的样子。

"把我们赶出来，见鬼，"乔治不满地说，"是我们自己逃跑的。他们倒是追我们来着，但没能逮着。"

伦尼开心地咯咯笑了起来。"这我可忘不掉。"

乔治仰卧在沙地上，双手交叉垫在脑袋后。伦尼学着他的样子躺下，抬起脑袋看看自己的姿势是否标准。"天哪，你这个人真麻烦，"乔治说，"我要是没有你这个尾巴，准会过得轻轻松松的，而且过得舒舒服服的。我会活得轻松如意，说不定还能找到个女人呢。"

伦尼静静地躺了一会儿，然后满怀希望地说："我们要在一座农场上干活儿了，乔治。"

"说得对啊。这一点你记着了。但是，今晚我们得在这儿睡了，我有我的理由。"

此时暮色四合。谷地里已经完全没有了阳光，只有加比兰山脉顶端仍然闪烁着落日的余晖。一条水蛇悄无声息地游过静水，头部犹如一副小潜望镜一般探出了水面。芦苇在水流中轻微地晃动着。远处公路那边，有个人在高声喊着什么话，另外一个人高声回应着。悬铃木树的枝丫在微风中飒飒作响，但没一会儿微风便停息了。

"乔治——我们为什么不继续往前走，到农场去吃点儿晚饭呢？农场上有晚饭的。"

got supper at the ranch."

George rolled on his side. "No reason at all for you. I like it here. **Tomorra**[①] we're gonna go to work. I seen **thrashin' machines**[②] on the way down. That means we'll be **buckin'**[③] **grain**[④] bags, **bustin' a gut**[⑤]. Tonight I'm gonna lay right here and look up. I like it."

Lennie got up on his knees and looked down at George. "Ain't we gonna have no supper?"

"Sure we are, if you gather up some dead willow sticks. I got three cans of beans in my bindle. You get a fire ready. I'll give you a match when you get the sticks together. Then we'll heat the beans and have supper."

Lennie said, "I like beans with ketchup."

"Well, we ain't got no ketchup. You go get wood. An' don't you **fool around**[⑥]. It'll be dark before long."

Lennie **lumbered**[⑦] to his feet and disappeared in the brush. George lay where he was and whistled softly to himself. There were sounds of splashings down the river in the direction Lennie had taken. George stopped whistling and listened.

"Poor bastard," he said softly, and then went on whistling again.

In a moment Lennie came **crashing**[⑧] back through the brush. He carried one small willow stick in his hand. George sat up. "Awright," he said **brusquely**[⑨]. "**Gi'me**[⑩] that mouse!"

But Lennie made an **elaborate**[⑪] **pantomime**[⑫] of innocence. "What mouse, George? I ain't got no mouse."

George held out his hand. "Come on. Give it to me. You ain't **puttin' nothing over**[⑬]."

Lennie hesitated, backed away, looked wildly at the brush line as though he **contemplated**[⑭] running for his freedom. George said coldly, "You gonna give me that mouse or do I have to **sock**[⑮] you?"

"Give you what, George?"

"You know God damn well what. I want that mouse."

Lennie reluctantly reached into his pocket. His voice **broke**[⑯] a little. "I

① tomorra = tomorrow
② thrashing machine 脱粒机，脱谷机
③ buck [bʌk] v. 传递，搬动（或装载）（重物）
④ grain [grein] n. 谷（物）
⑤ bust a gut〈口〉努力做

⑥ fool around〈口〉闲荡
⑦ lumber ['lʌmbə] v. 笨拙地移动，缓慢吃力（发出响声）地移动

⑧ crash [kræʃ] v. 哗啦啦地猛冲直闯
⑨ brusquely ['brʌskli] ad. （言语、态度上）粗鲁地，简慢地，生硬无礼地
⑩ gi'me [gimi:]〈口〉=give me（或 give it to me）
⑪ elaborate [i'læb(ə)rət] a. 精心计划（或制作的）
⑫ pantomime ['pæntəmaim] n. 形体动作，示意动作，手势
⑬ put over（用欺骗手段）使信以为真，使接受
⑭ contemplate ['kɔntempleit; -təm-] v. 盘算，打算
⑮ sock [sɔk] v.〈俚〉（尤指）用拳头猛击
⑯ broke [brəuk] v.（break 的过去式）（嗓音）突变

乔治翻了个身。"对你而言，是没有任何理由的。我喜欢这处地方。我们明天就要开始干活儿了。我一路上看到不少脱粒机。这就意味着，我们要扛大麦包，拼着命去扛。今晚我准备躺在这儿，看看天空。我喜欢这样。"

伦尼爬起来，双膝跪地，低头看着乔治。"我们不吃晚饭吗？"

"我们当然要吃晚饭啦，你去捡一些柳树枝来吧。我的铺盖卷里还有三个豆子罐头。你去准备生火，等你捡来了树枝我就把火柴给你。我们把豆子罐头热一热，然后就吃晚饭。"

伦尼说："我喜欢豆子拌番茄酱吃。"

"得了吧，我们可没有番茄酱。你去捡柴火来，别到处瞎跑啊。天很快就要黑了。"

伦尼笨手笨脚地慢慢站起来，然后消失在灌木丛中。乔治躺在原地不动，自个儿轻轻吹着口哨。从伦尼刚去的那个方向传来了河水哗啦啦的声音。乔治收住声，仔细听了一阵。

"可怜的笨蛋。"他轻声说着，然后又吹起了口哨。

过了一会儿，伦尼从灌木丛中闯了出来，一只手上拿着一根细柳树枝。乔治坐起身子。"好了，"他语气生硬地说，"把老鼠给我！"

但伦尼做出一副无辜样儿，装得还挺像那么回事。"什么老鼠啊，乔治？我没有老鼠啊。"

乔治伸出一只手。"快点儿，把老鼠给我。你瞒不了我的。"

伦尼一面迟疑，一面后退，眼珠子往那一排灌木所在的地方乱瞄，似乎在盘算溜走的可能。乔治语气冷漠地说："你是打算把老鼠给我呢，还是让我揍你一顿？"

"给你什么啊，乔治？"

"该死的，给什么你再清楚不过了。我要那只老鼠。"

伦尼不情不愿地把手伸进衣服口袋，说话间声音都

don't know why I can't keep it. It ain't nobody's mouse. I didn't steal it. I found it lyin' right beside the road."

George's hand remained outstretched **imperiously**①. Slowly, like a **terrier**② who doesn't want to bring a ball to its master, Lennie approached, **drew back**③, approached again. George **snapped**④ his fingers sharply, and at the sound Lennie laid the mouse in his hand.

"I wasn't doin' nothing bad with it, George. Jus' **strokin'**⑤ it."

George stood up and threw the mouse as far as he could into the darkening brush, and then he stepped to the pool and washed his hands. "You crazy fool. Don't you think I could see your feet was wet where you went **acrost**⑥ the river to get it?" He heard Lennie's **whimpering**⑦ cry and **wheeled**⑧ about. "**Blubberin'**⑨ like a baby! Jesus Christ! A big guy like you." Lennie's lip **quivered**⑩ and tears started in his eyes. "Aw, Lennie!" George put his hand on Lennie's shoulder. "I ain't takin' it away jus' for meanness. That mouse ain't fresh, Lennie; and besides, you've broke it pettin' it. You get another mouse that's fresh and I'll let you keep it a little while."

Lennie sat down on the ground and hung his head **dejectedly**⑪. "I don't know where there is no other mouse. I remember a lady used to give 'em to me—**ever'**⑫ one she got. But that lady ain't here."

George **scoffed**⑬. "Lady, huh? Don't even remember who that lady was. That was your own Aunt Clara. An' she stopped givin' 'em to ya. You always killed 'em."

Lennie looked sadly up at him. "They was so little," he said, apologetically. "I'd pet 'em, and pretty soon they bit my fingers and I **pinched**⑭ their heads a little and then they was dead—because they was so little.

"I **wisht**⑮ we'd get the rabbits pretty soon, George. They ain't so little."

"The hell with the rabbits. An' you ain't to be trusted with no live mice.

① imperiously [im'piriəsli] ad. 专横地
② terrier ['teriə] n.【动】㹴
③ drew back 向后移动，后退，后缩（drew [dru:] v. draw 的过去式）
④ snap [snæp] v. 捻（手指）发嚯啪声
⑤ stroke [strəuk] v.（用手等）轻抚
⑥ acrost = across
⑦ whimper ['wimpə] v. 抽搭，抽泣
⑧ wheel [wi:l] v. 转弯，转变方向
⑨ blubber ['blʌbə] v. 放声哭，抽泣
⑩ quiver ['kwivə] v. 颤抖，发抖
⑪ dejectedly [di'dʒektidli] ad. 沮丧地，垂头丧气地，情绪低落地，泄气地
⑫ ever' ['evə(r)] a.〈方〉每一的（=every）
⑬ scoff [skɔf] v. 嘲弄，嘲笑，讥笑
⑭ pinch [pin(t)ʃ] v. 捏，拧
⑮ wisht = wished

有点儿变了。"我不明白，我为什么就不能留着它呢，它又不是谁的。也不是我偷来的。我是在路边捡到它的。"

乔治的那只手仍然还伸着，毫不通融。伦尼慢慢接近乔治，随即又后退，然后再接近，恰如一只不愿意把球还回自己主人的㹴犬。乔治打了个清脆的响指。这声音一响，伦尼就把老鼠放到了乔治手上。

"我并没有拿着老鼠做什么坏事呀，乔治，就只是摸摸它。"

乔治站起身，使出浑身力气，把老鼠扔到了远处昏暗的灌木丛中，然后迈步走向河畔，洗了洗手。"你这个笨蛋疯子。你蹚水过河去捡老鼠，双脚都湿了，你以为我看不见吗？"他听见伦尼抽抽搭搭哭泣的声音，于是转过身。"哭得像个婴儿似的！天哪！亏你长了这么大的个子！"伦尼嘴唇微颤，眼眶里涌出泪水。"噢，伦尼！"乔治把一只手搭到伦尼的肩膀上，"我扔掉老鼠，不是出于什么坏心眼儿，而是因为老鼠不新鲜了，伦尼。还有，你摸老鼠摸得太用力，都戳破了。下次你若是捡到一只新鲜的老鼠，我就同意你保留一阵子。"

伦尼坐到地上，沮丧地垂下头。"我不知道什么地方还有老鼠呢。我记得，有位太太以前常送老鼠给我——凡是她找到的都会送给我。但是，那位太太又不在这儿。"

乔治嘲弄道："太太，嗯？连那位太太是谁都不记得了。那是你的亲姨妈克拉拉啊。还有，她早就不再送老鼠给你了，因为你老是弄死它们。"

伦尼悲伤地抬头看着他。"老鼠太小了，"他内疚地说，"每回我去摸老鼠，摸了没一会儿，它们就咬我的手指，我便会稍稍捏一捏它们的脑袋，结果就捏死了——因为老鼠太小了。

"我真希望，我们能尽快养些兔子，乔治。兔子的个头可不小。"

"让那些兔子见鬼去吧。反正活老鼠绝不能给你。"

Your Aunt Clara give you a rubber mouse and you wouldn't have nothing to do with it."

"It wasn't no good to pet," said Lennie.

The **flame**① of the sunset lifted from the mountaintops and dusk came into the valley, and a half darkness came in among the willows and the sycamores. A big **carp**② rose to the surface of the pool, **gulped**③ air and then sank mysteriously into the dark water again, leaving widening rings on the water. Overhead the leaves **whisked**④ again and little **puffs**⑤ of willow **cotton**⑥ blew down and landed on the pool's surface.

"You gonna get that wood?" George **demanded**⑦. "There's plenty right up against the back of that sycamore. Floodwater wood. Now you get it."

Lennie went behind the tree and brought out a **litter**⑧ of dried leaves and twigs. He threw them in a **heap**⑨ on the old ash pile and went back for more and more. It was almost night now. A dove's wings **whistled**⑩ over the water. George walked to the fire pile and lighted the dry leaves. The flame **cracked**⑪ up among the twigs and **fell to**⑫ work. George **undid**⑬ his bindle and brought out three cans of beans. He **stood**⑭ them **about**⑮ the fire, close in against the **blaze**⑯, but not quite touching the flame.

"There's enough beans for four men," George said.

Lennie watched him from over the fire. He said patiently, "I like 'em with ketchup."

"Well, we ain't got any," George exploded. "Whatever we ain't got, that's what you want. God **a'mighty**⑰, if I was alone I could live so easy. I could go get a job an' work, an' no trouble. No mess at all, and when the end of the month come I could take my fifty **bucks**⑱ and go into town and get whatever I want. Why, I could stay in a **cat house**⑲ all night. I could eat any place I want, hotel or any place, and order any damn thing I could think of. An' I could do all that every damn month. Get a gallon of whisky, or set in a **pool room**⑳ and play cards or **shoot**㉑ pool." Lennie knelt and looked over the fire at the

① flame [fleim] n. 光辉，光泽，闪光，光亮
② carp [kɑ:p] n. 鲤鱼
③ gulp [gʌlp] v. 大口大口地吸（气）
④ whisk [wisk] v. 迅速地移动
⑤ puff [pʌf] n.（空气、烟雾、气味等的）一股
⑥ cotton ['kɔt(ə)n] n.（其他植物产的）似棉花般柔软的纤维
⑦ demand [di'mɑ:nd] v. 询问
⑧ litter ['litə] n.（一堆）杂乱的东西
⑨ heap [hi:p] n.（一）堆
⑩ whistle ['wis(ə)l] v.（风、炮弹等）发啸叫声，呼啸而行
⑪ crack [kræk] v. 噼啪地响，发出爆裂声
⑫ fall to 开始（fell [fel] v. fall 的过去式）
⑬ undid [ʌn'did] v.（undo 的过去式）解开，打开，松开
⑭ stood [stud] v.（stand 的过去式和过去分词）竖放
⑮ about [ə'baut] prep.（空间上）在……附近
⑯ blaze [bleiz] n. 火焰，火堆
⑰ a'mighty = almighty [ɔ:l'maiti] a. 全能的，万能的，有无限权力的，有强大力量的
⑱ buck [bʌk] n.〈美口〉（一）元
⑲ cat house〈美俚〉妓院
⑳ pool room〈美〉台球房，弹子房，桌球房
㉑ shoot [ʃu:t] v.（将球、弹子等）击向目标

克拉拉姨妈给了你一只橡皮老鼠，但你不要。"

"橡皮老鼠抚摸起来不舒服呀。"伦尼说。

落日的余晖从山顶上消失了，暮色降临谷地，杨柳树和悬铃木树丛笼罩在半明半暗之中。一条大鲤鱼浮上静水面，吸了吸气，随即又神秘莫测地潜回昏暗的水中，只在水面上留下一圈圈四散开的涟漪。头顶上的树叶又飒飒作响起来，细小的一团团柳絮飘落下来，落在静水面上。

"你去拾柴火吗？"乔治问。"那棵悬铃木树后面有很多漂流木柴。你现在去拾吧。"

伦尼走到那棵树后面，拾回了一堆干树叶和细枝。他把这些堆在前人留下的那堆灰烬上，又转身去拾，如此数次。现在夜幕将至。一只野鸽展翅呼啸着掠过水面。乔治走到火堆旁，点燃了干树叶。小树枝噼噼啪啪地燃烧起来，火开始起作用了。乔治解开自己的铺盖卷，从里面取出三个豆子罐头。他把罐头立在火堆周围，既靠得近，又碰不到火焰。

"这豆子都够四个人吃的了。"乔治说。

伦尼在火堆另一侧看着乔治。他耐着性子说："我喜欢豆子拌番茄酱吃。"

"得了吧，我们可没有番茄酱啊，"乔治火了，"我们没有的东西，你偏偏想要。天哪，我要是一个人过，得多轻松自如啊。我可以去找一份差事干起来，轻而易举，什么麻烦的事情都没有。等到月底，我可以领到五十块钱，然后进城去，想买什么买什么。可不是嘛，我可以整宿待在窑子里。我可以想去哪儿吃饭就去哪儿吃饭，旅馆也行，别的任何地方也行，点他妈的我想得到的任何东西。而且，我他妈的每个月都可以这样干。买一加仑威士忌酒，或者待在某个台球室里，玩玩扑克，或打打台球。"伦尼双膝跪地，隔着火堆看着愤怒的乔治，因为惊恐，脸绷得紧紧的。"而我得到什么啦？"乔治火气正旺，接着说，"我得到了你！你一份差事都保不住，弄得我也跟着丢差事。让我四

• 019 •

Of Mice and Men

angry George. And Lennie's face was **drawn**① with terror. "An' **whatta**② I got," George went on **furiously**③. "I got you! You can't keep a job and you lose me ever' job I get. Jus' keep me **shovin'**④ all over the country all the time. An' that ain't the worst. You get in trouble. You do bad things and I got to get you out." His voice rose nearly to a shout. "You crazy son-of-a-bitch. You keep me **in hot water**⑤ all the time." He took on the elaborate manner of little girls when they are **mimicking**⑥ one another. "Jus' wanted to feel that girl's dress—jus' wanted to pet it like it was a mouse—Well, how the hell did she know you jus' wanted to feel her dress? She jerks back and you hold on like it was a mouse. She yells and we got to hide in a **irrigation**⑦ **ditch**⑧ all day with guys lookin' for us, and we got to **sneak**⑨ out in the dark and get outa the country. All the time somethin' like that—all the time. I wisht I could put you in a cage with about a million mice an' let you have fun." His anger left him suddenly. He looked across the fire at Lennie's **anguished**⑩ face, and then he looked ashamedly at the flames.

It was quite dark now, but the fire lighted the trunks of the trees and the **curving**⑪ branches overhead. Lennie crawled slowly and cautiously around the fire until he was close to George. He sat back on his heels. George turned the bean cans so that another side faced the fire. He pretended to be unaware of Lennie so close beside him.

"George," very softly. No answer. "George!"

"Whatta you want?"

"I was only **foolin'**⑫, George. I don't want no ketchup. I wouldn't eat no ketchup if it was right here beside me."

"If it was here, you could have some."

"But I wouldn't eat none, George. I'd leave it all for you. You could cover your beans with it and I wouldn't touch none of it."

George still stared morosely at the fire. "When I think of the swell time I could have without you, I **go nuts**⑬. I never get no peace."

Lennie still knelt. He looked **off**⑭ **into**⑮ the darkness across the river. "George, you want I should go away and leave you alone?"

① drawn [drɔ:n] *a.*（脸等）扭歪的，紧张的
② whatta = what have
③ furiously ['fjuəriəsli] *ad.* 狂怒地，暴怒地
④ shove [ʃʌv] *v.* 推，猛推
⑤ in hot water 有麻烦，惹麻烦
⑥ mimic ['mimik] *v.* 模仿，学……的样子
⑦ irrigation [,iri'geiʃn] *n.* 灌溉
⑧ ditch [ditʃ] *n.* 水道，渠道
⑨ sneak [sni:k] *v.* 偷偷地走，溜
⑩ anguished ['æŋgwiʃt] *a.* 感到极度痛苦的，表示出极度痛苦的
⑪ curve [kə:v] *v.* 使弯曲

⑫ fool [fu:l] *v.* 开玩笑

⑬ go nuts 发疯
⑭ off [ɔf] *ad.* 向一边
⑮ into ['intu; 'intə] *prep.* 朝，向

乡八镇地跑，不得消停。这还不是最糟糕的呢。你还惹麻烦。你做了坏事，我还得领着你逃跑。"他提高嗓门，话几乎是吼着出来的，"你这个狗娘养的疯子。我天天得给你收拾烂摊子。"乔治随即摆出小姑娘相互模仿对方时那种夸张的样子，"只是想摸一摸那个姑娘的衣裙——只是想要像抚摸老鼠那样摸一摸——你得了吧，真是见鬼了，她怎么知道你只是想摸一摸她的衣裙呢？她猛然后退，而你却像对待一只老鼠一样抓住不放。她大喊大叫起来，我们只得藏到灌溉水沟里去，白天那些家伙一直都在寻找我们。趁天黑了我们才偷偷溜出来，离开那个地方。回回都是这种事——回回都是。我真是巴不得把你放进一只笼子里，与一百来万只老鼠做伴，让你玩个够。"他的怒气来得快，消得也快。他看了一眼火堆对面伦尼痛苦的表情，随即低头看着火苗，一脸愧疚。

　　天现在已经很黑了，但火焰照亮了一根根树干和上方弯曲着的枝丫。伦尼绕着火堆，缓慢而谨慎地爬到乔治身边跪坐下来。乔治让豆子罐头转了个面对着火焰。他假装着没有注意到伦尼就在自己身边。

　　"乔治。"喊的声音很柔和，但对方没有回应，"乔治！"

　　"你想要干什么？"

　　"我只是说着玩玩的，乔治。我其实不想吃番茄酱，即便番茄酱摆在我身边，我也不会吃的。"

　　"假如现在有番茄酱，你还是可以吃一点儿的。"

　　"但我不会吃的，乔治。我会全部留给你。你可以在豆子上面盖满番茄酱，我连尝都不会尝一下。"

　　乔治依旧阴郁地盯着火堆。"一想到没有你在身边自己能够享受快乐的时光，我就心烦意乱。我的生活从来没平静过。"

　　伦尼继续跪着，他朝着远处河对岸的黑暗处看去。"乔治，你想要我离开，你一个人独自待着吗？"

Of Mice and Men

"Where the hell could you go?"

"Well, I could. I could go off in the hills there. Some place I'd find a cave."

"Yeah? How'd you eat? You ain't got sense enough to find nothing to eat."

"I'd find things, George. I don't need no nice food with ketchup. I'd lay out in the sun and nobody'd hurt me. An' if I **foun'**① a mouse, I could keep it. Nobody'd take it away from me."

George looked quickly and **searchingly**② at him. "I been mean, ain't I?"

"If you don' want me I can go off in the hills an' find a cave. I can go away any time."

"No—look! I was jus' foolin', Lennie. 'Cause I want you to stay with me. Trouble with mice is you always kill 'em." He paused. "Tell you what I'll do, Lennie. First chance I get I'll give you a **pup**③. Maybe you wouldn't kill *it*. That'd be better than mice. And you could pet it harder."

Lennie avoided the **bait**④. He had sensed his advantage. "If you don't want me, you only jus' got to say so, and I'll go off in those hills right there—right up in those hills and live by myself. An' I won't get no mice stole from me."

George said, "I want you to stay with me, Lennie. Jesus Christ, somebody'd shoot you for a **coyote**⑤ if you was by yourself. No, you stay with me. Your Aunt Clara wouldn't like you running off by yourself, even if she is dead."

Lennie spoke **craftily**⑥, "Tell me—like you done before."

"Tell you what?"

"About the rabbits."

George **snapped**⑦, "You ain't gonna put nothing over on me."

Lennie pleaded, "Come on, George. Tell me. Please, George. Like you done before."

① foun'= found

② searchingly ['sə:tʃiŋli] ad. 敏锐地，锐利地，洞察地

③ pup [pʌp] n. 小狗，幼犬

④ bait [beit] n.〈喻〉诱饵，诱惑（物）

⑤ coyote [kai'əuti] n.【动】丛林狼，郊狼

⑥ craftily ['krɑ:ftli] ad. 狡猾地，诡计多端地

⑦ snap [snæp] v. 厉声说话

"见鬼，你能去哪儿呢？"

"这个嘛，我有地方去的，我可以跑到那边山上去，总能找到一个洞穴的。"

"是吗？你吃什么呢？你这个人没有脑子，找不到东西吃的。"

"我找得到东西的，乔治。我不需要吃拌了番茄酱的好东西。我可以躺在阳光下，谁都不会伤害我。假如我发现了一只老鼠，我可以把它留下来。没有人会从我手上把老鼠夺走。"

乔治快速地用探究的目光看了他一眼。"我对你不好，是吧？"

"你要是不想要我了，我可以跑到山上去，找个洞穴住。我随时都可以离开的。"

"不——你听好啦！我只是说着玩玩的，伦尼，因为我想要你和我待在一块儿。老鼠带来的问题是，你总是把老鼠弄死。"他停顿了一下，"告诉你我的打算吧，伦尼。只要有了机会，我便会给你弄条小狗崽来。你或许不会把小狗崽弄死的。跟老鼠比起来，小狗崽更加理想一些。你可以用更大的劲儿抚摸小狗崽。"

伦尼不为诱惑所动。他意识到，目前形势对自己有利。"假如你不要我了，你尽管直说，我这就到那些山上去——就是那边的山上，一个人谋生去。而且我不会让人从我身边偷走老鼠的。"

乔治说："我想要你和我待在一块儿，伦尼。天哪，你要是一个人待着，有人会把你当成丛林狼，一枪崩了你的。不，你要和我待在一块儿。你克拉拉姨妈不愿让你独自一人离开，即使她去世了也会这样想的。"

伦尼趁机说："给我讲一讲吧——像你先前那样讲一讲吧。"

"给你讲一讲什么啊？"

"讲一讲那些兔子吧。"

乔治厉声说："你休想把我糊弄过去。"

伦尼恳求道："求你了，乔治，给我讲一讲呗，求你啦，乔治，像你先前那样讲一讲吧。"

Of Mice and Men

"You get a **kick**① outa that, don't you? Awright, I'll tell you, and then we'll eat our supper . . ."

George's voice became deeper. He repeated his words **rhythmically**② as though he had said them many times before. "Guys like us, that work on ranches, are the loneliest guys in the world. They got no family. They don't belong no place. They come to a ranch an' **work up**③ a **stake**④ and then they go **inta**⑤ town and **blow**⑥ their stake, and the first thing you know they're poundin' their tail on some other ranch. They ain't got nothing to look ahead to."

Lennie was delighted. "That's it—that's it. Now tell how it is with us."

George went on. "With us it ain't like that. We got a future. We got somebody to talk to that **gives a damn about**⑦ us. We don't have to sit in no bar room **blowin' in**⑧ our **jack**⑨ jus' because we got no place else to go. If them other guys gets in jail they can **rot**⑩ **for all anybody gives a damn**⑪. But not us."

Lennie **broke in**⑫. "*But not us! An' why? Because . . . because I got you to look after me, and you got me to look after you, and that's why.*" He laughed delightedly. "Go on now, George!"

"You got it by heart. You can do it yourself."

"No, you. I forget some **a'**⑬ the things. Tell about how it's gonna be."

"O.K. Someday—we're gonna get the jack together and we're gonna have a little house and a couple of acres an' a cow and some pigs and—"

"*An' live off the fatta the lan'*⑭," Lennie shouted. "An' have *rabbits*. Go on, George! Tell about what we're gonna have in the garden and about the rabbits in the cages and about the rain in the winter and the **stove**⑮, and how thick the cream is on the milk like you can hardly cut it. Tell about that, George."

"**Why'n't**⑯ you do it yourself? You know all of it."

"No . . . you tell it. It ain't the same if I tell it. Go on . . . George. How I get to **tend**⑰ the rabbits."

"Well," said George, "we'll have a big vegetable **patch**⑱ and a rabbit **hutch**⑲ and chickens. And when it rains in the winter, we'll just say the hell

① kick [kik] n.〈口〉极大的乐趣
② rhythmically ['riðmikli] ad. 有节奏地，有韵律地
③ work up 逐步建立，逐步发展；up [ʌp] ad.（数量等）由小到大
④ stake [steik] n.（投机生意等的）股本，股份
⑤ inta = into
⑥ blow [bləu] v.〈口〉挥霍，把钱花在……身上
⑦ not give a damn〈口〉毫不在乎
⑧ blow in〈美口〉挥霍，花光
⑨ jack [dʒæk] n.〈美俚〉钱
⑩ rot [rɔt] v.〈喻〉（因被幽禁、缺乏活动等而）变得憔悴，失去活力，走向毁灭
⑪ for all sb. gives a damn= for all sb. cares 与某人全然不相干，不关某人的事
⑫ break in 打断，插嘴
⑬ a'= of
⑭ live off the fatta the lan'= live off the fat of the land; live off the land 靠地吃饭，靠狩猎或耕种生活；fat [fæt] n. 积蓄，储备
⑮ stove [stəuv] n.（取暖或烹饪用的）炉
⑯ why'n't = why don't; 'n't [nt]〈口〉= not
⑰ tend [tend] v. 照顾，照料，照管
⑱ patch [pætʃ] n. 一小块地，（种有某种植物的）一块田地
⑲ hutch [hʌtʃ] n.（关兔等小动物的）笼，舍，棚

"你就爱听这个，对吧？好吧，我就给你讲一讲，然后，我们就吃晚饭……"

乔治说话的声音变得深沉起来，他抑扬顿挫地开了口，好像是在重复已经讲过许多遍的内容。"像我们一样在农场上干活儿的人，是世界上最孤独的人。他们没有家庭，不属于任何一个地方，到了农场上，靠干活儿攒下一笔钱，然后就进城花个精光。等你再去看时，他们又找了座农场干活儿去了，他们没有任何盼头。"

伦尼听后很高兴。"就是那样——就是那样。然后再讲一讲我们的情况吧。"

乔治接着说："我们的情况不一样。我们有未来。我们有个在乎自己的人可以说说话。我们不会因为没有其他任何地方可去，就坐在酒吧里把钱花得精光。那些人要是坐牢了，没有任何人会在乎他们。但我们不会这样。"

伦尼插话说："但我们不会这样！为什么呢？因为……因为我有你照顾我，你有我照顾你，这就是为什么。"他哈哈大笑起来，"现在接着讲吧，乔治！"

"你都已经记在心里了。你自己都可以讲了。"

"不行，你来讲。有些内容我忘了，你来讲一讲将来事情会怎么样吧。"

"好吧。有朝一日——我们会把挣到的钱积攒起来，买一幢小房子，购置几亩地，养头母牛，养几头猪，还有——"

"依靠那片土地谋生，"伦尼大声喊了起来，"还要养些兔子。接着讲吧，乔治！讲一讲我们的菜园里会种植什么菜，笼子里饲养的兔子，冬季里下雨的情况，还有火炉子，还有牛奶上的奶油有多么厚，你都切不动。讲一讲那些内容吧，乔治。"

"你怎么就不能自己讲，你全部都知道了。"

"不行……你来讲。我讲的效果不一样呢。接着讲吧，乔治。我是怎么照料那些兔子的？"

"好吧，"乔治说，"我们会开一大片菜地，盖一间兔舍，再养些鸡。冬季里下雨时，我们就会说，让干活儿见

· 025 ·

Of Mice and Men

with goin' to work, and we'll build up a fire in the stove and **set**① around it an' listen to the rain comin' down on the roof—**Nuts**②!" He took out his pocket knife. "I ain't got time for no more." He drove his knife through the top of one of the bean cans, **sawed**③ out the top and passed the can to Lennie. Then he opened a second can. From his side pocket he brought out two spoons and passed one of them to Lennie.

They sat by the fire and filled their mouths with beans and **chewed**④ **mightily**⑤. A few beans **slipped**⑥ out of the side of Lennie's mouth. George **gestured**⑦ with his spoon. "What you gonna say tomorrow when the boss asks you questions?"

Lennie stopped chewing and swallowed. His face was concentrated. "I . . . I ain't gonna . . . say a word."

"Good boy! That's fine, Lennie! Maybe you're gettin' better. When we get the **coupla**⑧ acres I can let you tend the rabbits all right. 'Specially if you remember as good as that."

Lennie **choked**⑨ with pride. "I can remember," he said.

George **motioned**⑩ with his spoon again. "Look, Lennie. I want you to look around here. You can remember this place, can't you? The ranch is about a quarter mile up that way. Just follow the river?"

"Sure," said Lennie. "I can remember this. **Di'n't**⑪ I remember about not gonna say a word?"

"'**Course**⑫ you did. Well, look. Lennie—if you jus' happen to get in trouble like you always done before, I want you to come right here an' hide in the brush."

"Hide in the brush," said Lennie slowly.

"Hide in the brush till I come for you. Can you remember that?"

"Sure I can, George. Hide in the brush till you come."

"But you ain't gonna get in no trouble, because if you do, I won't let you tend the rabbits." He threw his empty bean can off into the brush.

"I won't get in no trouble, George. I ain't gonna say a word."

"O.K. Bring your bindle over here by the fire. It's gonna be nice sleepin'

① set = sat
② nuts [nʌts] *int.* 〔表示憎恶、失望、惊讶、不赞成、拒绝、藐视等〕呸！胡说！混蛋！
③ saw [sɔː] *v.* 拉锯般地来回移动

④ chew [tʃuː] *v.* 咀嚼，咬
⑤ mightily ['maitili] *ad.* 竭尽全力地，猛烈
⑥ slip [slip] *v.* 滑落，脱落
⑦ gesture ['dʒestʃə] *v.* 做手势，用动作示意

⑧ coupla = couple of

⑨ choke [tʃəuk] *v.* （因感情激动而）哽得说不出话来

⑩ motion ['məuʃ(ə)n] *v.* 做手势

⑪ di'n't = didn't

⑫ 'course = of course

鬼去吧。我们在炉子里生起火来，围坐在火炉边，听雨水从房顶上落下来——哎呀！"他从衣服口袋里拿出折叠刀。"我没有时间再讲了。"他用刀刃插入一个豆子罐头，割开顶盖，递给伦尼。接着他又开了一个罐头。他从一个侧兜里掏出两把勺子，递了一把给伦尼。

他们坐在火堆旁，嘴里塞满了豆子，用力咀嚼着。伦尼一边的嘴角里掉出了几颗豆子。乔治用手上的勺子示意了一下。"场主明天向你提问时，你准备怎么说呢？"

伦尼停止咀嚼，吞下豆子，表情专注。"我……我不会……吭一声。"

"好孩子！很棒啊，伦尼！或许你真的变听话了呢。等到我们购置了几亩地后，我保证让你照料那些兔子，尤其你要是能记得像现在这样清楚的话。"

伦尼激动得噎了一下。"我记得。"他说。

乔治又用手上的勺子示意了一下。"听着，伦尼。我要你把这附近好好看一看。你能够记住这个地方，对吧？农场在那边，四五百米远的样子。只需要顺着河流走就行，对吧？"

"没错，"伦尼说，"这个我能记得。我不是已经记得到时候不吭一声这事了吗？"

"你当然记住了。好了，听着，伦尼——你要是碰巧跟以前似的，又惹上什么麻烦了，我要你直接到这儿来，藏到灌木丛里。"

"藏到灌木丛里。"伦尼慢慢说道。

"藏到灌木丛里，一直等到我来找你。你能记住这一点吗？"

"当然能啦，乔治。藏到灌木丛里，一直等到你来找我。"

"但是，你不会再去惹麻烦了，因为你一旦惹了麻烦，我便不会让你照料那些兔子了。"他把手上空了的豆子罐头扔进灌木丛。

"我不会惹麻烦的，乔治，我不会吭一声的。"

"好吧，把你的铺盖卷拿到火堆旁边来。睡在这儿

· 027 ·

here. Lookin' up, and the leaves. Don't build up no more fire. We'll let **her**① die down."

They made their beds on the sand, and as the blaze dropped from the fire the **sphere**② of light grew smaller; the **curling**③ branches disappeared and only a **faint**④ **glimmer**⑤ showed where the tree trunks were. From the darkness Lennie called, "George—you asleep?"

"No. Whatta you want?"

"Let's have different color rabbits, George."

"Sure we will," George said sleepily. "Red and blue and green rabbits, Lennie. Millions of 'em."

"Furry ones, George, like I seen in the **fair**⑥ in Sacramento."

"Sure, furry ones."

"'Cause I can **jus' as well**⑦ go away, George, an' live in a cave."

"You can jus' as well go to hell," said George. "Shut up now."

The red light **dimmed**⑧ on the **coals**⑨. Up the hill from the river a coyote **yammered**⑩, and a dog answered from the other side of the stream. The sycamore leaves whispered in a little night **breeze**⑪.

① her 指 fire

② sphere [sfiə] *n.* 范围，领域

③ curling [kə:liŋ] *a.* 弯曲的

④ faint [feint] *a.* 不清楚的，模糊的，隐约的，暗淡的

⑤ glimmer ['glimə] *n.* 微光，微弱的闪光

⑥ fair [fɛə] *n.* 定期集市

⑦ jus' as well = just as well 不必遗憾，正好，幸好，不妨

⑧ dim [dim] *v.* 变暗淡，变模糊

⑨ coal [kəul] *n.* 余火，灰烬

⑩ yammer ['jæmə] *v.*〈口〉〈方〉哀号，呜咽

⑪ breeze [bri:z] *n.* 微风，轻风

会很舒服的。抬头能看到天空，还有树叶。不要再添加柴火了，让火慢慢熄灭掉吧。"

他们在沙地上铺好床，火焰的势头减弱了，火光照亮的范围缩小了。弯曲着的枝丫不见了，只有树干若隐若现。黑暗中伦尼喊了一声："乔治——你睡着了吗？"

"没有啊，干什么？"

"我们养一些不同颜色的兔子吧，乔治。"

"当然会养的，"乔治困倦地说道，"红、蓝和绿色兔子。伦尼，养他几百万只呢。"

"要毛茸茸的兔子，乔治，像我在萨克拉门托¹集市上看到的那种。"

"好的，毛茸茸的兔子。"

"因为我可以离开，乔治，住到山上的洞穴里去。"

"你也可以下地狱去，"乔治说，"现在闭嘴。"

灰烬堆上红光慢慢暗了下来。河畔的山上有一只丛林狼在嗥叫着，河流对岸一只狗在回应着。黑夜的微风中，悬铃木树叶在飒飒作响。

---

1 萨克拉门托是美国加利福尼亚州的首府。

The bunk house was a long, rectangular building. Inside, the walls were **whitewashed**[1] and the floor unpainted. In three walls there were small, square windows, and in the fourth, a solid door with a wooden **latch**[2]. Against the walls were eight **bunks**[3], five of them made up with blankets and the other three showing their **burlap**[4] **ticking**[5]. Over each bunk there was nailed an apple box with the opening forward so that it made two shelves for the personal belongings of the **occupant**[6] of the bunk. And these shelves were loaded with little **articles**[7], soap and **talcum powder**[8], **razors**[9] and those Western magazines ranch men love to read and scoff at and secretly believe. And there were medicines on the shelves, and little **vials**[10], **combs**[11]; and from nails on the box sides, a few **neckties**[12]. Near one wall there was a black **cast-iron**[13] stove, its **stovepipe**[14] going straight up through the ceiling. In the middle of the room stood a big square table **littered with**[15] playing cards, and around it were grouped boxes for the players to sit on.

At about ten o'clock in the morning the sun threw a bright **dust-laden**[16] **bar**[17] through one of the side windows, and in and out of the **beam**[18] flies **shot**[19] like rushing stars.

The wooden latch raised. The door opened and a tall, stoop-shouldered old man came in. He was dressed in blue jeans and he carried a big **push-broom**[20] in his left hand. Behind him came George, and behind George, Lennie.

"The boss was expectin' you last night," the old man said. "He was **sore**[21] as hell when you wasn't here to go out this morning." He pointed with his right arm, and out of the sleeve came a round stick-like **wrist**[22], but no hand. "You can have them two beds there," he said, indicating two bunks near the stove.

· 030 ·

① whitewash ['waitwɔʃ] v. 用石灰水把……刷白，刷石灰水于……
② latch [lætʃ] n. 闩，门闩
③ bunk [bʌŋk] n.〈口〉睡觉处，床
④ burlap ['bə:læp] n. 粗麻布
⑤ ticking ['tikiŋ] n.（做垫套、褥套、枕芯套等的）竖质（条纹）棉布（或亚麻布）
⑥ occupant ['ɔkjup(ə)nt] n. 占用者，居住者
⑦ article ['ɑ:tik(ə)l] n.（物品的）一件，物件
⑧ talcum powder 滑石粉，爽身粉
⑨ razor ['reizə] n. 剃刀
⑩ vial ['vaiəl] n. 小瓶（尤指小药水瓶）
⑪ comb [kəum] n. 梳子
⑫ necktie ['nektai] n. 领带，领结
⑬ cast-iron 铸铁制的
⑭ stovepipe ['stəuvpaip] n.（从火炉通至烟囱或户外的）火炉管
⑮ littered with 使充满
⑯ dust-laden 充满尘埃的
⑰ bar [bɑ:] n.（光、颜色等形成的）线条，条纹，带
⑱ beam [bi:m] n.（日、月、灯等的）光线，光柱
⑲ shot [ʃɔt] v.（shoot 的过去式和过去分词）飞速通过，在……迅速穿过
⑳ push-broom 长柄阔扫帚
㉑ sore [sɔ:] a.〈主美〉生气的，恼火的，反感的
㉒ wrist [rist] n. 腕，腕关节

　　农工宿舍是一幢很长的方形建筑，室内的墙壁用石灰水刷成了白色，地板没有刷过油漆。房间里有三面墙壁上开着正方形的小窗户，第四面墙壁处开了一扇坚固的带木闩的房门。八张床铺靠墙壁摆放着，其中五张床上铺了毯子，另外三张露着粗麻布床单。每张床铺上方都用钉子固定了一只苹果箱，开口对外，形成两层搁板，供床铺的主人摆放个人物品用。搁板上摆满了各种小件物品，有肥皂和爽身粉、剃须刀，还有一些西部杂志，就是那种农工们一面爱读，一面嘲笑，私下里却又相信的杂志。搁板上还摆放着各种药品、小药瓶子、梳子。苹果箱两侧的钉子上挂着几条领带。一面墙壁附近摆放着一个黑色铁火炉，火炉的烟管笔直向上穿过天花板。房间的中央摆放着一张大方桌，上面乱糟糟地堆着扑克牌，桌子四周堆放着苹果箱，供玩牌的人当凳子坐。

　　上午十点钟左右，太阳从一扇边窗投入一道明亮的光柱，光柱中尘埃弥漫，趋光的苍蝇飞进飞出，犹如天空中快速滑过的流星一般。

　　木门闩向上一动，门开了，一个身材高大、肩背佝偻的老人进入室内。他穿着蓝色工装裤，左手拿着一根大扫把。乔治走在他的身后，伦尼走在乔治的身后。

　　"场主指望你们昨晚就到的，"老人说，"但你们没有到，今天上午出不了工，他可是肺都气炸了啊。"他用右臂指了指，袖管里面露出一截圆溜溜像棍子一样的手腕，但没有手掌。"你们睡这儿的两个床铺吧。"他说着，指了指火炉附近的两个床铺。

Of Mice and Men

George stepped over and threw his blankets down on the burlap **sack**① of **straw**② that was a mattress. He looked into his box shelf and then picked a small yellow can from it. "Say. What the hell's this?"

"I don't know," said the old man.

"Says 'positively kills **lice**③, **roaches**④ and other **scourges**⑤.' What the hell kind of bed you giving us, anyways. We don't want no **pants rabbits**⑥."

The old **swamper**⑦ **shifted**⑧ his broom and held it between his elbow and his side while he held out his hand for the can. He studied the label carefully. "Tell you what—" he said finally, "last guy that had this bed was a **blacksmith**⑨— hell of a nice **fella**⑩ and as clean a guy as you want to meet. Used to wash his hands even *after* he ate."

"Then how come he got **graybacks**⑪?" George was **working up** a slow **anger**⑫. Lennie put his bindle on the neighboring bunk and sat down. He watched George with open mouth.

"Tell you what," said the old swamper. "This here blacksmith—name of Whitey—was the kind of guy that would put that stuff around even if there wasn't no bugs—just to make sure, see? Tell you what he used to do—At meals he'd peel his **boil'**⑬ potatoes, an' he'd take out ever' little spot, no matter what kind, before he'd eat it. And if there was a red **splotch**⑭ on an egg, he'd **scrape** it **off**⑮. Finally **quit**⑯ about the food. That's the **kinda**⑰ guy he was—clean. Used **ta**⑱ dress up Sundays even when he wasn't going no place, put on a necktie even, and then set in the bunk house."

"I ain't so sure," said George skeptically. "What did you say he quit for?"

The old man put the yellow can in his pocket, and he rubbed his **bristly**⑲ white whiskers with his **knuckles**⑳. "Why . . . he . . . just quit, the way a guy will. Says it was the food. Just wanted to move. Didn't give no other reason but the food. Just says '**gimme**㉑ my time' one night, the way any guy would."

George lifted his **tick**㉒ and looked underneath it. He leaned over and

① sack [sæk] *n.* 麻袋，粗布袋
② straw [strɔː] *n.* （谷类作物的）禾秆，稻草，麦秆
③ lice [lais] *n.* （louse 的复数）虱
④ roach [rəutʃ] *n.* 〈主美〉（=cockroach）【昆】蟑螂
⑤ scourge [skəːdʒ] *n.* 灾害
⑥ pants rabbits〈俚〉= crab lice［复］（crab louse［单］）毛虱，阴虱
⑦ swamper ['swɔmpə] *n.* 〈美〉干零星杂活的人，帮手，帮工
⑧ shift [ʃift] *v.* 转移，移动
⑨ blacksmith ['blæksmiθ] *n.* 铁匠，锻工
⑩ fella ['felə] *n.* 〈俚〉伙伴，伙计，小伙子
⑪ grayback ['greibæk] *n.* 〈美〉（=greyback）【昆】体虱，衣虱
⑫ work up sb's anger 发脾气
⑬ boil' = boiled
⑭ splotch [splɔtʃ] *n.* 斑点，污点，污渍
⑮ scrape off 刮落，擦去，削掉
⑯ quit [kwit] *v.* 〈口〉离职，辞职
⑰ kinda ['kaində]〈口〉（用在 this 等后面）……的一种，……的一类（=kind of）
⑱ ta = to
⑲ bristly ['brisli] *a.* 短而硬的，刚毛似的
⑳ knuckle ['nʌk(ə)l] *n.* 指节（尤指掌指关节）
㉑ gimme [gimiː]〈口〉= give me（或 give it to me）
㉒ tick [tik] *n.* （坚质棉布做的）垫套，褥套，枕芯套，褥子

乔治走了过去，一把将自己的铺盖卷扔在当床垫的稻草包上。他看了看那个苹果箱做成的搁物架，随即从上面拿起一个黄色的小罐子。"嘿，见鬼，这是什么东西啊？"

"我不知道。"老人说。

"上面写着'保证灭除虱子、蟑螂和其他害虫'。你都安排我们睡什么鬼床铺啊。我们可不想裤裆里生虫子。"

老清扫工把扫把夹在腋下，一边伸手去拿那个罐子。他把上面的标签仔仔细细地看了一番。"告诉你怎么回事吧——"他最后开口道，"上一个睡在这个床铺的人是个铁匠——一个少有的好人呢，可爱干净了，你见了准会喜欢的。他吃过东西后都要洗手的。"

"既然如此，他怎么身上还长虱子了？"乔治越说越气。伦尼把铺盖卷放在旁边的一个床铺上，然后坐了下来。他张着嘴，注视着乔治。

"告诉你怎么回事吧，"老清扫工说，"先前睡在这儿的那个铁匠——姓怀泰——就是那种人，即便身上没有生虱子，也要把这个东西放在旁边——只是为了做到万无一失，明白吗？告诉你他以前都干些什么事吧——吃饭时，他会先剥掉煮熟的土豆的皮，剔掉里面的每一个小黑点，无论那是什么黑点，然后才吃。假如鸡蛋上有个小红点，他也会把它刮掉。最后，因为伙食的原因，他辞职走了。他就是那种人——爱干净。到了星期天，他即便哪儿都不去，也会穿得妥妥当当，甚至还会打上领带，然后坐在宿舍里待着。"

"我可不那么相信呢，"乔治怀疑地说，"你刚才说他因为什么辞职走人了？"

老人把手上那只小黄罐子放进衣服口袋里，用指关节摩挲着自己的白胡茬。"呃……他……就是辞职走人了，跟别人辞职走人没什么两样，说是因为伙食。只是想要换个地方而已。除了说是因为伙食，没有说其他什么理由。那是某天晚上，他只说了'把我的工钱给我'，跟别人说的没什么差别。"

乔治掀起自己床上的粗麻布床单，检查床单下面的

inspected the **sacking**① closely. Immediately Lennie got up and did the same with his bed. Finally George seemed satisfied. He unrolled his bindle and put things on the shelf, his razor and bar of soap, his comb and bottle of pills, his **liniment**② and leather **wristband**③. Then he made his bed up neatly with blankets. The old man said, "I guess the boss'll be out here in a minute. He was sure **burned**④ when you wasn't here this morning. Come right in when we was eatin' breakfast and says, 'Where the hell's them new men?' An' he **give** the **stable**⑤ **buck**⑥ **hell**⑦, too."

George patted a wrinkle out of his bed, and sat down. "Give the stable buck hell?" he asked.

"Sure. Ya see the stable buck's a **nigger**⑧."

"Nigger, huh?"

"Yeah. Nice fella too. Got a **crooked**⑨ back where a horse kicked him. The boss gives him hell when he's mad. But the stable buck don't give a damn about that. He reads a lot. Got books in his room."

"What kind of a guy is the boss?" George asked.

"Well, he's a pretty nice fella. Gets pretty mad sometimes, but he's pretty nice. Tell ya what—know what he done Christmas? **Brang**⑩ a gallon of whisky right in here and says, 'Drink **hearty**⑪, boys. Christmas comes **but**⑫ once a year.'"

"**The hell**⑬ he did! Whole gallon?"

"Yes sir. Jesus, we had fun. They let the nigger come in that night. Little **skinner**⑭ name of Smitty took after the nigger. Done pretty good, too. The guys wouldn't let him use his feet, so the nigger got him. If he **coulda**⑮ used his feet, Smitty says he **woulda**⑯ killed the nigger. The guys said **on account of**⑰ the nigger's got a crooked back, Smitty can't use his feet." He paused in **relish**⑱ of the memory. "After that the guys went into Soledad and **raised hell**⑲. I didn't go in there. I ain't got the poop no more."

Lennie was just finishing making his bed. The wooden latch raised again and the door opened. A little **stocky**⑳ man stood in the open doorway. He wore blue jean trousers, a **flannel**㉑ shirt, a black, unbuttoned vest and a black coat.

① sacking ['sækiŋ] n. 袋布，麻袋布，粗麻布
② liniment ['linim(ə)nt] n.【药】搽剂，擦剂
③ wristband ['ris(t)bænd] n. 腕套
④ burn [bə:n] v. 激怒
⑤ stable ['steib(ə)l] n. 厩，马厩，牛棚，羊棚
⑥ buck [bʌk] n.〈贬〉青年男黑人（或印第安人）
⑦ give sb. hell 给某人吃苦头，使某人很不好受，狠揍某人
⑧ nigger ['nigə] n.〈俚〉〈贬〉老黑，黑人
⑨ crooked ['krukid] a. 变形了的，扭曲的，（因年老）而弯腰曲背的
⑩ brang [bræŋ] v.〈非规范〉（bring 的过去式）带来，拿来，取来
⑪ hearty ['hɑ:ti] a. 强烈的，有力的，尽情的
⑫ but [bʌt; bət] ad. 只，才，仅仅
⑬ the hell 用以加强语气，表示惊讶、不信、厌恶等
⑭ skinner ['skinə] n. 驱赶牲口队的人，驾驭役畜队的人
⑮ coulda = could have（-a [ə] suf.〈口〉代替助动词 have，下同）
⑯ woulda = would have
⑰ on account of 为了……的缘故，因为，由于
⑱ relish ['reliʃ] n.〈喻〉滋味，兴趣，兴味
⑲ raise hell〈口〉大闹起来，大吵大闹，引起骚动，制造麻烦
⑳ stocky ['stɔki] a. 低矮结实的，粗壮的
㉑ flannel ['flæn(ə)l] n. 法兰绒，绒布

情况。他俯下身子，仔细查看稻草垫子。伦尼立刻站起身，学着乔治的样子检查自己的床铺。最后，乔治似乎感到满意了。他打开自己的铺盖卷，把自己的东西摆放在搁物架上：有剃须刀和肥皂，梳子和药瓶，搽剂和皮护腕。他随后整理好床铺，铺上毯子。老人说："我寻思着，场主不一会儿便会来这儿了。他发现你们今天一大早没有出现，可是大动肝火来着。我们当时正在吃早饭，他走了进来，说：'真见鬼，那两个新来的哪儿去了？'还把那个管理马厩的家伙骂了一通。"

乔治轻轻抚平了床上的一道皱痕，然后坐了下来。"把管理马厩的家伙骂了一通？"他问道。

"可不是嘛，你知道吧，管理马厩的家伙是个黑鬼。"

"黑鬼，是吗？"

"是啊，也是个很好的人。背后给马踢了一脚，是个驼背。场主一不高兴就会冲着他骂。管理马厩的家伙才不在乎这个呢。他爱看书，屋子里有很多书呢。"

"场主是个什么样的人？"乔治问。

"他是个挺不错的人，有时候会生气冒火，但人挺不错。告诉你吧——你知道他圣诞节干了什么吗？搞了一加仑的威士忌酒来这儿，嘴里还说：'开怀畅饮吧，伙计们，圣诞节可是一年只有一次呢。'"

"真是不得了啊！整整一加仑吗？"

"可不是嘛，老兄。天哪，我们可有乐子了。他们当晚让那黑鬼也进来了。那个叫斯密蒂的赶牲口的小子与那黑鬼较量，打得可精彩了。大家不允许他用双脚踢，结果那黑鬼把他制服了。斯密蒂说，假如他能够用上双脚，他定会要了黑鬼的命。大家说，既然黑鬼是个驼背，斯密蒂就不能使用双脚了。"他停顿了一下，津津有味地回忆着，"玩完那个之后，大家去了索莱达，狂欢大闹了一场。我没跟着去，因为我没劲儿折腾了。"

这会儿伦尼刚刚铺好自己的床。木门闩又向上动了一下，门开了。一个矮墩墩的男子伫立在敞开着的门口。他穿着蓝色牛仔裤和法兰绒衬衫，敞开套着一件黑色马

· 035 ·

His thumbs were stuck in his belt, on each side of a square steel buckle. On his head was a **soiled**① brown Stetson hat, and he wore high-heeled boots and **spurs**② to prove he was not a **laboring**③ **man**④.

The old swamper looked quickly at him, and then **shuffled**⑤ to the door rubbing his whiskers with his knuckles as he went. "Them guys just come," he said, and shuffled past the boss and out the door.

The boss stepped into the room with the short, quick steps of a fat-legged man. "I wrote Murray and Ready I wanted two men this morning. You got your work **slips**⑥?" George reached into his pocket and **produced**⑦ the slips and handed them to the boss. "It wasn't Murray and Ready's fault. Says right here on the slip that you was to be here for work this morning."

George looked down at his feet. "Bus driver give us **a bum steer**⑧," he said. "We **hadda**⑨ walk ten miles. Says we was here when we wasn't. We couldn't get no rides in the morning."

The boss **squinted**⑩ his eyes. "Well, I had to send out the grain teams **short**⑪ two **buckers**⑫. Won't do any good to go out now till after dinner." He pulled his time book out of his pocket and opened it where a pencil was stuck between the **leaves**⑬. George scowled meaningfully at Lennie, and Lennie nodded to show that he understood. The boss licked his pencil. "What's your name?"

"George Milton."

"And what's yours?"

George said, "His name's Lennie Small."

The names were entered in the book. "Le's see, this is the twentieth, noon the twentieth." He closed the book. "Where you boys been working?"

"**Up**⑭ around Weed," said George.

"You, too?" to Lennie.

"Yeah, him too," said George.

The boss pointed a playful finger at Lennie. "He ain't **much of a**⑮ talker, is he?"

① soil [sɔil] v. 弄脏，弄污
② spur [spə:] n. 踢马刺，靴刺
③ laboring ['leibəriŋ] a. 劳动的，从事劳动的
④ laboring man 体力劳动者，工人
⑤ shuffle ['ʃʌf(ə)l] v. 拖着脚走
⑥ slip [slip] n.（布、纸、金属等的）条
⑦ produce [prə'dju:s] v. 出示，拿出
⑧ a bum steer 错误的指导；bum [bʌm] a. 假的，错误的；steer [stiə] n.〈美口〉关于驾驶（或引路）的指示
⑨ hadda = had to
⑩ squint [skwint] v. 眯（起）眼，眨（眼）
⑪ short [ʃɔ:t] a. 短缺的，不足的
⑫ bucker ['bʌkə(r)] n.（煤、农产品等的）装运工
⑬ leaf [li:f] n.（书刊等的）张
⑭ up [ʌp] ad. 在北方
⑮ much of a〈口〉[通常用于否定句或疑问句]了不起的，十分好的

甲和一件黑色外套。他把两个大拇指插在腰部的皮带内，一边靠着一个正方形的不锈钢皮带扣。他头上戴着一顶脏兮兮的棕色斯泰森毡帽[1]，脚上穿着高跟的靴子，还带了马刺，这表明他不是个干活儿的农工。

老清扫工飞快地看了他一眼，随即拖着脚步走向门口，一边走一边用指关节摩挲着自己的胡须。"这两个人刚来。"他边说边拖着脚步从场主身边走过，出门去了。

场主走进房间，迈着两腿粗壮的那种人特有的又小又快的步子。"我给默里-雷迪写信说我今天上午需要两个人。你们领到了工作卡吗？"乔治伸手从衣服口袋里掏出了两张工作卡，递给场主。"看来并不是默里-雷迪公司的过错。这工卡上说了，你们今天上午该在此地上工的。"

乔治低头看着自己的双脚。"但公交车司机给我们指错了路，"他说，"我们不得不走了十英里路呢。他说我们到了目的地，但其实并没有到。我们早上也搭不到车。"

场主眯起了双眼。"好嘛，我只得让收麦子的人马在缺少两个人的情况下出发了。现在去也没有用了，等到吃了午饭再说吧。"他从衣服口袋里掏出记工本，翻到了夹着一支铅笔的那一页。乔治别有意味地向伦尼皱起眉头，伦尼点了点头，心领神会。场主舔了一下铅笔。"你叫什么名字？"

"乔治·米尔顿。"

"你又叫什么名字呢？"

乔治说："他叫伦尼·斯莫尔。"

场主把两个人的名字记在了记工本上。"让我瞧瞧，今天是20日，20日中午。"他合上了本子。"你们两个人先前在哪儿干活儿来着？"

"北方威德一带。"乔治说。

"你也是吗？"他问伦尼。

"不错，他也是。"乔治说。

场主伸出一根手指，玩儿闹似的指向伦尼。"他不爱说话，对吧？"

---
1 一种美国西部牛仔戴的宽边高顶毡帽。

"No, he ain't, but he's sure **a hell of**① a good worker. Strong as a bull."

Lennie smiled to himself. "Strong as a bull," he repeated.

George scowled at him, and Lennie dropped his head in shame at having forgotten.

The boss said suddenly, "Listen, Small!" Lennie raised his head. "What can you do?"

In a panic, Lennie looked at George for help. "He can do anything you tell him," said George. "He's a good skinner. He can **rassel**② grain bags, drive a **cultivator**③. He can do anything. Just give him a try."

The boss turned on George. "Then why don't you let him answer? What you trying to put over?"

George broke in loudly, "Oh! I ain't saying he's bright. He ain't. But I say he's a God damn good worker. He can put up a four hundred pound **bale**④."

The boss deliberately put the little book in his pocket. He **hooked**⑤ his thumbs in his belt and squinted one eye nearly closed. "Say—what you sellin'?"

"Huh?"

"I said what **stake**⑥ you got in this guy? You takin' his pay away from him?"

"No, 'course I ain't. Why ya think I'm sellin' him out?"

"Well, I never seen one guy take so much trouble for another guy. I just like to know what your interest is."

George said, "He's my . . . cousin. I told his old lady I'd take care of him. He got kicked in the head by a horse when he was a kid. He's awright. Just ain't bright. But he can do anything you tell him."

The boss turned half away. "Well, God knows he don't need any brains to buck **barley**⑦ bags. But don't you try to put nothing over, Milton. I **got my eye**⑧ on you. Why'd you quit in Weed?"

① a hell of a 极好的，极度的

② rassel ['ræsl] v.〈美〉〈非规范〉= wrestle 使劲搬动（或移动）

③ cultivator ['kʌltiveitə] n. 耕耘机

④ bale [beil] n.（打扎成的货物）大捆，大包

⑤ hook [huk] v. 使成钩状

⑥ stake [steik] n. 利害关系

⑦ barley ['bɑ:li] n. 大麦，大麦粒

⑧ get sb's eye on = have an eye on 注视，注意，留心观察，提防

"不错，他不爱说话，但他无疑是个很棒的农工，强壮如牛呢。"

伦尼自个儿笑了起来。"强壮如牛呢。"他重复了一声。

乔治朝着他皱眉头，伦尼因为自己忘记了嘱咐羞得耷拉下脑袋。

场主突然说："听着，斯莫尔！"伦尼抬起头，"你会干什么呢？"

伦尼慌了神，看向乔治寻求帮助。"无论您吩咐他干什么，他都会干，"乔治说，"他是个赶牲口的好手，扛得起大麦包，开得了耕作机。他什么活儿都会干。您就让他试试吧。"

场主朝乔治转过身。"那你为什么不让他自己回答呢？你想要耍什么滑头呢？"

乔治大声插话说："噢！我并没有说他很聪明。他确实不聪明。但是，我的意思是，他干起活儿来是一把好手。他一次能够扛起四百磅的大麦包呢。"

场主不慌不忙地把记工本放进衣服口袋里，勾起两只拇指重新插入皮带里，眯缝起一只眼睛。"我说——你在兜售什么呢？"

"啊？"

"我说，你从这个家伙身上能够捞到什么好处？你是不是要把他的报酬据为己有呢？"

"不，我当然不会做这样的事情。您为何会觉得我在兜售他呢？"

"哦，我从未见过哪个人会为了另外一个人这样劳心费神的。我只是想要知道，你能得到什么好处。"

乔治说："他是我……表弟。我对他老娘说过了，我会照顾好他的。他小时候被马踢到了脑袋。人倒没什么事儿，就是不够聪明。但无论您吩咐他干什么，他都干得了。"

场主转过半个身子。"好啦，老天都知道扛大麦包时用不着他动脑筋，但你不要耍滑头啊，米尔顿。我可是会留意你的。你们为什么不在威德干了？"

"Job was done," said George **promptly**①.

"What kinda job?"

"We . . . we was diggin' a **cesspool**②."

"All right. But don't try to put nothing over, 'cause you can't **get away with**③ nothing. I seen wise guys before. Go on out with the grain teams after dinner. They're pickin' up barley at the **threshing machine**④. Go out with Slim's team."

"Slim?"

"Yeah. Big tall skinner. You'll see him at dinner." He turned abruptly and went to the door, but before he went out he turned and looked for a long moment at the two men.

When the sound of his footsteps had **died away**⑤, George turned on Lennie. "So you wasn't gonna say a word. You was gonna leave your big **flapper**⑥ shut and leave me do the talkin'. Damn near lost us the job."

Lennie stared hopelessly at his hands. "I forgot, George."

"Yeah, you forgot. You always forget, an' I got to **talk** you **out of**⑦ it." He sat down heavily on the bunk. "Now he's got his eye on us. Now we got to be careful and not make no **slips**⑧. You keep your big flapper shut after this." He fell morosely silent.

"George."

"What you want now?"

"I wasn't kicked in the head with no horse, was I, George?"

"Be a damn good thing if you was," George said **viciously**⑨. "Save ever'body a hell of a lot of trouble."

"You said I was your cousin, George."

"Well, that was a lie. An' I'm **damn**⑩ glad it was. If I was a relative of yours I'd shoot myself." He stopped suddenly, stepped to the open front door and peered out. "Say, what the hell you doin' listenin'?"

The old man came slowly into the room. He had his broom in his hand. And at his heels there walked a **dragfooted**⑪ sheepdog, gray of **muzzle**⑫, and

① promptly ['prɔm(p)tli] ad. 敏捷地，及时地，迅速地

② cesspool ['sespu:l] n. 污水池，化粪池

③ get away with 〈口〉做成（坏事或错事而未被发觉或受处分）

④ threshing machine 脱粒机，脱谷机

⑤ die away 变弱，渐渐停止，逐渐消失

⑥ flapper ['flæpə] n. 嘴巴

⑦ talk out of 说服……放弃……

⑧ slip [slip] n. 疏漏，差错

⑨ viciously ['viʃəsli] ad. 恶毒地，凶残地

⑩ damn [dæm] = damned ad.〈口〉极，非常

⑪ dragfooted ['drægfutid] a. 拖沓着脚的

⑫ muzzle ['mʌzl] n.（四足动物的）口鼻部

"那儿的活儿都干完了。"乔治立刻回答说。
"干的什么活儿？"
"我们……我们挖了一个污水池。"
"好吧，不过，不要试图耍滑头，因为你们跑不掉的。聪明的人我以前可是见过的。吃过午饭后跟着收麦子的人马出工吧。他们在脱粒机旁拾大麦。你们跟斯利姆一组。"
"斯利姆？"
"对呀。赶牲口的大个子。你午饭时就能见到他了。"他突然转身朝着门口走去，但出门前又回过身，盯着两个人看了好一阵子。

等到听不见他的脚步声之后，乔治朝伦尼转过身。"还说你一声都不会吭呢。还说你会闭上你这张大臭嘴，让我来说。该死的，差点儿就把这差事弄丢了。"

伦尼失望地盯着自己的双手看。"我忘记了，乔治。"

"是啊，你忘记了。你总是会忘记，临了还要我来提醒你。"他重重地坐到床铺上，"看吧，他现在注意上我们啦，我们得小心谨慎点儿，别出任何差错。从今往后，你得闭上你这张大臭嘴。"他沉下脸，不说话了。

"乔治。"
"干什么？"
"我脑袋上没有被马踢过，对吧，乔治？"
"要是踢过，那才是天大的好事呢，"乔治恶狠狠地说，"给别人省了一大堆的麻烦。"
"你说我是你表弟，乔治。"
"这个嘛，那是句谎话。我他妈的真高兴这是句谎话，我若真有你这么个亲戚，我宁可一枪毙了自己。"他突然停住不说了，走到敞开着前门口，探着头朝外面看了看。"嘿，见鬼，你偷听什么呢？"

那个老人缓慢地走进房间。他手里拿着扫把，后面跟着一条牧羊犬，牧羊犬步伐拖沓，口鼻部位呈灰色，一双昏聩的老眼已经失明了。牧羊犬步履蹒跚，一瘸一拐地走到房间的一侧，躺下来，自顾自地轻声咕哝着，

with pale, blind old eyes. The dog struggled **lamely**① to the side of the room and lay down, **grunting**② softly to himself and licking his **grizzled**③, **moth-eaten coat**⑤. The swamper watched him until he was settled. "I wasn't listenin'. I was jus' standin' in the shade a minute scratchin' my dog. I jus' now finished **swampin'**⑥ out the **wash house**⑦."

"You was **pokin'**⑧ your big ears into our business," George said. "I don't like nobody to get **nosey**⑨."

The old man looked uneasily from George to Lennie, and then back. "I jus' come there," he said. "I didn't hear nothing you guys was sayin'. I ain't interested in nothing you was sayin'. A guy on a ranch don't never listen nor he don't **ast**⑩ no questions."

"Damn right he don't," said George, slightly **mollified**⑪, "not if he wants to stay workin' long." But he was reassured by the swamper's defense. "Come on in and set down a minute," he said. "That's a hell of an old dog."

"Yeah. I had **'im**⑫ ever since he was a pup. God, he was a good sheepdog when he was younger." He stood his broom against the wall and he rubbed his white **bristled**⑬ cheek with his knuckles. "How'd you like the boss?" he asked.

"Pretty good. Seemed awright."

"He's a nice fella," the swamper agreed. "You got to take him right."

At that moment a young man came into the bunk house; a thin young man with a brown face, with brown eyes and a head of tightly **curled**⑭ hair. He wore a work glove on his left hand, and, like the boss, he wore high-heeled boots. "Seen my old man?" he asked.

The swamper said, "He was here jus' a minute ago, Curley. Went over to the **cook house**⑮, I think."

"I'll try to catch him," said Curley. His eyes passed over the new men and he stopped. He glanced coldly at George and then at Lennie. His arms gradually bent at the elbows and his hands closed into fists. He **stiffened**⑯ and went into a slight **crouch**⑰. His glance was at once **calculating**⑱ and **pugnacious**⑲.

① lamely ['leimli] *ad.* 跛地，瘸地，残废地
② grunt [grʌnt] *v.* 像猪一样发呼噜声，咕哝，嘟哝
③ grizzled ['griz(ə)ld] *a.* 灰的，花白的，浅灰的，有灰斑的
④ moth-eaten ['mɔθ,i:tən] *a.* 虫蛀了似的，破烂的
⑤ coat [kəut] *n.*（动物的）皮毛
⑥ swamp [swɔmp] *v.* 淹没，浸没
⑦ wash house ['wɔʃhaus] *n.* 洗衣房
⑧ poke [pəuk] *v.* 把……指（或伸）向
⑨ nosey ['nəuzi] *a.* =nosy〈口〉爱打听的，好管闲事的
⑩ ast = ask
⑪ mollify ['mɔlifai] *v.* 使平静，抚慰
⑫ 'im = him
⑬ bristle ['brisl] *a.*（毛发等）直立
⑭ curl [kə:l] *v.* 使（头发）变鬈
⑮ cook house 厨房，伙房
⑯ stiffen ['stif(ə)n] *v.* 使僵硬，使绷紧
⑰ crouch [krautʃ] *n.* 蹲（伏）（的姿势），蜷伏（的姿势），弯腰屈膝（的姿势）
⑱ calculating ['kælkjuleitiŋ] *a.* 经过仔细分析（或打算）的，审慎的
⑲ pugnacious [pʌg'neiʃəs] *a.* 好斗的，好争吵的，好战的

舔着自己灰白而且生了虱子的皮毛。老清扫工注视着牧羊犬，直到它消停下来才移开目光。"我没有偷听，只是在背阴处站了一会儿，给我的狗梳理一下皮毛。我刚刚才打扫完洗涤房来着。"

"你刚刚竖起你的两只大耳朵偷听我们说话来着，"乔治说，"我不喜欢管闲事的人。"

老人局促地从乔治看向伦尼，又从伦尼看向乔治。"我刚刚才来，"他说，"你们两个人说的，我什么也没有听见。你们说了什么，我一点儿都不感兴趣。农场上干活儿的人绝不会偷听别人说话，也不会问人家问题。"

"这样做才他妈的对呢，"乔治说，态度稍稍平静了一点儿，"他们若是想要在农场上待得长久，就不能干那样的事情。"不过，老清扫工说明了情况后，乔治放下了心。"进来待一会儿吧，"他说，"这可是条老掉了牙的牧羊犬呢。"

"是呢，它还是幼崽时我就养着它啦。天哪，年轻力壮时，它可真是条优秀的牧羊犬啊。"老人把扫把靠墙放好，用指关节摩挲着自己留着白胡茬的脸颊。"你觉得场主人怎么样？"他问道。

"挺好的。看起来人挺不错啊。"

"他是个挺不错的人，"老清扫工赞同道，"你得对他忠诚老实。"

正说着，一个年轻人走进了宿舍。这年轻人身材单薄，脸庞黝黑，生了一双棕色的眼睛和一头浓密的鬈发。他左手戴着工作手套，脚上像场主一样，也穿着高跟的靴子。"看见我老爸了吗？"年轻人问。

老清扫工说："他刚才还在这儿呢，柯利。我估计，这会儿到厨房去了。"

"那我去找他。"柯利说。他的目光掠过两个新来的，然后停住不动了。他神情冷淡，看了看乔治，然后又看了看伦尼。他曲起胳膊肘，双手紧握成拳。他绷紧了身子，全身微蹲。他目光立刻流露出了挑衅的意味。伦尼被他看得局促不安，两只脚紧张地挪来挪去。

· 043 ·

Lennie **squirmed**① under the look and shifted his feet nervously. Curley stepped **gingerly**② close to him. "You the new guys the old man was waitin' for?"

"We just come in," said George.

"Let the big guy talk."

Lennie twisted with embarrassment.

George said, "**S'pose**③ he don't want to talk?"

Curley **lashed**④ his body around. "By Christ, he's gotta talk when he's spoke to. What the hell are you gettin' into it for?"

"We travel together," said George coldly.

"Oh, so it's that way."

George was tense, and motionless. "Yeah, it's that way."

Lennie was looking helplessly to George for instruction.

"An' you won't let the big guy talk, is that it?"

"He can talk if he wants to tell you anything." He nodded slightly to Lennie.

"We jus' come in," said Lennie softly.

Curley stared **levelly**⑤ at him. "Well, **nex'**⑥ time you answer when you're spoke to." He turned toward the door and walked out, and his elbows were still bent out a little.

George watched him out, and then he turned back to the swamper. "Say, what the hell's he got on his shoulder? Lennie didn't do nothing to him."

The old man looked cautiously at the door to make sure no one was listening. "That's the boss's son," he said quietly. "Curley's pretty **handy**⑦. He done quite a bit in the **ring**⑧. He's a **lightweight**⑨, and he's handy."

"Well, let him be handy," said George. "He don't have to take after Lennie. Lennie didn't do nothing to him. What's he got against Lennie?"

The swamper considered . . . "Well . . . tell you what. Curley's like a lot of little guys. He hates big guys. He's **alla time**⑩ **picking**⑪ **scraps**⑫ with big guys. Kind of like he's mad at 'em because he ain't a big guy. You seen little guys like that, ain't you? Always **scrappy**⑬?"

"Sure," said George. "I seen plenty tough little guys. But this Curley better

① squirm [skwə:m] v. 局促不安
② gingerly ['dʒindʒəli] ad. 极为谨慎地，小心翼翼地，轻手轻脚地

③ s'pose [spəuz] v.〈口〉= suppose
④ lash [læʃ] v. 驱使，激起

⑤ levelly ['levəli] ad. 坚定地，不动摇地
⑥ nex'= next

⑦ handy ['hændi] a. 灵敏的
⑧ ring [riŋ] n.（呈方形并由绳子拦隔的）拳击台
⑨ lightweight ['laitweit] n.（体重为57—60公斤的）轻量级（业余拳击手）
⑩ alla time = all the time
⑪ pick [pik] v. 寻找……的口实，寻（衅），找（毛病）
⑫ scrap [skræp] n.〈口〉争吵，打架
⑬ scrappy ['skræpi] a.〈美口〉爱吵架的，好斗的

柯利小心翼翼向前靠近他。"你们就是我老爸等待的新来的吗？"

"我们刚刚到的。"乔治说。

"让这个大个子说话。"

伦尼扭动着身子，显得很窘迫。

乔治说："假如他不想说呢？"

柯利猛地转过身。"天哪，别人跟他讲话，他就得回答。真见鬼，你从中掺和什么啊？"

"我们一块儿来的。"乔治说，语气很冷漠。

"噢，原来如此呢。"

乔治僵着身子，一动不动。"对呀，就是如此。"

伦尼一脸无助地看着乔治，等他吩咐。

"而你不让大个子开口说话，是这么回事吧？"

"他若是有什么事情要告诉你，他可以说。"他稍稍向伦尼点了点头。

"我们刚刚到的。"伦尼轻声说。

柯利一动不动地盯着对方。"那下次有人对你说话时，你要回应才是。"他转向门口，走了出去，两个胳膊肘仍然弯曲着。

乔治目送他走出房间，然后回身对着老清扫工。"嘿，他这到底是怎么啦？伦尼又没有招惹他。"

老人谨慎地看了看门口，确认没有人在偷听。"这是场主的儿子，"他悄声说，"柯利身手挺敏捷的，拳击场上有两下子，是个轻量级的，身手敏捷着呢。"

"得了吧，让他身手敏捷好啦，"乔治说，"他用不着与伦尼较量。伦尼又没有招惹他。他为什么要针对伦尼呢？"

老清扫工思忖着……"嗯……实话告诉你吧。柯利像许多身材矮小的人一样，痛恨大个子，总爱挑衅大个子，有点儿像是因为自己块头不大，所以才对人家发火似的。你以前见过他那样的小个子，对吧？总喜欢与别人干架。"

"肯定见过，"乔治说，"我见过许多强悍的小个子。

Of Mice and Men

not make no mistakes about Lennie. Lennie ain't handy, but this Curley **punk**① is gonna get hurt if he **messes around with**② Lennie."

"Well, Curley's pretty handy," the swamper said skeptically. "Never did seem right to me. S'pose Curley **jumps**③ a big guy an' **licks**④ him. Ever'body says what a **game**⑤ guy Curley is. And s'pose he does the same thing and gets licked. Then ever'body says the big guy oughtta pick somebody his own size, and maybe they **gang up on**⑥ the big guy. Never did seem right to me. Seems like Curley ain't givin' nobody a chance."

George was watching the door. He said **ominously**⑦, "Well, he better watch out for Lennie. Lennie ain't no fighter, but Lennie's strong and quick and Lennie don't know no rules." He walked to the square table and sat down on one of the boxes. He gathered some of the cards together and **shuffled**⑧ them.

The old man sat down on another box. "Don't tell Curley I said none of this. He'd **slough**⑨ me. He just don't give a damn. Won't ever get **canned**⑩ 'cause his old man's the boss."

George **cut**⑪ the cards and began turning them over, looking at each one and throwing it down on a pile. He said, "This guy Curley sounds like a son-of-a-bitch to me. I don't like mean little guys."

"Seems to me like he's worse lately," said the swamper. "He got married a couple of weeks ago. Wife lives over in the boss's house. Seems like Curley is **cockier**⑫ **'n**⑬ ever since he got married."

George grunted, "Maybe he's showin' off for his wife."

The swamper **warmed**⑭ to his **gossip**⑮. "You seen that glove on his left hand?"

"Yeah. I seen it."

"Well, that glove's **fulla**⑯ **vaseline**⑰."

"Vaseline? What the hell for?"

"Well, I tell ya what—Curley says he's keepin' that hand soft for his wife."

① punk [pʌŋk] n.〈主美口〉不中用的人
② mess around (with)〈美口〉烦扰, 惹
③ jump [dʒump] v.〈口〉猛地扑向, 突然袭击
④ lick [lik] v.〈口〉打败
⑤ game [geim] a. 斗鸡般的, 好斗的, 有精力的
⑥ gang up on 结成一伙, 联合起来
⑦ ominously ['ɔminəsli] a. 预示地, 预兆地
⑧ shuffle ['ʃʌf(ə)l] v. 洗（牌）
⑨ slough [slʌf] v. 使陷入泥坑, 使被泥潭吞没, 使沦入绝境
⑩ canned [kænd] a.〈美俚〉被解雇的, 被开除的
⑪ cut [kʌt] v. 切（牌）, 随意抽（一张牌）
⑫ cockier ['kɔkiə(r)] a. cocky ['kɔki] 的比较级,〈口〉骄傲自大的, 自以为是的, 趾高气扬的
⑬ 'n [ən] conj.〈口〉= than
⑭ warm [wɔ:m] v. 兴奋, 激动, 变得热情, 变得感兴趣（to）
⑮ gossip ['gɔsip] n. 流言蜚语, 闲言碎语的题材
⑯ fulla = full of
⑰ vaseline ['væsi,li:n] n. 凡士林

但是，这个柯利最好不要以为伦尼好欺负。伦尼身手不敏捷，但柯利要是故意去招惹他，受伤害的可是柯利自己呢。"

"得了吧，柯利的身手可是挺敏捷的。"老清扫工怀疑地说，"我一直觉得很不公平。假如柯利进攻某个大个子，而且打败了对方，那大家就会说，柯利真的很厉害。而假如他同样这么干，却被对方打败了，那么大家就会说，大个子应该与跟自己个头相当的人对阵才是，说不定他们还会合起来围攻那个大个子呢。我觉得这样做很不公平。看起来，柯利好像从来不给任何人机会似的。"

乔治注视着房门口。他带着警告的口气说："不管怎么说，他最好小心提防着点儿伦尼。伦尼不爱打架，但他身体强壮，行动迅速，完全不懂什么规矩。"说完，他走到那张方桌旁，坐到桌边的一个苹果箱上。他把上面的一些扑克牌拢到一起，洗起牌来。

老清扫工坐到另外一个苹果箱上。"别告诉柯利我说了这些话，否则，他会打死我的。他才不会在乎呢。谁也没法对他怎么样，因为他老爸是场主。"

乔治随意抽出一些牌，然后翻过来，每一张都看了看，再扔到一叠上面。他说："我觉得，那个柯利就是个狗娘养的。我不喜欢品性卑劣的小个子。"

"我觉得，他最近越来越变本加厉了，"老清扫工说，"他两个星期前结了婚。他老婆住在那边场主的住宅里。柯利婚后似乎越发目中无人了。"

乔治咕哝着说："他可能是想要在老婆面前逞威风吧。"

老清扫工听到他这句闲话，越发起劲了。"你看见他左手戴的那只手套了吗？"

"嗯，看见了。"

"哎呀，那手套上面涂满了凡士林呢。"

"凡士林？涂那玩意儿有什么用？"

"哈哈，告诉你怎么回事吧——柯利说了，他保养那只手是为了他老婆。"

· 047 ·

George studied the cards **absorbedly**①. "That's a dirty thing to tell around," he said.

The old man was reassured. He had drawn a **derogatory**② statement from George. He felt safe now, and he spoke more confidently. "Wait'll you see Curley's wife."

George cut the cards again and put out a **solitaire**③ **lay**④, slowly and deliberately. "**Purty**⑤?" he asked casually.

"Yeah. Purty . . . but—"

George studied his cards. "But what?"

"Well—she got the eye."

"Yeah? Married two weeks and got the eye? Maybe that's why Curley's pants is full of ants."

"I seen her **give** Slim **the eye**⑥. Slim's a **jerkline**⑦ skinner. Hell of a nice fella. Slim don't need to wear no high-heeled boots on a grain team. I seen her give Slim the eye. Curley never seen it. An' I seen her give Carlson the eye."

George pretended a lack of interest. "Looks like we was gonna have fun."

The swamper stood up from his box. "Know what I think?" George did not answer. "Well, I think Curley's married . . . a **tart**⑧."

"He ain't the first," said George. "There's plenty done that."

The old man moved toward the door, and his ancient dog lifted his head and peered about, and then got painfully to his feet to follow. "I gotta be settin' out the wash basins for the guys. The teams'll be in before long. You guys gonna buck barley?"

"Yeah."

"You won't tell Curley nothing I said?"

"Hell no."

"Well, you look her over, mister. You see if she ain't a tart." He stepped out the door into the brilliant sunshine.

George laid down his cards thoughtfully, turned his piles of three. He built

① absorbedly [əb'sɔ:bdli] *ad.* 极感兴趣地，全神贯注地

② derogatory [di'rɔgət(ə)ri] *a.* 减损的，毁损的，有辱人格的

③ solitaire ['sɔlitɛə; sɔli'tɛə] *n.* 单人纸牌戏

④ lay [lei] *n.* 放置方式，放置方向

⑤ purty ['pə:ti] *a.* 〈美〉〈方〉(非规范) = pretty

⑥ give sb. the eye 〈口〉对某人做媚眼，向某人送秋波

⑦ jerkline ['dʒə:klain] *n.* 原用于美国西部地区的一种单根缰绳

⑧ tart [tɑ:t] *n.* 〈俚〉〈贬〉妓女，娼妇，放荡的女人

乔治聚精会神地研究着扑克牌。"这样恶心的事情也到处炫耀。"他说。

老人终于安心了，因为他从乔治的嘴里套出了一句贬损人的话。他现在感觉安全了，于是更加推心置腹地说："等你见到柯利的老婆再说吧。"

乔治又开始随意抽出一些牌，慢条斯理，不慌不忙，一张一张摆成接龙状态。"漂亮吗？"他不经意地问了一声。

"嗯，漂亮着呢……不过——"

乔治研究着自己手上的扑克牌。"不过什么？"

"呃——她跟别人眉来眼去。"

"嗯？结婚才两个星期，就跟别人眉来眼去了？或许这便是为什么柯利像是裤裆里面爬满了蚂蚁似的吧。"

"我看见她给斯利姆抛媚眼。斯利姆是个驾驭牲口的高手，极好的一个人。斯利姆不用穿高跟靴子就能够管好收大麦的队伍。我看见她对着斯利姆抛媚眼。这种情形柯利是不可能看到的。我还看到她给卡尔森抛媚眼来着。"

乔治假装不感兴趣。"看起来我们有好戏看啦。"

老清扫工从坐着的箱子上起身。"知道我是怎么想的吗？"乔治没有接话。"这么说吧，我认为柯利娶了个……婊子。"

"他可不是第一个呢，"乔治说，"娶个婊子做老婆的人多了去了。"

老人走向门口，他那条老态龙钟的牧羊犬抬起头看了看四周，随即痛苦地爬起来跟了上去。"我得给那些家伙准备洗脸盆去了。收大麦的人马很快就要回来了。你们两个也是去扛大麦包的吧？"

"不错。"

"我说的话你不会告诉柯利吧？"

"当然不会了。"

"那好，你回头看看她吧，先生。你看看她是不是个婊子。"他出了门，走进明媚的阳光里。

乔治一边思索一边摆弄着手上的扑克牌，他把牌分

· 049 ·

four **clubs**① on his **ace**② pile. The sun square was on the floor now, and the flies **whipped**③ through it like sparks. A sound of **jingling**④ **harness**⑤ and the **croak**⑥ of heavy-laden **axles**⑦ sounded from outside. From the distance came a clear call. "Stable buck—ooh, sta-able buck!" And then, "Where the hell is that God damn nigger?"

George stared at his solitaire lay, and then he **flounced**⑧ the cards together and turned around to Lennie. Lennie was lying down on the bunk watching him.

"Look, Lennie! This here ain't no set up. I'm scared. You gonna have trouble with that Curley guy. I seen that kind before. He was kinda **feelin'** you **out**⑨. He figures he's got you scared and he's gonna take a **sock**⑩ at you the first chance he gets."

Lennie's eyes were frightened. "I don't want no trouble," he said **plaintively**⑪. "Don't let him sock me, George."

George got up and went over to Lennie's bunk and sat down on it. "I hate that kinda bastard," he said. "I seen plenty of 'em. Like the old guy says, Curley don't take no chances. He always wins." He thought for a moment. "If he **tangles**⑫ with you, Lennie, we're gonna get the can. Don't make no mistake about that. He's the boss's son. Look, Lennie. You try to keep away from him, will you? Don't never speak to him. If he comes in here you move clear to the other side of the room. Will you do that, Lennie?"

"I don't want no trouble," Lennie **mourned**⑬. "I never done nothing to him."

"Well, that won't do you no good if Curley wants to **plug**⑭ himself up for a fighter. Just don't have nothing to do with him. Will you remember?"

"Sure, George. I ain't gonna say a word."

The sound of the approaching grain teams was louder, **thud**⑮ of big **hooves**⑯ on hard ground, drag of brakes and the jingle of **trace**⑰ chains. Men were calling back and forth from the teams. George, sitting on the bunk beside Lennie, frowned as he thought. Lennie asked timidly, "You ain't mad, George?"

① club [klʌb] n.【牌】（一张）梅花
② ace [eis] n. A 纸牌
③ whip [wip] v. 一下子猛地移动
④ jingling ['dʒiŋliŋ] a. 叮当响的，发叮当声的
⑤ harness ['hɑ:nis] n. 马具，挽具
⑥ croak [krəuk] n.（蛙、鸦等的）呱呱叫声，低沉而沙哑的说话声
⑦ axle ['æks(ə)l] n.【机】轴，车轴
⑧ flounce [flauns] v. 急动
⑨ feel out 试探出……的意见（或态度），弄清楚
⑩ sock [sɔk] n. 打击，猛击
⑪ plaintively ['pleintivli] ad. 表示痛苦地，伤心地，表示悲伤地，悲哀地
⑫ tangle ['tæŋg(ə)l] v.〈口〉争吵，发生争论
⑬ mourn [mɔ:n] v. 悲哀地发出（或说出、唱出）
⑭ plug [plʌg] v.〈喻〉把……作插头般接入
⑮ thud [θʌd] n. 砰的一声，嘭的一声
⑯ hooves [hu:vz] n.（hoof 的复数形式）（马等有蹄动物的）蹄
⑰ trace [treis] n. 挽绳，缰绳

成三叠，在一叠 A 中摆了四张梅花。方形的太阳光柱现在移到了地板上，苍蝇像火花似的在光柱中蹿来蹿去。室外传来马具的叮当声和负重车轴的嘎吱声，远处还传来清晰的呼喊声。"马厩黑鬼——嗬，马——厩——黑鬼！"随后又是一声，"该死的，那黑鬼哪儿去啦？"

乔治盯着单人接龙牌戏的牌叠看了一会儿，随即把扑克牌拢到一块儿，朝伦尼转过身。伦尼正躺在床上注视着他。

"听着，伦尼！这个地方不好立足，我很害怕呢。你会跟那个柯利弄出麻烦来的。这样的事情我以前是见过的。他刚才是在试探你呢。他心里盘算着，先让你怕了他，日后一旦逮着了机会就会揍你一顿。"

伦尼眼中露出惧色。"我不想惹麻烦，"他痛苦地说，"别让他揍我，乔治。"

乔治站起身，走到伦尼的床边，坐了下去。"我痛恨那种混蛋，"他说，"那样的人我见得多呢。正如那个老清扫工说的，柯利不会让任何人有赢他的机会。他横竖是个赢。"乔治思忖了片刻，"假如他与你打起来，伦尼，我们会被解雇的。这一点千万不要搞错了。他可是场主的儿子。听好了，伦尼。你离他远点儿，好吗？绝不要和他说话。假如他来这儿，你就到房间的另一头去。你做得到吗，伦尼？"

"我不想惹麻烦，"伦尼悲伤地说，"我根本没有招惹他。"

"唉，假如柯利存心想要找人打架，你即便不招惹他也没有用。你只管不要和他有任何瓜葛。记住了吗？"

"记住了，乔治。我不会吭一声的。"

收大麦的队伍临近时传来的声音越来越响亮，那是牲口大蹄子踩踏在硬地面上的嘚嘚声，车闸拉动时发出的嘎吱声，系牲口的缰绳链子抖动时发出的叮当声。队伍中的农工们前呼后喊。乔治坐在床沿上伦尼的身边，眉头紧锁，想着心事。伦尼怯生生地问："你没有生气吧，乔治？"

"I ain't mad at you. I'm mad at this here Curley bastard. I hoped we was gonna get a little stake together—maybe a hundred dollars." His tone grew decisive. "You keep away from Curley, Lennie."

"Sure I will, George. I won't say a word."

"Don't let him **pull** you **in**①—but—if the son-of-a-bitch socks you—**let 'im have it**②."

"Let 'im have what, George?"

"Never mind, never mind. I'll tell you when. I hate that kind of a guy. Look, Lennie, if you get in any kind of trouble, you remember what I told you to do?"

Lennie raised up on his elbow. His face **contorted**③ with thought. Then his eyes moved sadly to George's face. "If I get in any trouble, you ain't gonna let me tend the rabbits."

"That's not what I meant. You remember where we **slep'**④ last night? Down by the river?"

"Yeah. I remember. Oh, sure I remember! I go there an' hide in the brush."

"Hide till I come for you. Don't let nobody see you. Hide in the brush by the river. Say that over."

"Hide in the brush by the river, down in the brush by the river."

"If you get in trouble."

"If I get in trouble."

A brake **screeched**⑤ outside. A call came, "Stable—Buck. Oh! Sta-able Buck."

George said, "Say it over to yourself, Lennie, so you won't forget it."

Both men glanced up, for the rectangle of sunshine in the doorway was cut off. A girl was standing there looking in. She had full, **rouged**⑥ lips and wide-spaced eyes, heavily made up. Her fingernails were red. Her hair hung in little rolled **clusters**⑦, like sausages. She wore a cotton house dress and red **mules**⑧,

① pull in 吸引
② let sb. have it〈口〉打击某人，向某人射击，用刀刺某人

③ contort [kən'tɔ:t] v.（剧烈地）扭曲，歪曲

④ slep' = slept

⑤ screech [skri:tʃ] v. 发出尖锐刺耳的声音

⑥ rouge [ru:ʒ] v. 在……上搽口红
⑦ cluster ['klʌstə] n.（果实、花等的）串，束，簇
⑧ mule [mju:l] n. 拖鞋，拖鞋式女鞋

"我不是冲你生气。我是冲着这儿的那个柯利笨蛋生气。我本来指望着我们能够在这儿积攒一点儿钱——也许能积攒到一百块。"说着，他的语气坚定了起来，"你离柯利远点儿，伦尼。"

"我一定做到，乔治。我不会吭一声的。"

"别让他缠上你——不过——假如那个狗娘养的揍你的话——你就让他受着。"

"让他受什么啊，乔治？"

"没什么，没什么。我到时候会告诉你的。我真恨那种人。听好了，伦尼，你要是惹上了什么麻烦，我告诉过你怎么办，你还记得吗？"

伦尼用胳膊肘支起身子，他思索着，想得五官都扭曲了。接着，他眼里露出悲伤，看向乔治的面庞。"我要是惹了什么麻烦，你就不会让我照料那些兔子了。"

"我指的不是这个。你记得我们昨晚睡在哪儿吗？河畔上游那里？"

"哎呀，我记得。噢，我当然记得！我得跑到那儿去，藏到灌木丛里。"

"藏在那儿，一直等到我去找你。不要让任何人看见你。藏到河畔的灌木丛里。你来复述一遍。"

"藏到河畔的灌木丛里，河畔上游的灌木丛里。"

"假如你惹了什么麻烦。"

"假如我惹了什么麻烦。"

室外传来车闸被扳动的刺耳摩擦声。有个声音喊道："马厩——黑鬼。嘿！马——厩——黑鬼。"

乔治说："你自个儿说几遍，伦尼，这样不至于又忘记了。"

阳光在门口投下的方形光柱忽然被人挡住，两人抬头看去。有个年轻女人伫立在门口朝室内看。只见她嘴唇丰满，涂着口红，两只眼睛的间距很宽，浓妆艳抹。她的指甲涂得通红，头发烫成一个个小卷儿，犹如香肠一般垂着。她身穿棉质便服[1]，脚蹬红色拖鞋。拖鞋覆盖

---

1 指女性从事家务劳动时穿的衣服。

Of Mice and Men

on the **insteps**① of which were little **bouquets**② of red ostrich feathers. "I'm lookin' for Curley," she said. Her voice had a **nasal**③, **brittle**④ quality.

George looked away from her and then back. "He was in here a minute ago, but he went."

"Oh!" She put her hands behind her back and leaned against the door frame so that her body was thrown forward. "You're the new fellas that just come, ain't ya?"

"Yeah."

Lennie's eyes moved down over her body, and though she did not seem to be looking at Lennie she **bridled**⑤ a little. She looked at her fingernails. "Sometimes Curley's in here," she explained.

George said brusquely. "Well he ain't now."

"If he ain't, I guess I better look some place else," she said playfully.

Lennie watched her, fascinated. George said, "If I see him, I'll pass the word you was looking for him."

She smiled **archly**⑥ and **twitched**⑦ her body. "Nobody can't blame a person for lookin'," she said. There were footsteps behind her, going by. She turned her head. "Hi, Slim," she said.

Slim's voice came through the door. "Hi, Good-lookin'."

"I'm tryin' to find Curley, Slim."

"Well, you ain't tryin' very hard. I seen him goin' in your house."

She was suddenly **apprehensive**⑧. "'Bye, boys," she called into the bunk house, and she hurried away.

George looked around at Lennie. "Jesus, what a **tramp**⑨," he said. "So that's what Curley picks for a wife."

"She's purty," said Lennie defensively.

"Yeah, and she's sure hidin' it. Curley got his work ahead of him. Bet she'd **clear out**⑩ for twenty bucks."

Lennie still stared at the doorway where she had been. "Gosh, she was purty." He smiled admiringly. George looked quickly down at him and then he

① instep ['instep] n.（鞋面的）覆盖足背部分
② bouquet [buˈkei; bəuˈkei; ˈbukei] n. 花束
③ nasal [ˈneiz(ə)l] a.（像）从鼻腔发出的，带鼻音的
④ brittle [ˈbrit(ə)l] a. 尖利的，绷紧的

⑤ bridle [ˈbraid(ə)l] v. 昂首收颔表示蔑视（或怨怼、高傲等）

⑥ archly [ˈɑːtʃli] ad. 调皮地，淘气地
⑦ twitch [twitʃ] v. 使抽搐，抽动

⑧ apprehensive [æpriˈhensiv] a. 忧虑的，担心的，疑惧的

⑨ tramp [træmp] n.〈美俚〉荡妇，妓女

⑩ clear out〈口〉走开，离开

足背的部分装饰着红色鸵鸟羽毛组成的小花束。"我找柯利。"她说，声音里带着尖锐的鼻音。

乔治的目光从她身上移开，没一会儿又移回来。"他刚才还在这儿呢，但已经走了。"

"噢！"她双手交在身后，身子倚靠在门框上，以便让身子前倾，"你们是新来的农工，对吧？"

"不错。"

伦尼的目光从上到下打量着她。她似乎没有朝着伦尼这边看，但还是昂首收颔了一点儿。她看了看自己的指甲。"柯利有时候会在这儿呢。"她解释着说。

乔治生硬地说："可他现在不在这儿。"

"他既然不在这儿，我寻思着，最好还是到别处去找吧。"她玩笑似的说。

伦尼注视着她，一副着迷的样子。乔治说："我要是见着他，就告诉他你在找他来着。"

她淘气地笑了笑，扭了扭身子。"没人能够责怪一个找人的人吧。"她说。她身后传来有人走过的脚步声，于是扭过头来。"你好，斯利姆。"她喊了一声。

门口传来了斯利姆的声音，"你好，美人儿。"

"我正在找柯利呢，斯利姆。"

"这样啊，你没有努力去找呢。我看见他回家去了。"

她突然紧张起来。"再见啦，小伙子们。"她朝宿舍里大喊了一声说，随即匆忙离开了。

乔治扭过头看着伦尼。"天哪，真是个荡妇啊，"他说，"柯利原来娶了这么个老婆啊。"

"她可真漂亮啊。"伦尼用维护的语气说。

"是啊，她可以一点儿没藏着掖着，柯利今后可有事情干了。我敢打赌，给她二十块钱她就能跟着别人跑了。"

伦尼仍然眼睁睁地看着她刚才伫立的门口。"天哪，她可真漂亮啊。"他一脸钦慕地笑着。乔治飞快

took him by an ear and shook him.

"Listen to me, you crazy bastard," he said **fiercely**①. "Don't you even take a look at that bitch. I don't care what she says and what she does. I seen 'em poison before, but I never seen no piece of jail bait worse than her. You leave her be."

Lennie tried to **disengage**② his ear. "I never done nothing, George."

"No, you never. But when she was standin' in the doorway showin' her legs, you wasn't lookin' the other way, neither."

"I never meant no harm, George. Honest I never."

"Well, you keep away from her, 'cause she's a **rattrap**③ if I ever seen one. You let Curley take the **rap**④. He **let** himself **in for it**⑤. Glove fulla vaseline," George said disgustedly. "An' I bet he's eatin' **raw**⑥ eggs and writin' to the **patent**⑦ medicine houses."

Lennie cried out suddenly—"I don't like this place, George. This ain't no good place. I wanna get outa here."

"We gotta keep it till we get a stake. We can't help it, Lennie. We'll get out jus' as soon as we can. I don't like it no better than you do." He went back to the table and set out a new solitaire **hand**⑧. "No, I don't like it," he said. "For two **bits**⑨ I'd shove out of here. If we can get jus' a few dollars in the **poke**⑩ we'll shove off and go up the American River and **pan**⑪ gold. We can make maybe a couple of dollars a day there, and we might **hit**⑫ a **pocket**⑬."

Lennie leaned eagerly toward him. "Le's go, George. Le's get outa here. It's mean here."

"We gotta stay," George said shortly. "Shut up now. The guys'll be comin' in."

From the washroom nearby came the sound of running water and **rattling**⑭ basins. George studied the cards. "Maybe we oughtta **wash up**⑮," he said. "But we ain't done nothing to get dirty."

A tall man stood in the doorway. He held a **crushed**⑯ Stetson hat under his arm while he combed his long, black, damp hair straight back. Like the others he wore blue jeans and a short denim jacket. When he had finished combing his

① fiercely ['fiəsli] ad. 凶猛地，残酷地，强烈地

② disengage [,disin'geidʒ; ,disen-] v. 使脱离，使松开

③ rattrap ['rættræp] n. 捕鼠夹

④ rap [ræp] n.〈美口〉行为恶果

⑤ let in for〈口〉使陷入，使卷入，惹起（麻烦等）

⑥ raw [rɔː] a. 生的，未经烹煮的

⑦ patent ['pæt(ə)nt; 'peit(ə)nt] a. 特许专卖（或生产的）

⑧ hand [hænd] n.（纸牌游戏中的）一手牌

⑨ bit [bit] n.〈美口〉[与双数连用] 一角两分半

⑩ poke [pəuk] n.〈口〉钱包，票伙

⑪ pan [pæn] v.（用淘选盘）淘（金等）

⑫ hit [hit] v.（无意中）碰上，（偶然）发现

⑬ pocket ['pɔkit] n.〈口〉钱

⑭ rattling ['rætliŋ] a. 格格作响的

⑮ wash up〈主美〉洗手洗脸

⑯ crushed [krʌʃt] a. 弄皱的

地低头瞥他一眼，然后扯住他的一只耳朵摇晃起来。

"听我说，你这个笨蛋疯子，"他严厉地说，"不准你再盯着那个婊子看。我不在乎她说了什么、做了什么。我见过这种女人祸害人，但还没有见过比她更厉害的祸水。你千万不要理睬她。"

伦尼挣扎着，试图让自己的耳朵解脱出来。"我可没有做什么呀，乔治。"

"不错，你是没有做什么。但是，她站在门口露大腿时，你也没躲开不看。"

"我没有要做坏事的意思，乔治。说老实话，绝对没有。"

"好啦，你离她远点儿，因为她是我见过的最厉害的陷阱了。你就让柯利受着吧，他反正是自找的。还往手套上涂满了凡士林。"乔治厌恶地说，"我敢打赌，他还会吃生鸡蛋，写信给特许药房购买药品呢[1]。"

伦尼突然大喊起来——"我不喜欢这个地方，乔治。这个地方不好，我想离开这儿。"

"我们得待在这儿，起码待到赚了钱再说。我们没有办法，伦尼。我们会尽快离开的。我和你一样不喜欢这儿。"他回到桌子边，重新开始一局单人接龙纸牌戏。"对，我不喜欢这儿，"他说，"只要挣到了几个钱，我们就离开这儿。假如我们口袋里面有了几块钱，我们就动身到河的上游去，去淘金。在那儿我们说不定每天可以挣两块钱。我们还有可能找到一个金矿穴呢。"

伦尼急切地向他探过身子去。"我们走吧，乔治。我们离开这儿。这儿令人不舒服。"

"我们得留下来，"乔治不耐烦地说，"现在闭嘴。有人来啦。"

一个身材高大的人站在门口，只见他腋下夹着一顶压瘪的斯泰森帽子，手里忙着把又黑又湿的长发直直地向后梳理。和其他人一样，他穿着蓝色牛仔裤和粗斜棉布短上衣。他梳完了头发，走进宿舍。他一身威严地走

---

1 当时民间助兴催情的偏方。

Of Mice and Men

hair he moved into the room, and he moved with a **majesty**① only achieved by royalty and **master**② **craftsmen**③. He was a jerkline skinner, the prince of the ranch, capable of driving ten, sixteen, even twenty **mules**④ with a single line to the leaders. He was capable of killing a fly on the **wheeler's**⑤ **butt**⑥ with a bull whip without touching the mule. There was a **gravity**⑦ in his manner and a **quiet**⑧ so **profound**⑨ that all talk stopped when he spoke. His authority was so great that his word was **taken**⑩ on any subject, be it politics or love. This was Slim, the jerkline skinner. His **hatchet face**⑪ was ageless. He might have been thirty-five or fifty. His ear heard more than was said to him, and his slow speech had **overtones**⑫ not of thought, but of understanding beyond thought. His hands, large and lean, were as delicate in their action as those of a temple dancer.

He smoothed out his crushed hat, **creased**⑬ it in the middle and put it on. He looked kindly at the two in the bunk house. "It's brighter'n a bitch outside," he said gently. "Can't hardly see nothing in here. You the new guys?"

"Just come," said George.

"Gonna buck barley?"

"That's what the boss says."

Slim sat down on a box across the table from George. He studied the solitaire hand that was upside down to him. "Hope you get on my team," he said. His voice was very gentle. "I gotta pair of punks on my team that don't know a barley bag from a blue ball. You guys ever bucked any barley?"

"Hell, yes," said George. "I ain't nothing to scream about, but that big bastard there can put up more grain alone than most pairs can."

Lennie, who had been following the conversation back and forth with his eyes, smiled **complacently**⑭ at the **compliment**⑮. Slim looked approvingly at George for having given the compliment. He leaned over the table and **snapped**⑯ the corner of a loose card. "You guys travel around together?" His tone was

① majesty ['mædʒisti] n. 庄重，威严
② master ['mɑ:stə] a. 能带学徒的，技术熟练的，精通的，优秀的
③ craftsmen ['krɑ:f(t)smən] n.（craftsman 的复数形式）工匠，手艺人，巧匠，工艺师
④ mule [mju:l] n. 骡，马骡
⑤ wheeler ['wi:lə] n. =wheel horse（马车的）辕马
⑥ butt [bʌt] n.〈美口〉屁股
⑦ gravity ['grævəti] n. 严肃，庄严
⑧ quiet ['kwaiət] n. 安静
⑨ profound [prə'faund] a. 根深蒂固的，深刻的
⑩ taken ['teikn] v.（take 的过去分词）接受，接纳
⑪ hatchet face 棱角分明的瘦削脸
⑫ overtone ['əuvətəun] n. 弦外之音，含蓄之意，暗示
⑬ crease [kri:s] v. 使起折痕，使起皱
⑭ complacently [kəm'pleisəntli] ad. 自满地，沾沾自喜地
⑮ compliment ['kɔmplim(ə)nt] n. 赞美（话），恭维（话）
⑯ snap [snæp] v. 使噼啪作响

了进来，那神态只有在皇室成员和工艺大师身上才能见到。他是个赶牲口的高手，是农场的王子。他能凭着一根缰绳驾驭十匹、十六匹，甚至二十匹骡子，让它们跟在领头的骡子身后。他能够用牛鞭消灭领头骡子屁股上的一只苍蝇，而又不会碰着牲口。他举止庄重，神态深沉，仿佛只要他一开口，周遭的声音便都会化为平静。他享有崇高的威信，谈及任何话题——无论是政治还是爱情，他的话都会被人接受。这就是斯利姆，一个赶牲口的高手。他脸部瘦削，棱角分明，令人无法判断其年龄。他可能是三十五岁，或者五十岁。他听得多，说得少。他缓慢的话语中充满了弦外之音，表达的不是思想，而是思想之外的同情。他双手又大又瘦，动作犹如寺庙舞者一般细腻。

他弄平了自己那顶压瘪了的帽子，在中间弄出一条折痕来，然后戴在头上。他友好地看着宿舍里的两个人。"室外光线太过强烈了，"他说着，语气和蔼，"进到室内后几乎看不见东西了。你们是新来的吧？"

"刚刚到的。"乔治说。

"准备扛大麦包吧？"

"场主是这么说来着。"

斯利姆在桌子边的苹果箱上坐下，正对着乔治，低头仔细看看那几叠倒对着他的单人接龙纸牌戏。"但愿你们分到我的组上，"他说，说话的声音很和蔼，"我组上有两个新手连大麦包和蓝色球都分不清楚。你们先前扛过大麦包吗？"

"瞧你说的，当然扛过，"乔治说，"我没有什么可以到处嚷嚷的，但这个大傻蛋扛起大麦包来可以一个顶俩呢。"

两个人交谈的时候，伦尼的目光来回移动着。听见了刚才乔治这句赞扬自己的话，他开心地笑了。斯利姆因为这句赞扬的话用欣赏的目光看着乔治。他从桌上探过身子，捻着一张散牌的一角发出啪啪声。"你们两个人是一块儿过来的吗？"他说话的语气很友好，自然而

· 059 ·

friendly. It **invited**① **confidence**② without demanding it.

"Sure," said George. "We kinda look after each other." He indicated Lennie with his thumb. "He ain't bright. Hell of a good worker, though. Hell of a nice fella, but he ain't bright. I've knew him for a long time."

Slim looked through George and beyond him. "Ain't many guys travel around together," he **mused**③. "I don't know why. Maybe ever'body in the whole damn world is scared of each other."

"It's a lot nicer to go around with a guy you know," said George.

A powerful, big-stomached man came into the bunk house. His head still dripped water from the **scrubbing**④ and **dousing**⑤. "Hi, Slim," he said, and then stopped and stared at George and Lennie.

"These guys jus' come," said Slim **by way of**⑥ introduction.

"Glad ta meet ya," the big man said. "My name's Carlson."

"I'm George Milton. This here's Lennie Small."

"Glad ta meet ya," Carlson said again. "He ain't very small." He chuckled softly at his joke. "Ain't small at all," he repeated. "Meant to ask you, Slim—how's your **bitch**⑦? I seen she wasn't under your wagon this morning."

"She **slang**⑧ her pups last night," said Slim. "Nine of 'em. I **drowned**⑨ four of 'em right off. She couldn't feed that many."

"Got five left, huh?"

"Yeah, five. I kept the biggest."

"What kinda dogs you think they're gonna be?"

"I **dunno**⑩," said Slim. "Some kinda shepherds, I guess. That's the most kind I seen around here when she **was in heat**⑪."

Carlson went on, "Got five pups, huh. Gonna keep all of 'em?"

"I dunno. Have to keep 'em a while so they can drink Lulu's milk."

① invite [in'vait] v. 引起
② confidence ['kɔnfid(ə)ns] n. 信任

③ muse [mju:z] v. 若有所思地说

④ scrub [skrʌb] v. 用力擦洗
⑤ douse [daus] v. 浇（或洒、泼）水在……上
⑥ by way of 当作，用作，作为

⑦ bitch [bitʃ] n. 母狗
⑧ slang [slæŋ] v.〈方〉〈古〉（sling 的过去式）抛，投，掷，扔
⑨ drown [draun] v. 使淹死，使溺死

⑩ dunno ['dʌnəu; dəˈnəu] v.〈口〉（我）不知道
⑪ be in heat 正在发情

然便赢得了对方的信任。

"当然，"乔治说，"我们相互照应来着。"他用大拇指指了指伦尼，"他脑袋瓜儿不怎么聪明，却是干活儿的好手。他人可好啦，就是不怎么聪明。我认识他很长时间了。"

斯利姆的目光顺着乔治看向他身后。"结伴同行的人不多啊，"他沉思着说，"我不知道为什么。莫非这个要不得的世界上人人都彼此惧怕不成。"

"有个你熟悉的人相伴一同上路，这样好多了。"乔治说。

有个身强力壮而又大腹便便的男子走进了宿舍。由于刚洗漱过，他的头上还在滴着水。"你好，斯利姆。"他打了声招呼，随即停住了脚步，盯着乔治和伦尼看。

"这两个是新来的。"斯利姆介绍着说。

"很高兴见到你们，"大个子说，"我叫卡尔森。"

"我叫乔治·米尔顿。这位是伦尼·斯莫尔。"

"很高兴见到你们。"卡尔森又说了一声，"他个头可不怎么小[1]啊。"他因为自己的玩笑话咯咯轻笑起来。"一点儿都不小呢，"他重复了一声。"我正想问你呢，斯利姆——你那条母狗怎么样了啊？我看今天上午它没待在你的大车底下嘛。"

"它昨晚生了小狗崽，"斯利姆说，"生了九条，我当即淹死了四条。它可喂不了那么多。"

"还剩下五条，是吗？"

"不错，五条。我留着那条最大的。"

"你觉得，它们将来会是什么品种的狗呢？"

"我不知道呢，"斯利姆说，"有点儿像牧羊犬吧，我猜。母狗发情的那段时间里，我看到周围最多的就是牧羊犬。"

卡尔森接着说："留下了五条，嗯。准备全部都养着吗？"

"我不知道呢，必须要养一段时间吧，等到它们把露露的奶吸干了再说呗。"

---

1 斯莫尔的原文为"small"，意思是"小"。

Of Mice and Men

Carlson said thoughtfully, "Well, looka here, Slim. I been thinkin'. That dog of Candy's is so God damn old he can't hardly walk. **Stinks**① **like hell**②, too. Ever' time he comes into the bunk house I can smell him for two, three days. Why'n't you get Candy to shoot his old dog and give him one of the pups to raise up? I can smell that dog a mile away. Got no teeth, damn near blind, can't eat. Candy feeds him milk. He can't chew nothing else."

George had been staring **intently**③ at Slim. Suddenly a **triangle**④ began to ring outside, slowly at first, and then faster and faster until the beat of it disappeared into one ringing sound. It stopped as suddenly as it had started.

"There she goes," said Carlson.

Outside, there was a burst of voices as a group of men went by.

Slim stood up slowly and with dignity. "You guys better come on while they's still something to eat. Won't be nothing left in a couple of minutes."

Carlson stepped back to let Slim **precede**⑤ him, and then the two of them went out the door.

Lennie was watching George excitedly. George **rumpled**⑥ his cards into a messy pile. "Yeah!" George said, "I heard him, Lennie. I'll ask him."

"A brown and white one," Lennie cried excitedly.

"Come on. Le's get dinner. I don't know whether he got a brown and white one."

Lennie didn't move from his bunk. "You ask him right away, George, so he won't kill no more of 'em."

"Sure. Come on now, get up on your feet."

Lennie rolled off his bunk and stood up, and the two of them started for the door. Just as they reached it, Curley **bounced**⑦ in.

"You seen a girl around here?" he demanded angrily.

George said coldly. "'**Bout**⑧ half an hour ago maybe."

① stink [stiŋk] v. 发出恶臭，有异味
② like hell 非常，猛烈地，过度地

③ intently [in'tentli] ad.（目光等）固定不动地
④ triangle ['traiæŋg(ə)l] n.【音】（打击乐器）三角铁

⑤ precede [pri'si:d] v.（顺序、位置或时间上）处在……之前，先于
⑥ rumple ['rʌmp(ə)l] v. 使凌乱

⑦ bounce [bauns] v. 急冲，猛闯

⑧ 'bout = about

卡尔森一边思索一边说："嗯，听我说，斯利姆。我一直在想，坎迪的那条狗都老掉牙了，路都走不了了，还臭气熏天的。那条狗进一回宿舍，身上那股臭味就够人闻上两三天的。你为何不让坎迪把那条狗给毙了，再送给他一条小狗崽养呢？我在一英里之外都能闻到那条狗的气味。那条狗牙齿都掉光了，几乎看不见东西，也吃不了东西。坎迪给它喂牛奶，因为别的它都嚼不动。"

乔治目不转睛地看着斯利姆。突然，室外传来有人击打一块三角铁的声音，速度先慢后快，而且越来越快。最后，一下一下的击打声汇成了一声回荡的声响。响着响着，这声音倏地停止，结束得与开始一般突然。

"要开饭啦。"卡尔森说。

室外突然传来一群人走过时的说话声音。

斯利姆不慌不忙地起身。"趁着现在还有吃的，你们还是赶紧过去吧，否则，再过几分钟可什么都没有了。"

卡尔森往后退了一点儿让斯利姆先走，接着两个人便都出门去了。

伦尼激动地注视着乔治。乔治草草把扑克牌拢成一堆。"好啦！"乔治说，"我听见他说的了，伦尼。我会去问他的。"

"要一条棕白色的。"伦尼激动地大声说。

"快走吧，我们先吃饭去。我还不知道他有没有棕白色的呢。"

伦尼赖在床上一动不动。"你这就去问他，乔治，这样他就不会再弄死小狗崽了。"

"那当然。现在快走吧，你赶紧起来。"

伦尼翻身下了床，站起身。两个人朝着房门口走去。他们刚走到门口，柯利就闯了进来。

"你们有没有在这儿看见一个女人？"他气呼呼地问道。

乔治冷冷地答道："约莫半个小时以前倒像是来过一个。"

· 063 ·

"Well what the hell was she doin'?"

George stood still, watching the angry little man. He said **insultingly**①, "She said—she was lookin' for you."

Curley seemed really to see George for the first time. His eyes **flashed**② over George, took in his height, measured his reach, looked at his **trim**③ **middle**④. "Well, which way'd she go?" he demanded at last.

"I dunno," said George. "I didn' watch her go."

Curley scowled at him, and turning, hurried out the door.

George said, "Ya know, Lennie, I'm scared I'm gonna tangle with that bastard myself. I **hate** his **guts**⑤. Jesus Christ! Come on. They won't be a damn thing left to eat."

They went out the door. The sunshine lay in a thin line under the window. From a distance there could be heard a rattle of dishes.

After a moment the ancient dog walked lamely in through the open door. He **gazed**⑥ about with **mild**⑦, half-blind eyes. He **sniffed**⑧, and then lay down and put his head between his paws. Curley **popped**⑨ into the doorway again and stood looking into the room. The dog raised his head, but when Curley jerked out, the grizzled head **sank**⑩ to the floor again.

① insultingly [in'sʌltiŋli] ad. 侮辱地，污蔑地，无礼地
② flash [flæʃ] v. 掠过
③ trim [trim] a. 苗条的，修长的
④ middle ['mid(ə)l] n.〈口〉身体的中部，腰部

⑤ hate sb.'s guts〈口〉对某人恨之入骨

⑥ gaze [geiz] v.（出神地）盯着看，凝视
⑦ mild [maild] a.（性情等）温和的，没劲的，没精打采的
⑧ sniff [snif] v.（吸着气）嗅，闻
⑨ pop [pɔp] v. 冷不防地出现（或发生），（突然）冒出
⑩ sank [sæŋk] v.（sink 的过去式）低落，落下

"啊，她来这儿干什么？"

乔治站着没动，盯着眼前这个满腔怒火的小个子。他带着捉弄的口吻说："她说——她在找你呢。"

柯利仿佛这才真正第一次看清楚了乔治。他瞥向乔治，将他的身高收入眼底，估摸着他能触及的范围，打量着他精瘦的腰身。"那么，她朝着哪个方向走了？"他最后开口问道。

"我不知道，"乔治说，"我又没看她往哪儿去。"

柯利恶狠狠地瞪了他一眼，转过身，匆匆忙忙出门去了。

乔治说："你知道吧，伦尼，我很害怕，害怕自己会与那个笨蛋纠缠上。我可是恨死他啦。天哪！快走吧。等下什么都没得吃了。"

他们出了门，阳光在窗户下面投下一道很窄的光线。远处传来了碟盘碰撞的声响。

过了一会儿，那条老迈的狗一瘸一拐地从敞开着的门口走了进来。那狗睁着没精打采又半瞎的眼睛，把四周打量了一番，嗅了嗅，然后躺了下去，把两个爪子放在脑袋两侧。柯利再次突然来，站在门口朝屋里张望。狗昂起了脑袋，不过柯利一走，它那灰白的脑袋就又垂回到地板上去了。

· 065 ·

Although there was evening brightness showing through the windows of the bunk house, inside it was dusk. Through the open door came the thuds and occasional **clangs**① of a **horseshoe**② game, and now and then the sound of voices raised in approval or **derision**③.

Slim and George came into the darkening bunk house together. Slim reached up over the card table and turned on the **tin-shaded**④ electric light. Instantly the table was brilliant with light, and the **cone**⑤ of the shade threw its brightness straight downward, leaving the corners of the bunk house still in dusk. Slim sat down on a box and George took his place opposite.

"It wasn't nothing," said Slim. "I **would of had to**⑥ drowned most of 'em anyways. No need to thank me about that."

George said, "It wasn't much to you, maybe, but it was a hell of a lot to him. Jesus Christ, I don't know how we're gonna get him to sleep in here. He'll want to sleep right out in the **barn**⑦ with 'em. We'll have trouble keepin' him from getting right in the box with them pups."

"It wasn't nothing," Slim repeated. "Say, you sure was right about him. Maybe he ain't bright, but I never seen such a worker. He damn near killed his partner buckin' barley. There ain't nobody can keep up with him. God **awmighty**⑧, I never seen such a strong guy."

George spoke proudly. "Jus' tell Lennie what to do an' he'll do it if it don't take no figuring. He can't think of nothing to do himself, but he sure can take orders."

① clang [klæŋ] n.（金属相击的）铿锵声，当当声
② horseshoe ['hɔːsʃuː; -ʃʃ-] n. 马蹄铁，马掌
③ derision [di'riʒ(ə)n] n. 嘲笑，嘲弄
④ tin-shaded 铁皮灯罩的 tin [tin] n. 镀锡铁皮，马口铁；shade [ʃeid] v.（用罩等）遮（发光体）
⑤ cone [kəun] n.（空心或实心的）圆锥形东西
⑥ would of had to = would have had to
⑦ barn [bɑːn] n. 谷仓，粮仓
⑧ awmighty = almighty

尽管有黄昏时的光线透过窗户照进室内，宿舍里面还是一片昏暗。房门敞开着，外面传来掷蹄铁游戏[1]的砰砰声，偶尔有当当声，时不时还有人们赞赏或者嘲笑的声音。

斯利姆和乔治一起走进光线渐暗的宿舍。斯利姆伸手探到牌桌上方，打开罩着铁皮灯罩的电灯。牌桌上立刻亮堂了起来。灯光被灯罩阻挡，直直往下投去一片圆形的光亮，而宿舍的四个角落仍然黑暗一片。斯利姆坐在一个苹果箱上，乔治坐在他的正对面。

"这不是什么大不了的事情，"斯利姆说，"不管怎么说，我都得淹死掉其中的大部分。你用不着谢我。"

乔治说："对你来说或许不是什么大事，但对他来说，这事可大啦。天哪，我真不知道该如何说服他回来睡觉呢。他定是会想在牲口棚那边与小狗崽一块儿睡呢。他要是往狗窝里钻，我们可得费老大的劲儿才能拦得住呢。"

"这不是什么大不了的事情。"斯利姆重复了一声，"嗯，他那人你真是说对了，他可能不大聪明，但我从未见过这样能干活儿的人。他在扛大麦包时差点儿要了他搭档的命呢。没有任何人能够赶得上他。上帝做证，我从未见过如此身强力壮的人。"

乔治自豪地开口，"但凡不需要动脑子的事情，你只要告诉伦尼怎么做，他就会怎么做。他自己想不出怎么去做事情，但他肯定会遵命行事。"

---

1 掷蹄铁游戏的玩法是：游戏者将马蹄铁或马蹄铁形的金属块扔向一根柱子，套住柱子或比其他游戏者更接近柱子获胜。

There was a clang of horseshoe on iron **stake**① outside and a little cheer of voices.

Slim moved back slightly so the light was not on his face. "Funny how you an' him **string along**② together." It was Slim's calm invitation to confidence.

"What's funny about it?" George demanded defensively.

"Oh, I dunno. Hardly none of the guys ever travel together. I hardly never seen two guys travel together. You know how the **hands**③ are, they just come in and get their bunk and work a month, and then they quit and go out alone. Never seem to give a damn about nobody. It jus' seems kinda funny a **cuckoo**④ like him and a smart little guy like you travelin' together."

"He ain't no cuckoo," said George. "He's dumb as hell, but he ain't crazy. An' I ain't so bright neither, or I wouldn't be buckin' barley for my fifty and **found**⑤. If I was bright, if I was even a little bit smart, I'd have my own little place, an' I'd be **bringin' in**⑥ my own crops, **'stead**⑦ of doin' all the work and not getting what comes up outa the ground." George fell silent. He wanted to talk. Slim neither encouraged nor discouraged him. He just sat back quiet and **receptive**⑧.

"It ain't so funny, him an' me goin' **aroun'**⑨ together," George said at last. "Him and me was both born in Auburn. I knowed his Aunt Clara. She took him when he was a baby and raised him up. When his Aunt Clara died, Lennie just come along with me out workin'. Got kinda used to each other after a little while."

"Umm," said Slim.

George looked over at Slim and saw the calm, Godlike eyes fastened on him. "Funny," said George. "I used to have a hell of a lot of fun with 'im. Used to play jokes on **'im**⑩ 'cause he was too dumb to take care of **'imself**⑪. But he was too dumb even to know he had a joke played on him. I had fun.

① stake [steik] *n.* 桩，标桩

② string along（忠实地）跟随

③ hand [hænd] *n.* 人手，雇员（指工人、船员等）

④ cuckoo ['kuku:] *n.*〈俚〉傻子，怪人，疯子

⑤ found [faund] *n.*（除工资外供应的）免费膳宿

⑥ bring in 生出……作为收益，挣得

⑦ 'stead = instead

⑧ receptive [ri'septiv] *a.*（对建议等）愿接受的，易接受的

⑨ aroun' = around

⑩ 'im = him

⑪ 'imself = himself

室外传来蹄铁打住铁柱发出的当当声，还有一阵零星的喝彩声。

斯利姆身子稍稍后移了一点儿，免得让灯光直射在自己的脸上。"你和他会拴在一块儿，这件事情真是很有意思呢。"斯利姆语气平静，落入对方耳中仿佛是吐露心声的邀请。

"这有什么有意思的？"乔治反问道。

"噢，我说不好。农工们不怎么会结伴同行的。我几乎从未见过有两个人结伴同行的。你知道那些做工的是些什么样的人。他们只是跑来落脚，占上一个床位，干上个把月，然后便辞工独自离开。他们好像从来都不会关心其他什么人。因此，他那样的一个疯子和你这样的一个聪明人一路结伴而行，看起来挺有意思的。"

"他绝不是个疯子，"乔治说，"他只是笨得要命，但并不是个疯子。而我也不聪明，否则，我也不会为了五十块钱加上免费食宿跑来扛大麦包。我要是聪明，我要是哪怕有一丁点儿聪明，我也会拥有属于自己的一小片地方，那样庄稼的收成便我自个儿的了，而不是像现在这样，干了地里的活儿，却得不到地里的收成。"乔治打住不说了。他本来想要说下去的，但斯利姆既没有鼓励他，也没有打扰他，只是后仰着身子坐在那儿，一言不发，静静倾听。

"我和他一路结伴而行，四面八方到处走，这事也不那么有意思吧，"乔治最后说，"我和他两个人都出生在奥本。我认识他姨妈克拉拉。他还是个婴儿时，姨妈就把他接去养了，一直到他长大成人。克拉拉姨妈去世后，伦尼就跟着我出来找活儿干，过了一阵子，我们彼此便习惯了。"

斯利姆"嗯"了一声。

乔治看着桌子对面的斯利姆，看到那双平静如神灵般的眼睛落在自己身上。"有意思的是，"乔治说，"以前和他在一块儿的时候我真是其乐无穷啊。我常常对他开玩笑，因为他笨得连自己都顾不好。但是，他实在太

· 069 ·

Made me seem God damn smart alongside of him. Why he'd do any damn thing I tol' him. If I **tol'**① him to walk over a **cliff**②, over he'd go. That wasn't so damn much fun after a while. He never got mad about it, neither. I've **beat the hell**③ outa him, and he coulda **bust**④ every bone in my body jus' with his **han's**⑤, but he never lifted a finger against me." George's voice was **taking on**⑥ the tone of **confession**⑦. "Tell you what made me stop that. One day a bunch of guys was standin' around up on the Sacramento River. I was feelin' pretty smart. I turns to Lennie and says, 'Jump in.' An' he jumps. Couldn't swim a **stroke**⑧. He damn near drowned before we could get him. An' he was so damn nice to me for pullin' him out. **Clean**⑨ forgot I told him to jump in. Well, I ain't done nothing like that no more."

"He's a nice fella," said Slim. "Guy don't need no sense to be a nice fella. Seems to me sometimes it jus' works the other way around. Take a real smart guy and he ain't hardly ever a nice fella."

George **stacked**⑩ the **scattered**⑪ cards and began to lay out his solitaire hand. The shoes thudded on the ground outside. At the windows the light of the evening still made the window squares bright.

"I ain't got no people," George said. "I seen the guys that go around on the ranches alone. That ain't no good. They don't have no fun. After a long time they get mean. They get wantin' to fight all the time."

"Yeah, they get mean," Slim agreed. "They get so they don't want to talk to nobody."

"'Course Lennie's a God damn **nuisance**⑫ most of the time," said George. "But you get used to goin' around with a guy an' you can't get rid of him."

"He ain't mean," said Slim. "I can see Lennie ain't a bit mean."

"'Course he ain't mean. But he gets in trouble alla time because he's so God damn dumb. Like what happened in Weed—" He stopped, stopped in the

① tol'=told
② cliff [klif] n.（尤指海边的）悬崖，峭壁
③ beat the hell outa=beat the hell out of 猛击，痛打
④ bust [bʌst] v. 使断裂，打破，打碎
⑤ han's = hands
⑥ take on 呈现
⑦ confession [kən'feʃ(ə)n] n. 承认，坦白
⑧ stroke [strəuk] n.（游泳的）两臂划水一周
⑨ clean [kli:n] ad. 完全地，全部地

⑩ stack [stæk] v. 把……叠成堆，把……筑成垛
⑪ scattered ['skætəd] a. 分散的，散布的

⑫ nuisance ['nju:s(ə)ns] n. 讨厌的人，讨厌鬼

笨了，甚至都不知道我在跟他开玩笑。我找着了乐子。跟他一处，倒是显得我真他妈的聪明啊。是啊，我叫他干什么，他就会干什么。假如我要他走到悬崖上去，他便会走过去。过了一段时间后，这样的事情便没有什么好玩的了。他倒也从来都不会生气上火。我揍他的次数可多啦。而他只要还手，我全身的骨头都会断掉，但他从未伤过我一根指头。"乔治说话的声音里渐渐流露出忏悔之意，"我告诉你，我为何不再捉弄他了吧。有一天，一群人站在萨克拉门托河岸边。我当时感觉自己挺聪明，就转身对伦尼说：'跳下去吧。'他于是便跳下去了。他不会游泳，我们把他捞上来的时候，他差点儿就没气儿了。我把他救上岸来，他对我感激不已，把我叫他跳下去的事情忘得一干二净了。唉，从那以后，我便再也不干那种事情了。"

"他是个很好的人啊，"斯利姆说，"不一定非得聪明才能成为一个好人呢。依我看吧，有时候，事情倒是反过来的呢。比如说，一个头脑精明的人却不一定总是好人。"

乔治把桌上散乱的纸牌拢了起来，开始玩单人接龙牌戏。室外传来脚步声。窗口处，窗户的方框在黄昏的暮色中仍然清晰可见。

"我没有任何亲人，"乔治说，"我见过那些独自一人四处奔波，在各家农场上干活儿的人。那样真不好。他们享受不到任何乐趣。时间过久了，人心就变得卑劣起来，每时每刻都想着寻衅斗殴来着。"

"是啊，他们会变得卑劣的，"斯利姆表示认同，"他们变成那样，也就不想和别人说话了。"

"当然啦，大部分时候，伦尼烦人透顶，"乔治说，"但你一旦习惯了与某个人同行，你便不可能甩掉他不管。"

"他的人品并不卑劣，"斯利姆说，"我可以看得出，伦尼的人品一点儿都不卑劣。"

"他当然不卑劣。但他总是惹麻烦，因为他是个少见的笨蛋。就拿在威德的那件事说吧——"他住了口，

middle of turning over a card. He looked alarmed and peered over at Slim. "You wouldn't tell nobody?"

"What'd he do in Weed?" Slim asked calmly.

"You wouldn' tell? . . . No, 'course you wouldn'."

"What'd he do in Weed?" Slim asked again.

"Well, he seen this girl in a red dress. Dumb bastard like he is, he wants to touch ever'thing he likes. Just wants to feel it. So he reaches out to feel this red dress an' the girl **lets out**[①] a **squawk**[②], and that gets Lennie all **mixed up**[③], and he holds on **'cause**[④] that's the only thing he can think to do. Well, this girl **squawks**[⑤] and squawks. I was jus' a little bit off, and I heard all the yellin', so I comes running, an' by that time Lennie's so scared all he can think to do is jus' hold on. I socked him over the head with a fence **picket**[⑥] to make him let go. He was so **scairt**[⑦] he couldn't let go of that dress. And he's so God damn strong, you know."

Slim's eyes were **level**[⑧] and **unwinking**[⑨]. He nodded very slowly. "So what happens?"

George carefully built his line of solitaire cards. "Well, that girl **rabbits**[⑩] in an' tells the **law**[⑪] she been **raped**[⑫]. The guys in Weed start a **party**[⑬] out to **lynch**[⑭] Lennie. So we sit in a irrigation ditch under water all the rest of that day. Got on'y our heads sticking out from the side of the ditch. An' that night we **scrammed**[⑮] outa there."

Slim sat in silence for a moment. "Didn't hurt the girl none, huh?" he asked finally.

"Hell, no. He just scared her. I'd be scared too if he grabbed me. But he never hurt her. He jus' wanted to touch that red dress, like he wants to pet them pups all the time."

"He ain't mean," said Slim. "I can tell a mean guy a mile off."

"'Course he ain't, and he'll do any damn thing I—"

Lennie came in through the door. He wore his blue denim coat over his shoulders like a **cape**[⑯], and he walked **hunched**[⑰] way **over**[⑱].

① let out 发出
② squawk [skwɔːk] n. 响而粗的叫声
③ mix up 混淆，弄混，使弄不清，把……弄糊涂
④ 'cause [kɔːz, kəz] conj.〈口〉= because
⑤ squawk [skwɔːk] v. 发出响而粗的叫声
⑥ picket ['pikit] n.（拴牲口、作篱栅等用的）尖木桩，尖板条
⑦ scairt = scared
⑧ level ['lev(ə)l] a. 平稳的，稳定的，坚定的，不动摇的
⑨ unwinking [ʌn'wiŋkiŋ] a. 不眨眼的，不动摇的
⑩ rabbit ['ræbit] v.〈美俚〉一溜烟逃跑
⑪ law [lɔː] n.［常作 the law］〈口〉执法者，警察，警官，（美国的）民选县治安官，探员
⑫ rape [reip] v. 强奸
⑬ party ['pɑːti] n.（共同工作或活动的）队，组，群
⑭ lynch [lin(t)ʃ] v.（暴民）以私刑（通常为绞刑）处死某人
⑮ scram [skræm] v. 快速离去，走开
⑯ cape [keip] n. 斗篷，披肩
⑰ hunch [hʌn(t)ʃ] v. 弯成弓状，耸着肩（或弯着背）走动
⑱ over ['əʊvə(r)] ad. 从一方至另一方

那只翻牌的手停在半途。他神色惊恐地朝斯利姆看去。"你不会告诉别人吧？"

"他在威德干了什么？"斯利姆平静地问。

"你不会说出去吧？……不，你当然不会说出去的。"

"他在威德干了什么？"斯利姆又问了一遍。

"嗯，他看见了一个穿红裙子的女人。像他那样的傻瓜笨蛋，碰到喜欢的任何东西都想去摸一把。只是想去摸一下。就这么着，他伸出手去摸那个女人的红裙子，那个女的发出了一声尖叫，倒把伦尼吓得慌了神。他抓住衣裙不放手，因为这是他能够想到的唯一可做的事情。就这样，那个女人叫个不停。我当时正好在附近不远处，听见了一连串的尖叫声，便跑了过去。那时候，伦尼吓得惊恐万状，脑子里只想着牢牢抓住那衣裙不放。我抄起一根篱栅木敲他的脑袋，他才松了手。他太害怕了，根本无法主动松开那衣裙。他那么身强力壮，这你是知道的。"

斯利姆目光平静，双眼眨都不眨。他缓慢地点了点头。"后来情况如何呢？"

乔治细心地摆着手上扑克牌。"后来啊，那个女的跑了，告诉警察说，她被强奸了。威德的一帮人跑出来想把伦尼弄死。因此，我们躲到一条灌溉渠里，在水下坐了一整天，只有脑袋在水渠边伸出来。我们当晚便从那儿跑出来了。"

斯利姆坐着沉默了一会儿。"没有伤害那个女的，对吧？"他最后开口问道。

"对啊，根本没有。他只是吓着她了。他若是揪住我，我也会被吓着的。但他根本没有伤着她。他只是想要摸一下那条红裙子罢了，就跟他总是想要抚摸小狗崽子一样。"

"他并不人品卑劣，"斯利姆说，"一个人品卑劣的家伙，即便在一英里之外，我都能认出来。"

"他当然不卑劣，但他会做任何事情，只要我——"

伦尼从门口走了进来。他把身上穿的蓝色斜纹粗布外套像斗篷一样披在肩上，佝偻着身子走路。

Of Mice and Men

"Hi, Lennie," said George. "How you like the pup now?"

Lennie said breathlessly, "He's brown an' white jus' like I wanted." He went directly to his bunk and lay down and turned his face to the wall and **drew up**① his knees.

George put down his cards very deliberately. "Lennie," he said sharply.

Lennie **twisted**② his neck and looked over his shoulder. "Huh? What you want, George?"

"I tol' you you couldn't bring that pup in here."

"What pup, George? I ain't got no pup."

George went quickly to him, grabbed him by the shoulder and rolled him over. He reached down and picked the tiny puppy from where Lennie had been concealing it against his stomach.

Lennie sat up quickly. "Give **'um**③ to me, George."

George said, "You get right up an' take this pup back to the nest. He's gotta sleep with his mother. You want to kill him? Just born last night an' you take him out of the nest. You take him back or I'll tell Slim not to let you have him."

Lennie held out his hands pleadingly. "Give 'um to me, George. I'll take 'um back. I didn't mean no harm, George. Honest I didn't. I jus' wanted to pet 'um a little."

George handed the pup to him. "Awright. You get him back there quick, and don't you take him out no more. You'll kill him, the first thing you know." Lennie **fairly**④ **scuttled**⑤ out of the room.

Slim had not moved. His calm eyes followed Lennie out the door. "Jesus," he said. "He's jus' like a kid, ain't he?"

"Sure he's jes' like a kid. There ain't no more harm in him than a kid neither, except he's so strong. I bet he won't come in here to sleep tonight. He'd sleep right alongside that box in the barn. Well—let 'im. He ain't doin' no harm out there."

It was almost dark outside now. Old Candy, the swamper, came in and went to his bunk, and behind him struggled his old dog. "Hello, Slim. Hello, George. Didn't neither of you play horseshoes?"

① draw up 拉起，提起
（drew [dru:] draw 的过去式）

② twist [twist] v. 使转动，旋动

③ 'um = them

④ fairly ['fɛəli] ad. 完全，简直

⑤ scuttle ['skʌt(ə)l] v. 急促奔跑，急赶，疾走

"嘿，伦尼，"乔治说，"你现在觉得那条小狗崽怎么样啊？"

伦尼气喘吁吁地说："小狗崽棕白相间，正是我想要的呢。"他径直走向自己床边，躺了下来，侧脸对着墙壁，架起双腿。

乔治慢条斯理地放下手上的扑克牌。"伦尼。"他厉声道。

伦尼扭过脖子，侧着头看过来。"嗯，干什么呀，乔治？"

"我告诉过你，不能把小狗崽带到宿舍里来。"

"什么小狗崽呀，乔治？我没带小狗崽来呀。"

乔治快步朝他走过去，揪住他的一个肩膀，让他翻过身，伸手从伦尼腹部的衣服下面取出一只小狗崽。

伦尼急忙坐了起来。"把小狗崽还给我，乔治。"

乔治说："你赶紧起来，把小狗崽送回到窝里去。小狗崽必须得和母狗睡在一起，你这是想要弄死它吗？昨晚才出生的，你却把它从窝里拿出来。你赶快送回去，否则我就跟斯利姆说，不让你养了。"

伦尼恳求着伸出双手。"把小狗崽还给我吧，乔治。我会送回去的。我不想伤害它，乔治。说老实话，我不想伤害它。我只是想要摸一会儿。"

乔治把小狗崽还给了他。"好吧，你赶紧送回去，不要再拿出来了。否则，没等你回过神来，你就已经弄死它了。"伦尼差不多是快跑出了房间。

这期间斯利姆一动不动，目光平静地看着伦尼跑出房门。"天哪，"他说，"他简直就像个孩子啊。"

"确实如此，他就像个孩子。他能做的坏事与孩子差不多，只是他格外强壮罢了。我敢打赌，他今晚不会回来睡觉了。他会睡在牲口棚里的狗窝旁边。嗯——随他去吧。他不会在那边闯什么祸的。"

室外现在已经差不多全黑了。老坎迪，也就是那个清扫工，进了屋，走到他的床边，那条老牧羊犬颤颤巍巍地走在他身后。"嘿，斯利姆。嘿，乔治。你们没有去玩掷蹄铁游戏吗？"

Of Mice and Men

"I don't like to play ever' night," said Slim.

Candy went on, "Either you guys got a **slug**① of whisky? I gotta **gut**② ache."

"I ain't," said Slim. "I'd drink it myself if I had, an' I ain't got a gut ache neither."

"Gotta bad gut ache," said Candy. "Them God damn **turnips**③ give it to me. I knowed they was going to before I ever eat 'em."

The thick-bodied Carlson came in out of the darkening yard. He walked to the other end of the bunk house and turned on the second shaded light. "Darker'n hell in here," he said. "Jesus, how that nigger can **pitch**④ shoes."

"He's **plenty**⑤ good," said Slim.

"Damn right he is," said Carlson. "He don't give nobody else a chance to win—" He stopped and sniffed the air, and still sniffing, looked down at the old dog. "God awmighty, that dog stinks. Get him outa here, Candy! I don't know nothing that stinks as bad as an old dog. You gotta get him out."

Candy rolled to the edge of his bunk. He reached over and patted the ancient dog, and he apologized, "I been around him so much I never notice how he stinks."

"Well, I can't stand him in here," said Carlson. "That stink **hangs around**⑥ even after he's gone." He walked over with his heavy-legged **stride**⑦ and looked down at the dog. "Got no teeth," he said. "He's all **stiff**⑧ with **rheumatism**⑨. He ain't no good to you, Candy. An' he ain't no good to himself. Why'n't you shoot him, Candy?"

The old man squirmed uncomfortably. "Well—hell! I had him so long. Had him since he was a pup. I **herded**⑩ sheep with him." He said proudly, "You wouldn't think it to look at him now, but he was the best damn sheep dog I ever seen."

George said, "I seen a guy in Weed that had an **Airedale**⑪ could herd sheep. Learned it from the other dogs."

① slug [slʌg] n.（酒等的）一口，一小杯
② gut [gʌt] n. 肠，胃，〈口〉肚子，腹部
③ turnip ['tə:nip] n.【植】芜菁

④ pitch [pitʃ] v.（游戏中）把（硬币、铁圈等）掷向目标
⑤ plenty ['plenti] ad.〈口〉充分地，完全地，十分

⑥ hang around 待在（某处）附近，围集在……周围
⑦ stride [straid] n. 步态，步法
⑧ stiff [stif] a.（手足等）僵硬的，僵直的，活动时疼痛的，难以活动的，不灵活的
⑨ rheumatism ['ru:mətiz(ə)m] n. 风湿病
⑩ herd [hə:d] v. 放牧
⑪ Airedale ['ɛədeil] n. = Airedale terrier 万能㹴（一种有黑斑的棕色粗毛大猎犬）

"我不喜欢每晚都玩。"斯利姆说。

坎迪接着说："你们两个谁有威士忌吗？我胃痛。"

"我没有，"斯利姆说，"假如我有，我早就喝掉了，不过我胃也不痛。"

"我胃痛得厉害，"坎迪说，"都是吃了那些该死的萝卜给闹的，我就知道吃了萝卜准会胃痛。"

大个子卡尔森从光线越来越暗的院子里走了进来。他走到宿舍的另一端，打开了另一盏带灯罩的电灯。"这儿比地狱都更加黑暗哩，"他说，"天哪，那个黑鬼可真会玩掷蹄铁游戏呢。"

"他手段可高明啦。"斯利姆说。

"他妈的真厉害，"卡尔森说，"他不给任何人获胜的机会——"他话没有说完便打住了，闻了闻空气中的气味，边闻边低头去看那条老牧羊犬。"万能的上帝啊，这狗臭死了。把它给弄出去，坎迪！要我说这世上最臭的就属老狗了。你一定得把它给弄出去。"

坎迪翻了个身，从床沿伸出一只手，轻轻拍了拍老迈的牧羊犬，抱歉地说道："我一直都跟他待在一块儿，所以都闻不出。"

"不管怎么说吧，狗待在房间里，我可是受不了呢，"卡尔森说，"它即便离开了房间，臭味还在呢。"他迈着沉重的脚步走了过去，低头看着那条狗，"牙齿都没有啦，"他说，"患了风湿病，全身活动不灵。这狗对你没有什么用途了，坎迪，就是活着它自己也做不了什么。何不一枪毙了它呢，坎迪？"

老人局促不安地蠕动了一下身子。"得了吧——真见鬼！我养了它那么长时间。它还是幼崽时，我便开始养着了。我和它一块儿放过羊呢。"他说，语气中洋溢着自豪感，"你别看它现在不怎么样，以前却是我见过的最好的牧羊犬来着。"

乔治说："我在威德看见一个人养了一条能够牧羊的万能㹴，那狗从别的狗那儿学来了这本事。"

Carlson was not to be **put off**①. "Look, Candy. This ol' dog jus' suffers **hisself**② all the time. If you was to take him out and shoot him right in the back of the head—" he leaned over and pointed, "— right there, why he'd never know what hit him."

Candy looked about unhappily. "No," he said softly. "No, I couldn't do that. I had 'im too long."

"He don't have no fun," Carlson insisted. "And he stinks **to beat hell**③. Tell you what. I'll shoot him for you. Then it won't be you that does it."

Candy threw his legs off his bunk. He scratched the white **stubble**④ whiskers on his cheek nervously. "I'm so used to him," he said softly. "I had him from a pup."

"Well, you ain't bein' kind to him keepin' him alive," said Carlson. "Look, Slim's bitch got a **litter**⑤ right now. I bet Slim would give you one of them pups to raise up, wouldn't you, Slim?"

The skinner had been studying the old dog with his calm eyes. "Yeah," he said. "You can have a pup if you want to." He seemed to **shake**⑥ himself free for speech. "Carl's right, Candy. That dog ain't no good to himself. I wisht somebody'd shoot me if I get old an' a **cripple**⑦."

Candy looked helplessly at him, for Slim's opinions were law. "Maybe it'd hurt him," he suggested. "I don't mind takin' care of him."

Carlson said, "The way I'd shoot him, he wouldn't feel nothing. I'd put the gun right there." He pointed with his toe. "Right back of the head. He wouldn't even quiver."

Candy looked for help from face to face. It was quite dark outside by now. A young laboring man came in. His **sloping**⑧ shoulders were bent forward and he walked heavily on his **heels**⑨, as though he carried the **invisible**⑩ grain bag. He went to his bunk and put his hat on his shelf. Then he picked a **pulp magazine**⑪ from his shelf and brought it to the light over the table. "Did I show you this,

① put off 使分心，使心乱
② hisself [hi'self] *pron.*〈非规范〉〈方〉= himself

③ to beat hell〈美口〉起劲地

④ stubble ['stʌb(ə)l] *a.* 须茬

⑤ litter ['litə] *n.*（猪、狗等多产动物生下的）一窝（仔畜）

⑥ shake [ʃeik] *v.* 以摇动（或扭动等）使处于特定状态

⑦ cripple ['krip(ə)l] *n.* 跛子，跛足的动物，伤残的人（或动物）

⑧ sloping [sləupiŋ] *a.* 倾斜的
⑨ heel [[hi:l]] *n.*（足）跟
⑩ invisible [in'vizib(ə)l] *a.* 看不见的，无形的
⑪ pulp magzaine〈主美〉（纸质低劣、内容庸俗或耸人听闻的）低级黄色书刊

卡尔森不甘心被岔开话头。"听我说，坎迪。这条老牧羊犬自己也一直在受罪。不如你把它领出去，在它的后脑勺上来一枪就完事了——"他探过身子指了指，"——就这儿，来不及知道被什么东西打中了的。"

坎迪环顾了一番四周，一副很不开心的样子。"不行，"他轻声说，"不行，我不能那样做。我都养了它那么久了。"

"它过得不快活，"卡尔森坚持不懈地说，"而且臭气熏天。告诉你吧，我来替你一枪毙了它。那样便不需要你自己动手了。"

坎迪把两条腿伸到床下，不安地挠了挠脸颊上的白色胡茬。"我已经完全习惯它了，"他轻声道，"从小狗崽时便开始养着了。"

"得了吧，你让它这样活着，那才是对它不仁慈呢，"卡尔森说，"听我说，斯利姆饲养的那条母狗刚下了一窝小崽子。我敢打赌，斯利姆会愿意送给你一条小狗养着的，是不是，斯利姆？"

这位赶牲口人刚刚一直在平静地审视那老牧羊犬。"是啊，"他说，"你若想要，我可以给你一条小狗崽。"他似乎想要把话说透，"卡尔[1]说得对，坎迪。这条狗活着也是在受罪。等到我人老行动不便了，我也希望有人一枪把我结果了。"

坎迪无助地看着对方，因为斯利姆的看法等于法律。"它或许会感到痛苦的，"他提示说，"我愿意照料它。"

卡尔森说："按我的办法一枪毙了它，它是不会有任何感觉的。我会用枪对准这儿打。"他用脚趾比画了一下，"正中后脑勺上。它连抖都不会抖一下。"

坎迪用求助的目光挨个看着大家。室外现在已经很黑了。有个年轻的农工进入室内。他倾斜着肩膀向前佝着，拖着沉重的脚步，仿佛扛着个看不见的大麦包。他走到自己床边，把帽子放在搁物架上。他随即从架子上拿起一本廉价杂志，拿到亮灯的桌旁。"我给你看过这

---

1 卡尔是卡尔森的昵称。

Slim?" he asked.

"Show me what?"

The young man turned to the back of the magazine, put it down on the table and pointed with his finger. "Right there, read that." Slim bent over it. "Go on," said the young man. "Read it out loud."

"'Dear Editor,'" Slim read slowly. "'I read your **mag**① for six years and I think it is the best on the market. I like stories by Peter Rand. I think he is a **whing-ding**②. Give us more like the Dark Rider. I don't write many letters. Just thought I would tell you I think your mag is the best **dime's**③ worth I ever spent.'"

Slim looked up questioningly. "What you want me to read that for?"

Whit said, "Go on. Read the name at the bottom."

Slim read, "'Yours for success, William Tenner.'" He glanced up at Whit again. "What you want me to read that for?"

Whit closed the magazine impressively. "Don't you remember Bill Tenner? Worked here about three months ago?"

Slim thought. . . "Little guy?" he asked. "Drove a cultivator?"

"That's him," Whit cried. "That's the guy!"

"You think he's the guy wrote this letter?"

"I know it. Bill and me was in here one day. Bill had one of them books that just come. He was lookin' in it and he says, 'I wrote a letter. Wonder if they put it in the book!' But it wasn't there. Bill says, 'Maybe they're **savin'**④ it for later.' An' that's just what they done. There it is."

"Guess you're right," said Slim. "Got it right in the book."

George held out his hand for the magazine. "Let's look at it?"

Whit found the place again, but he did not **surrender**⑤ his hold on it. He pointed out the letter with his forefinger. And then he went to his box shelf and laid the magazine carefully in. "I wonder if Bill seen it," he said. "Bill and me

个了吗，斯利姆？"他问。

"给我看什么啊？"

年轻人翻到杂志的封底，放在桌子上，手指着某处。"就在这儿，看看这个。"斯利姆俯下身子看他指着的内容。"念吧，"年轻人说，"念出声音来。"

"'尊敬的编辑：'"斯利姆缓慢地念着，"'我阅读你们的杂志已经长达六年了，感觉这份杂志是市面上最优秀的。我喜爱阅读彼得·兰德的小说。我觉得，他是个顶呱呱的小说家。给我们多登载一些诸如《黑暗骑士》那样的作品。我不怎么写信，只是觉得，我要告诉您，我觉得你们的杂志价廉物美，钱花得值。'"

斯利姆疑惑地抬起头。"你要我念这个做什么啊？"

惠特说："接着念。把结尾处的署名念出来。"

斯利姆念道："'祝您成功，威廉·特纳。'"他抬头瞥了惠特一眼，"你要我念这个做什么啊？"

惠特郑重其事地合上了杂志。"你不记得比尔·特纳了吗？大概三个月前，在这儿干过活儿的那个？"

斯利姆思忖着……"一个小个子？"他问道，"开耕种机的那个？"

"正是他，"惠特大声说，"正是那家伙呢。"

"你认为是他写的这封信吗？"

"我知道是他写的。有一天，我和比尔[1]在这儿待着。比尔收到了一本新出的杂志。他一边看着杂志里面的内容，一边说：'我写了一封信，不知道他们是否会登载出来！'但那一期上面没有登载。比尔就说：'他们或许放到以后登载吧。'结果就是那么回事，这一期果然登出来了。"

"看来你说对了，"斯利姆说，"正是在这一期登载出来了。"

乔治伸手去拿那本杂志。"让我看看吧？"

惠特又找到了那处地方，但捏住了杂志不松手。他用食指指出信的位置，然后走向他那苹果箱制成的搁物架，小心翼翼地把杂志放到里面。"我不知道比尔看见

1　比尔是威廉的昵称。

① mag [mæg] n.〈口〉= magazine

② whing-ding ['wiŋdiŋ] n. = wingding〈美俚〉非常引人注目（或紧张激烈的）事物

③ dime [daim] n.〈口〉小钱，少量的钱

④ save [seiv] v. 保留，留下

⑤ surrender [sə'rendə] v. 放弃，交出，让出

worked in that patch of field peas. Run cultivators, both of us. Bill was a hell of a nice fella."

During the conversation Carlson had refused to be **drawn in**①. He continued to look down at the old dog. Candy watched him uneasily. At last Carlson said, "If you want me to, I'll put the old devil out of his misery right now and **get it over with**②. Ain't nothing left for him. Can't eat, can't see, can't even walk without hurtin'."

Candy said hopefully, "You ain't got no gun."

"The hell I ain't. Got a **Luger**③. It won't hurt him none at all."

Candy said, "Maybe tomorra. Le's wait till tomorra."

"I don't see no reason for it," said Carlson. He went to his bunk, pulled his bag from underneath it and took out a Luger **pistol**④. "Let's get it over with," he said. "We can't sleep with him stinkin' around in here." He put the pistol in his **hip**⑤ pocket.

Candy looked a long time at Slim to try to find some **reversal**⑥. And Slim gave him none. At last Candy said softly and hopelessly, "Awright—take 'im." He did not look down at the dog at all. He lay back on his bunk and crossed his arms behind his head and stared at the ceiling.

From his pocket Carlson took a little leather **thong**⑦. He stooped over and tied it around the old dog's neck. All the men except Candy watched him. "Come boy. Come on, boy," he said gently. And he said apologetically to Candy, "He won't even feel it." Candy did not move nor answer him. He twitched the thong. "Come on, boy." The old dog got slowly and stiffly to his feet and followed the gently pulling **leash**⑧.

Slim said, "Carlson."

"Yeah?"

"You know what to do."

"What ya mean, Slim?"

"Take a shovel," said Slim **shortly**⑨.

"Oh, sure! I get you." He led the dog out into the darkness.

① draw in（诱）使……进入（或参加）

② get over with 熬过，做完，结束（一件不愉快但必须做的事）

③ Luger ['luːgə] n. 卢格尔手枪（一种德国半自动手枪）

④ pistol ['pɪst(ə)l] n. 手枪
⑤ hip [hɪp] n.【解】臀（部），髋（部）

⑥ reversal [rɪ'vɜːs(ə)l] n. 反向，倒转，颠倒

⑦ thong [θɒŋ] n. 皮带子，条带，（皮）鞭

⑧ leash [liːʃ] n.（系狗、鹰等的）皮带，绳子，链条

⑨ shortly ['ʃɔːtlɪ] ad. 简短地，简要地，扼要地

了没，"他说，"我和比尔在那片豌豆地里干过活儿。驾驶耕种机来着，我们两个人是。比尔是个可好的人啦。"

这场谈话卡尔森始终没有参与，而是一直低头看着老牧羊犬。坎迪不安地注视着他。卡尔森最后说："你要是想的话，我可以马上帮助这老畜生解脱痛苦，一了百了。它活着毫无意义，看不见，吃不了，就连走路都疼。"

坎迪满怀着希望说："可你没有枪啊。"

"谁说我没有，我有好吧，有一把卢格尔手枪。它不会感到痛苦的。"

坎迪说："明天吧，明天再说吧。"

"我看没必要。"卡尔森说。他走到自己床边，从床底下拖出一个袋子，从袋子里拿出一把卢格尔手枪。"了结了拉倒，"他说，"它待在这宿舍里，臭气熏天，我们都睡不了觉了。"他把手枪放进屁股后面的裤子口袋里。

坎迪久久地看着斯利姆，企图找到某种逆转的办法。但斯利姆没有给他提出任何办法。坎迪最后开了口，声音又轻又绝望，"好吧——你领它走吧。"他没有低头看一眼牧羊犬。他躺回床上，两臂相交垫着脑袋，直直地盯着天花板看。

卡尔森从衣服口袋里掏出一根小皮带，俯下身子，拴在老牧羊犬的脖子上。除了坎迪之外，所有人都注视着他。"走吧，孩子，走吧，孩子。"他和蔼地说。接着他满怀着歉意对坎迪说："它不会有一点儿感觉的。"坎迪躺着一动不动，也没有给出回应。卡尔森拉了拉皮带。"走吧，孩子。"老牧羊犬动作迟缓，身子僵硬，好不容易站立起来，顺着轻轻拉着它的皮带走了。

斯利姆说："卡尔森。"
"嗯？"
"你知道怎么办吗？"
"这话什么意思，斯利姆？"
"带把铁锹。"斯利姆简短地说。
"噢，那当然！我明白你的意思啦。"他牵着老牧

George followed to the door and shut the door and set the latch gently **in its place**①. Candy lay **rigidly**② on his bed staring at the ceiling.

Slim said loudly, "One of my **lead**③ mules got a bad hoof. Got to get some **tar**④ on it." His voice **trailed off**⑤. It was silent outside. Carlson's footsteps died away. The silence came into the room. And the silence lasted.

George **chuckled**⑥, "I bet Lennie's right out there in the barn with his pup. He won't want to come in here no more now he's got a pup."

Slim said, "Candy, you can have any one of them pups you want."

Candy did not answer. The silence fell on the room again. It came out of the night and **invaded**⑦ the room. George said, "Anybody like to play a little **euchre**⑧?"

"I'll **play out**⑨ a few with you," said Whit.

They took places opposite each other at the table under the light, but George did not shuffle the cards. He **rippled**⑩ the edge of the **deck**⑪ nervously, and the little snapping noise drew the eyes of all the men in the room, so that he stopped doing it. The silence fell on the room again. A minute passed, and another minute. Candy lay still, staring at the ceiling. Slim gazed at him for a moment and then looked down at his hands; he **subdued**⑫ one hand with the other, and held it down. There came a little **gnawing**⑬ sound from under the floor and all the men looked down toward it gratefully. Only Candy continued to stare at the ceiling.

"Sounds like there was a rat under there," said George. "We ought to get a trap down there."

Whit **broke out**⑭, "What the hell's takin' him so long? **Lay out**⑮ some cards, why don't you? We ain't going to get no euchre played this way."

George brought the cards together tightly and studied the backs of them.

① in place 在合适的（或常处的、原来的、指定的）位置
② rigidly ['ridʒidli] ad. 僵硬地
③ lead [li:d] a. 被牵引的，受指引的
④ tar [tɑ:] n. 煤焦油沥青
⑤ trail off 逐渐减弱，缩小
⑥ chuckle ['tʃʌk(ə)l] v. 暗笑，咯咯地轻声笑
⑦ invade [in'veid] v. 渗入，渗透，遍布，充溢
⑧ euchre ['ju:kə] n.〈美〉尤克牌戏
⑨ play out 把（比赛）进行到底
⑩ ripple ['rip(ə)l] v. 使呈波状
⑪ deck [dek] n.〈主美〉一副纸牌
⑫ subdue [səb'dju:] v. 抑制，克制
⑬ gnaw [nɔ:] v. 咬，啃，啮
⑭ break out（因感情冲动而）发作
⑮ lay out 摊开（衣物等）

羊犬，走到室外的黑暗中。

乔治跟着走到门口，关上房门，轻轻地落下闩子。坎迪直挺挺地躺在床上，眼睛盯着天花板。

斯利姆大声说："我看管的那些领头的骡子中有一匹的蹄子裂了。得涂抹一些沥青上去。"他的声音越来越低。室外一片寂静。卡尔森的脚步声渐渐消失了。寂静降临室内，持续着。

乔治咯咯笑着说："我敢打赌，伦尼正在牲口棚那边和他的小狗崽待在一块儿呢。他现在有了小狗崽，才不会想到来这儿呢。"

斯利姆说："坎迪，我那些小狗崽你想要哪条都行。"

坎迪没有回话。寂静再次降临在宿舍里。这氛围来源于黑夜，然后袭入宿舍间。乔治说："有谁想要玩几把尤克牌戏¹吗？"

"我来跟你玩几把吧。"惠特说。

他们两个人面对面坐在灯光下的桌子边，但乔治没有洗牌。他神情紧张地摆弄着一副牌，牌叠的边沿在他手下如波浪般起伏，发出轻微的哗啦啦的声音，引来屋里所有人的目光，于是，他停止了手上的动作。沉寂的气氛再次笼罩了宿舍。一分钟过去了，又是一分钟过去了。坎迪仍然躺着，眼睛盯着天花板。斯利姆注视了他片刻，然后低头看着自己的双手。他伸出一只手按住另一只，然后把这手压了下去。地板下面传来细微的啃咬声，大家都低下头朝着发出声音的地方看，心中充满感激。只有坎迪一如既往地注视着天花板。

"听声音，地板下面好像有老鼠呢，"乔治说，"我们应该在那下面放一个捕鼠器。"

惠特脱口说："真是的，怎么磨蹭这么长时间啊？发牌呀，愣着干什么啊？这样我们还玩什么尤克牌戏啊。"

乔治把扑克牌紧紧地拢在一起，仔细查看牌的背

---

1 尤克牌戏是轻松有趣的纸牌游戏，需要四个玩家存在固定的合作伙伴关系，合作伙伴（即对家）坐在对面，只有五张牌，每个玩家和他的对家至少要赢三到五招，赢得越多获得的奖励就越多。

Of Mice and Men

The silence was in the room again.

A shot sounded in the distance. The men looked quickly at the old man. Every head turned toward him.

For a moment he continued to stare at the ceiling. Then he rolled slowly over and faced the wall and lay silent.

George shuffled the cards noisily and **dealt**① them. Whit **drew**② a scoring board to him and set the **pegs**③ to start. Whit said, "I guess you guys really come here to work."

"How do ya mean?" George asked.

Whit laughed. "Well, ya come on a Friday. You got two days to work till Sunday."

"I don't see how you figure," said George.

Whit laughed again. "You do if you been around these big ranches much. Guy that wants to **look over**④ a ranch comes in **Sat'day**⑤ afternoon. He gets Sat'day night supper an' three meals on Sunday, and he can quit Monday mornin' after breakfast without turning his hand. But you come to work Friday noon. You got to **put in**⑥ a day an' a half no matter how you figure."

George looked at him levelly. "We're gonna **stick aroun'**⑦ a while," he said. "Me an' Lennie's gonna **roll up**⑧ a stake."

The door opened quietly and the stable buck put in his head; a lean **negro**⑨ head, **lined**⑩ with pain, the eyes patient. "Mr. Slim."

Slim took his eyes from old Candy. "Huh? Oh! Hello, Crooks. **What's a matter**⑪?"

"You told me to warm up tar for that mule's foot. I got it warm."

"Oh! Sure, Crooks. I'll come right out an' **put** it **on**⑫."

"I can do it if you want, Mr. Slim."

"No. I'll come do it myself." He stood up.

Crooks said, "Mr. Slim."

"Yeah."

"That big new guy's messin' around your pups out in the barn."

① dealt [delt] v.（deal 的过去式和过去分词）发（纸牌）
② drew [dru:] v.（draw 的过去式）拉，拖，拉动，拖动
③ peg [peg] n. 标度钉，得分枚（一种木制或象牙制小钉）
④ look over 把……看一遍
⑤ Sat'day = Saturday
⑥ put in 度过，消磨（时间等）；花费，付出（时间、精力等）
⑦ stick aroun' = stick around 逗留，留下
⑧ roll up 积累，渐次增加（或扩大）
⑨ negro ['ni:grəu] n. 黑人的
⑩ line [lain] v. 使布满纹路，使起皱纹
⑪ what's a matter = what's the matter
⑫ put on 把……放上去

面。宿舍再次笼罩着沉寂的氛围。

远处传来一声枪响。房间里其他人都急忙看向老清扫工。每个人都朝他扭过头去。

他继续盯着天花板看了一会儿，然后慢慢地翻过身去，脸朝着墙壁，一声不吭地躺着。

乔治大声地洗好了牌，然后发牌。惠特把一块计分板拉到自己身边，把木丁挪回到起点。惠特说："我估摸着，你们两个人是真正来干活儿的。"

"你这话是什么意思？"乔治问。

惠特哈哈笑了起来。"嗯，你们是星期五到的，干上两天的活儿才是星期天呢。"

"我不明白你是怎么算的。"乔治说。

惠特又哈哈笑了起来。"假如你在这些大农场上干得久了，你就会明白的。想在农场上混日子的人会星期六下午来。如此一来，他可以享用星期六的晚饭，星期天还有三顿饭。星期一早餐后，他就可以辞职不干了，连手都不用动一下。但你们是星期五中午来的，无论你怎样计算，你们也得干上一天半的活儿。"

乔治一动不动地盯着对方。"我们准备要待上一段时间的，"他说，"我和伦尼想要积攒一笔钱呢。"

有人轻轻地推开了房门，马厩的黑鬼探进脑袋，那是一颗瘦小的黑脑袋，脸上因疼痛显露出皱纹，目光中充满了耐性。"斯利姆先生。"

斯利姆把目光从老坎迪身上移开。"嗯？噢！嘿，克鲁克斯。什么事？"

"您嘱咐我给沥青加热好涂在那匹骡子的蹄子上。我已经热好了。"

"噢，那好哇，克鲁克斯。我这就去涂上。"

"假如您需要，我可以涂的，斯利姆先生。"

"不用，我自己去涂吧。"说完他站起了身。

克鲁克斯说："斯利姆先生。"

"嗯？"

"那个新来的大个子正在牲口棚那边折腾您的小狗崽呢。"

"Well, he ain't doin' no harm. I give him one of them pups."

"Just thought I'd tell ya," said Crooks. "He's takin' 'em outa the nest and **handlin'**① them. That won't do them no good."

"He won't hurt 'em," said Slim. "I'll come along with you now."

George looked up. "If that crazy bastard's foolin' around too much, jus' **kick** him **out**②, Slim."

Slim followed the stable buck out of the room.

George dealt and Whit picked up his cards and examined them. "Seen the new kid yet?" he asked.

"What kid?" George asked.

"Why, Curley's new wife."

"Yeah, I seen her."

"Well, ain't she a **looloo**③?"

"I ain't seen that much of her," said George.

Whit laid down his cards impressively. "Well, stick around an' keep your eyes open. You'll see plenty. She ain't **concealin'**④ nothing. I never seen nobody like her. She got the eye goin' all the time on everybody. I bet she even gives the stable buck the eye. I don't know what the hell she wants."

George asked **casually**⑤, "Been any trouble since she got here?"

It was obvious that Whit was not interested in his cards. He laid his hand down and George **scooped**⑥ it in. George laid out his **deliberate**⑦ solitaire hand—seven cards, and six on top, and five on top of those.

Whit said, "I see what you mean. No, they ain't been nothing yet. Curley's got **yella-jackets**⑧ in his **drawers**⑨, but that's all so far. Ever' time the guys is around she shows up. She's lookin' for Curley, or she thought she **lef'**⑩ somethin' layin' around and she's lookin' for it. Seems like she can't keep away from guys. An' Curley's pants is just crawlin' with ants, but they ain't nothing come of it yet."

George said, "She's gonna make a mess. They's gonna be a bad mess about

① handle ['hænd(ə)l] v. 触，摸，拿，弄，抓

② kick out 撵走

③ looloo ['lu:lu:] n.〈俚〉漂亮的女人

④ conceal [kən'si:l] v. 隐藏，掩盖

⑤ casually ['kæʒjuəli] ad. 随便地，漫不经心地

⑥ scoop [sku:p] v.〈口〉急速地（或挥动着）捡起，拾起，抱起

⑦ deliberate [di'lib(ə)rət] a. 不慌不忙的，从容的，悠闲的

⑧ yella-jacket = yellow jacket〈美口〉小黄蜂（一种体黑且具鲜黄条纹的胡蜂科小蜂）

⑨ drawer [drɔ:(r)] n. [~s]〈长〉内裤

⑩ lef' = left

"噢，他不是搞破坏，我给了他一条小狗崽。"

"我只是觉得要告诉您一声，"克鲁克斯说，"他把小狗崽从狗窝里拿出来了，这样做对小狗崽不好啊。"

"他不会伤害小狗崽的，"斯利姆说，"我现在就随你一块儿去。"

乔治抬起了头，"假如那个笨蛋疯子玩得过分了，你尽管一脚把他踹出来，斯利姆。"

斯利姆跟随着马厩的黑鬼走出了房间。

乔治发完牌，惠特拿起自己的牌研究了起来。"见过那个新来的小娘儿们了吗？"他问。

"什么小娘儿们？"乔治反问。

"嘿，就是柯利刚娶的老婆啊。"

"嗯，我见过她了。"

"那么，你不觉得她是个骚娘儿们吗？"

"我没见过她几次。"乔治说。

惠特慢条斯理地放下手上的牌。"这么着吧，你在附近转一转，睁大眼睛瞧好了，到时就见得多了。她连遮遮掩掩的功夫都不做。我从未见过有谁像她一样的。她随时随地不分对象地抛媚眼。我敢打赌，她甚至都会对着马厩的黑鬼抛媚眼。我真搞不懂她到底想要干什么。"

乔治随口问道："她来到这儿之后惹了什么麻烦吗？"

很显然，惠特对手上的扑克牌并没有什么兴趣。他放下了牌，乔治把他手上的牌收了过去。乔治不慌不忙，摆起了他的单人接龙牌戏——七张牌，上面叠加六张，六张上面再叠加五张。

惠特说："我明白你的意思。不，还没有怎么样呢。柯利一直像内裤里爬进了小黄蜂似的焦躁不安，但仅此而已。每次只要有男人在场，那女的就出现了。她不是来找柯利，就是觉得自己落下了什么东西，跑过来寻找。她似乎离不开男人似的。而柯利的裤裆里像是爬满了蚂蚁。但他们还没有闹出什么事情。"

乔治说："她会惹出麻烦来的，要是出了大麻烦，

her. She's a jail bait all set on the **trigger**①. That Curley got his work **cut out**② for him. Ranch with a bunch of guys on it ain't no place for a girl, specially like her."

Whit said, "If you got **idears**③, you ought ta come in town with us guys tomorra night."

"Why? What's doin'?"

"Jus' the usual thing. We go in to old Susy's place. Hell of a nice place. Old Susy's a **laugh**④—always **crackin'**⑤ jokes. Like she says when we come up on the front porch las' Sat'day night. Susy opens the door and then she yells over her shoulder, 'Get yor coats on, girls, here comes the **sheriff**⑥.' She never talks **dirty**⑦, neither. Got five girls there."

"What's it **set** you **back**⑧?" George asked.

"Two an' a half. You can get a **shot**⑨ for two bits. Susy got nice chairs to set in, too. If a guy don't want a **flop**⑩, **why**⑪ he can just set in the chairs and have a couple or three shots and pass the time of day and Susy don't give a damn. She ain't **rushin'** guys **through**⑫ and kickin' 'em out if they don't want a flop."

"Might go in and look the **joint**⑬ **over**⑭," said George.

"Sure. Come along. It's a hell of a lot of fun—her crackin' jokes all the time. Like she says one time, she says, 'I've knew people that if they got a **rag**⑮ rug on the floor an' a **kewpie**⑯ **doll**⑰ lamp on the **phonograph**⑱ they think they're running a **parlor house**⑲.' That's Clara's house she's talkin' about. An' Susy says, 'I know what you boys want,' she says. 'My girls is clean,' she says, 'an' there ain't no water in my whisky,' she says. 'If any you guys wanta look at a kewpie doll lamp an' take your own chance gettin' burned, why you know where to go.' An' she says, 'There's guys around here walkin' **bow-legged**⑳ 'cause they like to look at a kewpie doll lamp.'"

George asked, "Clara **runs**㉑ the other house, huh?"

"Yeah," said Whit. "We don't never go there. Clara gets three bucks a

① trigger ['trigə] n. 启动装置
② cut out 安排，计划
③ idears = ideas
④ laugh [lɑ:f]〈口〉有趣的人（或同伴）
⑤ crack [kræk] v. 说（笑话等）
⑥ sheriff ['ʃerif] n.〈美〉（大多由民选产生的）县治安官
⑦ dirty ['də:ti] ad.〈口〉肮脏地，下流地，卑鄙地，奸诈地
⑧ set back〈口〉使花费
⑨ shot [ʃɔt] n.〈口〉（烈酒等的）一口，一小杯
⑩ flop [flɔp] n.〈美口〉睡眠，此处指交媾
⑪ why [wai] int. [表示惊讶、不耐烦、赞成、异议犹豫或引出另一种想法] 哎呀！
⑫ rush through 赶紧做，匆匆完成
⑬ look over 察看，参观
⑭ joint [dʒɔint] n.〈口〉地方，处所
⑮ rag [ræg] n. 破布，碎布
⑯ kewpie ['kju:pi] n. 丘比特仙童［Cupid 的变体］
⑰ kewpie doll 丘比特娃娃（有双翅的胖脸赛璐珞或塑料制娃娃，形似爱神 Cupid）
⑱ phonograph ['fəunəgrɑ:f; -græf] n.〈美〉留声机，唱机
⑲ parlor house（尤指陈设考究的）妓院
⑳ bow-legged ['bəu,legid] a. 弓形腿的，膝内翻的
㉑ run [rʌn] v. 经营，管理，开办

一定和她脱不了干系。她就是个祸水妞儿，正等着人上钩呢。柯利真是给自己找了个大麻烦。农场上住着那么些男人，就不是女人该待的地方啊，尤其像她那样的女人。"

惠特说："你要是有想法，那明天晚上就随我们一块儿进城去吧。"

"怎么了？进城干什么？"

"也就平常的事情而已。我们到老苏茜的窑子去，那可是个好去处呢。老苏茜可逗人笑啦——总爱开玩笑打趣。就说上个星期六晚上吧，我们到了她门口，苏茜开了门，接着便扭过头大声喊：'姑娘们，快把衣服穿上，治安官来啦。'她也从来不说脏话，窑子里有五个女的。"

"得花多少钱呢？"乔治问。

"两块五。你可以花两角五分买杯酒喝。苏茜的窑子里还有坐着很舒适的椅子。假如光顾窑子的客人不想找姑娘，嗯，他们可以就只是坐在里面喝上两三杯酒，打发时光，苏茜对此毫不在乎。客人们即便不找姑娘，她也不会撵他们出去的。"

"倒是可以去见识一番那个地方呢。"乔治说。

"没有问题，一起去吧。真是其乐无穷啊——她总爱开玩笑打趣。比如有一次，她说：'我认识一些人，在地上铺上一块破布一样的地毯，在留声机上放上一盏像丘比特娃娃形状的台灯，就觉得自己拥有了高级窑子了。'她那是在说克拉拉的窑子呢。苏茜又说：'我知道你们小伙子们想要什么，'她说，'我这里的姑娘很干净的，'她说，'我这里的威士忌没有掺水。'她说，'你们当中要是有谁想要看一看丘比特娃娃形状的台灯，准备冒险让自己烧着，你们知道该往哪儿走。'她还说，'这儿有些人走路迈着罗圈腿，就是因为他们想要看一看丘比特娃娃形状的台灯是什么样的[1]。'"

乔治问："克拉拉经营了另外一家窑子，是吧？"

"是啊，"惠特说，"我们从来都不光顾那儿。克拉

---

1 暗示迈罗圈腿走路的人患有性病。

Of Mice and Men

crack[1] and thirty-five cents a shot, and she don't crack no jokes. But Susy's place is clean and she got nice chairs. Don't let no **goo-goos**[2] in, neither."

"Me an' Lennie's rollin' up a stake," said George. "I might go in an' set and have a shot, but I ain't **puttin' out**[3] no two and a half."

"Well, a guy got to have some fun sometime," said Whit.

The door opened and Lennie and Carlson came in together. Lennie crept to his bunk and sat down, trying not to attract attention. Carlson reached under his bunk and brought out his bag. He didn't look at old Candy, who still faced the wall. Carlson found a little cleaning **rod**[4] in the bag and a can of oil. He laid them on his bed and then brought out the pistol, took out the magazine and snapped the **loaded**[5] **shell**[6] from the **chamber**[7]. Then he fell to cleaning the **barrel**[8] with the little rod. When the **ejector**[9] snapped, Candy turned over and looked for a moment at the gun before he turned back to the wall again.

Carlson said casually, "Curley been in yet?"

"No," said Whit. "What's **eatin'**[10] on Curley?"

Carlson squinted down the barrel of his gun. "Lookin' for his **old lady**[11]. I seen him going round and round outside."

Whit said sarcastically, "He spends half his time lookin' for her, and the rest of the time she's lookin' for him."

Curley burst into the room excitedly. "Any you guys seen my wife?" he demanded.

"She ain't been here," said Whit.

Curley looked threateningly about the room. "Where the hell's Slim?"

"Went out in the barn," said George. "He was gonna put some tar on a **split**[12] hoof."

Curley's shoulders **dropped**[13] and **squared**[14]. "How long ago'd he go?"

"Five—ten minutes."

Curley jumped out the door and **banged**[15] it after him.

Whit stood up. "I guess maybe I'd like to see this," he said. "Curley's just **spoilin'**[16] or he wouldn't start for Slim. An' Curley's handy, God damn handy.

① crack [kræk] n.〈美俚〉愉快,刺激
② goo-goo ['gu:gu:] a.〈口〉色情的,勾引的
③ put out 拿出,取出

④ rod [rɔd] n.(木质、金属或塑料)杆,竿,棒条
⑤ load [ləud] v. 把弹药装填(枪炮)
⑥ shell [ʃel] n. 弹药筒
⑦ chamber ['tʃeimbə] n.(枪的)弹膛,药室
⑧ barrel ['bær(ə)l] n. 枪管
⑨ ejector [i'dʒektə(r)] n.【机】推出器
⑩ eat [i:t] v.〈美口〉烦扰,打扰
⑪ old lady〈口〉妻子

⑫ split [split] a. 裂开的
⑬ drop [drɔp] v. 下垂
⑭ square [skwɛə] v. 成直角
⑮ bang [bæŋ] v. 砰地敲(或推、扔)
⑯ spoil [spɔil] v. 指 spoiling for fight; be spoiling for 一心想,切望

人鼠之间

拉那儿快活一次收三块,喝一杯收三角五分。她还不会说俏皮话儿。但是,苏茜的窑子干净,还有坐着舒适的椅子。她也不会让举止轻佻的人进入。"

"我和伦尼正要积攒一笔钱来着,"乔治说,"我可以进去坐一坐,喝一杯,但我不会掏两块五的。"

"哎呀,人有时候得享受一番才是呢。"惠特说。

宿舍的门开了,伦尼和卡尔森一块儿走了进来。伦尼蹑手蹑脚地走到床边坐了下来,尽量不引起其他人的注意。卡尔森把手伸到床底下,拿出他的袋子。老坎迪依然把脸对着墙壁,卡尔森也并不去看他。卡尔森从袋子里拿出一根很细的通条和一罐油,把东西放到了床上,随即拿出手枪,取出弹仓,咔嗒一声把子弹从膛内退出。然后他开始用通条清洗枪膛。枪的推出器发出咔嗒的响声时,坎迪转过身看了一会儿那把枪,然后又翻身对着墙壁。

卡尔森不经意地问:"柯利到过这儿吗?"

"没有,"惠特说,"柯利怎么啦?"

卡尔森眯着眼睛朝枪管里看。"找他老婆呢。我看见他在外面到处找。"

惠特带着讥讽的口气说:"他把一半时间用在寻找她上面了,剩下的时间被她找。"

柯利冲进了宿舍,情绪很激动。"你们中有谁看见我老婆了吗?"他问。

"她没来过这儿。"惠特说。

柯利面露威胁地把整个房间环顾了一番。"真见鬼,斯利姆哪儿去啦?"

"到牲口棚那边去了,"乔治说,"有匹骡子的蹄子开裂了,他要去涂些沥青。"

柯利垂下肩膀,随即又挺直了。"他出去多长时间了?"

"五分——十分钟吧。"

柯利奔了出去,砰的一声关上了身后的门。

惠特站了起来。"我想我还是去看看吧,"他说,"柯利这是成心想打架,否则,他不会跑去找斯利姆。而柯

· 093 ·

Got in the finals for the **Golden Gloves**①. He got newspaper **clippings**② about it." He considered. "But jus' the same, he better leave Slim alone. Nobody don't know what Slim can do."

"Thinks Slim's with his wife, don't he?" said George.

"Looks like it," Whit said. "'Course Slim ain't. Least I don't think Slim is. But I like to see the **fuss**③ if it **comes off**④. Come on, le's go."

George said, "I'm stayin' right here. I don't want to get mixed up in nothing. Lennie and me got to make a stake."

Carlson finished the cleaning of the gun and put it in the bag and pushed the bag under his bunk. "I guess I'll go out and look her over," he said. Old Candy lay still, and Lennie, from his bunk, watched George cautiously.

When Whit and Carlson were gone and the door closed after them, George turned to Lennie. "What you got on your mind?"

"I ain't done nothing, George. Slim says I better not pet them pups so much for a while. Slim says it ain't good for them; so I come right in. I been good, George."

"I coulda told you that," said George.

"Well, I wasn't hurtin' 'em none. I jus' had mine in my **lap**⑤ pettin' it."

George asked, "Did you see Slim out in the barn?"

"Sure I did. He tol' me I better not pet that pup no more."

"Did you see that girl?"

"You mean Curley's girl?"

"Yeah. Did she come in the barn?"

"No. Anyways I never seen her."

"You never seen Slim talkin' to her?"

"Uh-uh. She ain't been in the barn."

"O.K.," said George. "I guess them guys ain't gonna see no fight. If there's any fightin', Lennie, you keep out of it."

① Golden Gloves 指 National Golden Gloves 或其他包括区域性比赛在内的业余拳击比赛
② clipping ['klipiŋ] n.（从报纸、杂志等）剪下的资料，简报
③ fuss [fʌs] n. 忙乱，大惊小怪，小题大做
④ come off 发生，举行

⑤ lap [læp] n.（人坐着时）腰以下到膝为止的大腿部

利身手敏捷，真他妈身手敏捷。他打进过'金手套'拳王赛的决赛。他还保存着相关报道的剪报呢。"他想了想，"但是，他最好还是不要去惹斯利姆。谁都不知道斯利姆会干出什么事情来。"

"他认为斯利姆和他老婆在一块儿对吧？"乔治问。

"看起来是这么回事，"惠特说，"斯利姆当然不会做这样的事情。至少我觉得斯利姆不会。但是，万一发生了争执，我倒是想要去看一看。走吧，我们看看去。"

乔治说："我就待在这儿吧。我不想掺和进什么事情去。我和伦尼还有一笔钱要攒呢。"

卡尔森清理好手枪，放进那个袋子里，又把袋子推回到床底下。"我出去找找她吧。"他说。老坎迪仍然一动不动躺着。伦尼躺在自己床上，谨慎地盯着乔治看。

惠特和卡尔森出去关上了房门后，乔治朝伦尼转过身。"你心里想什么呢？"

"我什么都没有做啊，乔治。斯利姆说，我最好暂时不要总去摸那些小狗崽。斯利姆说，摸了对小狗崽不好。所以我就进来了。我一直很乖的，乔治。"

"我正要告诉你这一点呢。"乔治说。

"嗯，我没有伤着任何一条小狗崽。我只是把我那一条捧在膝上摸了摸。"

乔治问："你在牲口棚那边看见斯利姆了吗？"

"我当然看见了啦。他告诉我说，最好不要再摸小狗崽了。"

"你看见那个女的了吗？"

"你指的是柯利的老婆吗？"

"是啊，她去牲口棚了吗？"

"没有，反正我没有看见她的人影儿。"

"你从来没有看见过斯利姆和她说话吗？"

"没，没，她没有到过牲口棚。"

"好吧，"乔治说，"我猜那两个家伙看不到打架的场面了。假如他们打起来，伦尼，你离现场远一点儿。"

Of Mice and Men

"I don't want no fights," said Lennie. He got up from his bunk and sat down at the table, across from George. Almost automatically George shuffled the cards and laid out his solitaire hand. He used a deliberate, thoughtful slowness.

Lennie reached for a **face card**① and studied it, then turned it upside down and studied it. "Both ends the same," he said. "George, why is it both ends the same?"

"I don't know," said George. "That's jus' the way they make 'em. What was Slim doin' in the barn when you seen him?"

"Slim?"

"Sure. You seen him in the barn, an' he tol' you not to pet the pups so much."

"Oh, yeah. He had a can a' tar an' a paint brush. I don't know what for."

"You sure that girl didn't come in like she come in here today?"

"No. She never come."

George sighed. "You give me a good **whore house**② every time," he said. "A guy can go in an' get drunk and get ever'thing outa his **system**③ all at once, an' no messes. And he knows how much it's gonna set him back. These here jail baits is just set on the trigger of the **hoosegow**④."

Lennie followed his words admiringly, and moved his lips a little to keep up. George continued, "You remember Andy Cushman, Lennie? Went to grammar school?"

"The one that his old lady used to make hot cakes for the kids?" Lennie asked.

"Yeah. That's the one. You can remember anything if there's anything to eat in it." George looked carefully at the solitaire hand. He put an ace up on his scoring **rack**⑤ and piled a two, three and four of **diamonds**⑥ on it. "Andy's in San Quentin right now on account of a tart," said George.

Lennie **drummed**⑦ on the table with his fingers. "George?"

"Huh?"

"George, how long's it gonna be till we get that little place an' live on the

① face card〈主美〉=court card 人头牌，花牌（纸牌的 K、Q、J）

② whore house〈口〉妓院
③ system ['sistəm] n.（机体内多个器官组成的）系统，身体

④ hoosegow ['hu:sgau] n.〈美俚〉监牢，班房

⑤ rack [ræk] n.（一般设有挂钩、搁板或横档等的）架子，挂架，支架，搁架

⑥ diamond ['daiəmənd] n.（一张）方块牌
⑦ drum [drʌm] v. 有节奏地敲击（鼓等）

"我根本不想打架。"伦尼说。他从床上起身，坐到桌子边，面对着乔治。乔治几乎下意识地洗着牌，玩起了他的单人接龙牌戏。他手法娴熟，深思熟虑，慢条斯理。

伦尼伸手拿起一张带人脸的扑克牌，仔细观察了起来，然后又掉过头来仔细观察。"两头都是一样呢，"他说，"乔治，为什么扑克牌两头都是一样的呢？"

"我不知道，"乔治说，"扑克牌就是制作成这样的。你在牲口棚那边看见斯利姆时，他在干什么呢？"

"斯利姆吗？"

"对呀。你在牲口棚里看见他的，他还嘱咐你不要总去摸小狗崽来着。"

"噢，是啊。他拿了一罐沥青和一把刷油漆用的刷子。我不知道他要干什么去。"

"你确定那个女人没有到牲口棚那边去吗，就像她今天白天到这儿来一样？"

"对，她绝对没有去。"

乔治叹息了一声。"说来说去还是窑子好啊，"他说，"男人可以进去醉一场，来一次痛快的，什么麻烦也不会有。他花钱花在明处，心里清楚。这些祸水妞儿啊，上了她们的钩就只能进班房了。"

伦尼一字一句地听着，一脸崇敬，嘴唇稍稍蠕动着，好跟上对方说话的节拍。乔治接着说："你还记得安迪·库什曼吗，伦尼？上过文法学校的？"

"是从前他老婆给孩子们做热蛋糕的那个吧？"伦尼问。

"是啊，就是那个。只要是和吃的有关，你什么事情都记得住。"乔治仔细看着单人接龙牌戏。他在计分板上放了一张 A，又在上面垒了方块二、三和四。"安迪现在待在圣昆丁监狱呢，为了一个荡妇。"乔治说。

伦尼用手指击打着桌面。"乔治？"

"嗯？"

"乔治，还要过多长时间，我们才能拥有那一小块

fatta the lan'—an' rabbits?"

"I don't know", said George. "We gotta get a big stake together. I know a little place we can get cheap, but they ain't givin' it away."

Old Candy turned slowly over. His eyes were wide open. He watched George carefully.

Lennie said, "Tell about that place, George."

"I jus' tol' you, jus' las' night."

"Go on—tell again, George."

"Well, it's ten acres," said George. "Got a little **win'mill**①. Got a little **shack**② on it, an' a chicken **run**③. Got a kitchen, **orchard**④, cherries, apples, peaches, **'cots**⑤, **nuts**⑥, got a few berries. They's a place for **alfalfa**⑦ and plenty water to **flood**⑧ it. They's a pig **pen**⑨—"

"An' rabbits, George."

"No place for rabbits now, but I could **easy**⑩ build a few hutches and you could feed alfalfa to the rabbits."

"Damn right, I could," said Lennie. "You God damn right I could."

George's hands stopped working with the cards. His voice was growing warmer. "An' we could have a few pigs. I could build a **smoke house**⑪ like the one **gran'pa**⑫ had, an' when we kill a pig we can **smoke**⑬ the bacon and the hams, and make sausage an' all like that. An' when the **salmon**⑭ **run**⑮ **up**⑯ river we could catch a hundred of 'em an' **salt**⑰ 'em down or smoke 'em. We could have them for breakfast. They ain't nothing so nice as **smoked**⑱ salmon. When the fruit come in we could **can**⑲ it— and tomatoes, they're easy to can. Ever' Sunday we'd kill a chicken or a rabbit. Maybe we'd have a cow or a goat, and the cream is so God damn thick you got to cut it with a knife and take it out with a spoon."

Lennie watched him with wide eyes, and old Candy watched him too.

① win'mill = windmill ['win(d)mil] n. 风车房，风车
② shack [ʃæk] n. 简陋木屋，棚屋
③ run [rʌn] n. 饲养场
④ orchard ['ɔ:tʃəd] n. 果园
⑤ 'cots = apricots（apricot ['eiprikɔt] n.【植】杏，杏树）
⑥ nut [nʌt] n.【植】坚果
⑦ alfalfa [æl'fælfə] n.【植】苜蓿，紫苜蓿
⑧ flood [flʌd] v. 浇灌水于
⑨ pen [pen] n.（围养禽畜的）圈，栏
⑩ easy ['i:zi] ad. 容易地，轻松地，顺利地
⑪ smoke house〈主美〉（熏制鱼、肉等的）烟熏室
⑫ gran'pa = grandpa
⑬ smoke [sməuk] v. 熏制（鱼、肉等）
⑭ salmon ['sæmən] n.【鱼】鲑，大麻哈鱼
⑮ run [rʌn] v.（鱼在产卵期）洄游
⑯ up [ʌp] prep. 往……的上游
⑰ salt [sɔ:lt; sɔlt] v. 用盐给……调味，用盐腌，盐渍
⑱ smoked [sməukt] a. 用烟处理的
⑲ can [kæn] v. 把（食品等）装罐（或听、坛瓶）保存

土地，然后依靠土地过日子——还能饲养兔子呢？"

"我不知道，"乔治说，"我们得合起来积攒一大笔钱才行。我知道一块土地，可以很便宜买到，但人家不会不要钱白送的。"

老坎迪缓慢翻过身来，眼睛睁得大大的，仔细地注视着乔治。

伦尼说："说说那个地方吧，乔治。"

"我才对你说过，就在昨天晚上。"

"接着说呗——再说一遍吧，乔治。"

"好吧，那地方面积十英亩[1]，"乔治说，"里面有架小风车，有幢小木屋，有间鸡舍，有间厨房，有座果园——果园里有樱桃树、苹果树、桃子树、杏子树、坚果树，还有一些草莓树。还有一片苜蓿地，水量充足。还有一座猪圈——"

"还有兔子呢，乔治。"

"那儿现在还没有饲养兔子的地方，但我不费什么劲儿就能做出几个兔笼子，你可以给兔子喂苜蓿。"

"说得太对啦，我可以的，"伦尼说，"你说得真是太对啦，我可以的。"

乔治的双手不再摆弄扑克牌了，说话的声音也慢慢变得热络起来。"我们还可以饲养几头猪。我可以盖一间过去爷爷盖过的那种熏肉房，宰杀了猪后，我们可以熏肉，熏火腿，制作香肠，还有诸如此类的食品。等到大马哈鱼逆流而上时，我们可以捕他个上百条，用盐腌起来，或者用烟熏好。我们早饭时就可以吃了。若论吃的，没有什么比得上烟熏的大马哈鱼味道鲜美了。到了水果收获的季节，我们可以制作水果罐头——还有番茄，番茄罐头制作起来很容易。每个星期天，我们都可以宰杀一只鸡或者一只兔子。我们或许还可以饲养一头母牛或者一只山羊，奶汁那可都是上等品质啊，很稠的，你得用刀去切，然后用勺子舀出来呢。"

伦尼睁大眼睛注视着他，老坎迪也注视着他。伦尼

1　一英亩约等于 4047 平方米。

· 099 ·

Lennie said softly, "We could live offa the fatta the lan'."

"Sure," said George. "All **kin's**① **a**② vegetables in the garden, and if we want a little whisky we can sell a few eggs or something, or some milk. We'd jus' live there. We'd belong there. There wouldn't be no more runnin' round the country and gettin' fed by a **Jap**③ cook. No, sir, we'd have our own place where we belonged and not sleep in no bunk house."

"Tell about the house, George," Lennie begged.

"Sure, we'd have a little house an' a room to **ourself**④. Little **fat**⑤ iron stove, an' in the winter we'd keep a fire goin' in it. It ain't enough land so we'd have to work too hard. Maybe six, seven hours a day. We wouldn't have to buck no barley eleven hours a day. An' when we **put in**⑥ a crop, why, we'd be there to **take** the crop **up**⑦. We'd know what come of our planting."

"An' rabbits," Lennie said eagerly. "An' I'd take care of 'em. Tell how I'd do that, George."

"Sure, you'd go out in the alfalfa patch an' you'd have a sack. You'd fill up the sack and bring it in an' put it in the rabbit cages."

"They'd **nibble**⑧ an' they'd nibble," said Lennie, "the way they do. I seen 'em."

"Ever' six weeks or so," George continued, "them **does**⑨ would **throw**⑩ a litter so we'd have plenty rabbits to eat an' to sell. An' we'd keep a few **pigeons**⑪ to go flyin' around the win'mill like they done when I was a kid." He looked **raptly**⑫ at the wall over Lennie's head. "An' it'd be our own, an' nobody could **can**⑬ us. If we don't like a guy we can say, 'Get the hell out,' and **by God**⑭ he's got to do it. An' if a **fren'**⑮ come along, why we'd have an extra bunk, an' we'd say, 'Why don't you spen' the night?' an' by God he would. We'd have a **setter**⑯ dog and a couple stripe cats, but you gotta watch out them cats don't get the little rabbits."

Lennie breathed hard. "You jus' let 'em try to get the rabbits. I'll break

① kin's = kinds
② a = of

③ Jap [dʒæp] a.〈口〉〈贬〉日本的，日本佬的

④ ourself = ourselves
⑤ fat [fæt] a. 巨大的

⑥ put in 种植
⑦ take up 拿走

⑧ nibble ['nɪb(ə)l] v. 啃，一点儿一点儿地咬（或吃）
⑨ doe [dəʊ] n. 雌兔
⑩ throw [θrəʊ] v.（母畜）下（仔）
⑪ pigeon ['pɪdʒɪn; 'pɪdʒ(ə)n] n. 鸽子（泛指野鸽和家鸽）
⑫ raptly [ræptlɪ] ad. 着迷地，痴迷地，狂喜地，全神贯注地，出神地，神情痴迷地
⑬ can [kæn] v.〈美口〉解雇（职工）
⑭ by God 老天作证
⑮ fren'= friend
⑯ setter ['setə] n. 赛特犬（一种捕猎用的长毛狗，经过训练能站定用鼻指示猎物的所在）

轻声说："我们可以靠那片土地过日子呢。"

"可不是嘛，"乔治说，"菜园子里面种着各种各样的蔬菜。假如我们想要来点儿威士忌，那就卖上几个鸡蛋，或者卖点儿牛奶，诸如此类吧。我们就这样住在那儿，我们属于那儿。我们再也不需要四乡八镇到处奔波，靠吃日本厨师做的饭过日子了。不，兄弟啊，我们会有一片属于我们自己的土地，不用再睡在集体宿舍里。"

"说说我们那幢房子吧，乔治。"伦尼恳求道。

"没问题，我们会拥有一幢小住宅，一个属于我们自己的房间。里面有一个小型的大肚子铁炉，到了冬天，我们就把炉子生起来。土地面积不怎么大，我们用不着过于劳累。或许一天干个六七个小时就够了。我们不用再每天背十一个小时的大麦包了。等到我们在土里种了庄稼后，嘿，我们便待那儿等着收获。我们会知道，自己种植的东西能有什么收获。"

"还有兔子呢，"伦尼热切地说，"我来照料那些兔子。说说我会怎么照料吧，乔治。"

"没问题，你会到外面的苜蓿地里去，手里拿着个袋子，你会往袋子里面装满苜蓿，然后扛回家，放到兔笼里面去。"

"兔子们会啃呀啃的，"伦尼说，"兔子吃东西就是那个样子的，我见识过。"

"每过六个星期左右吧，"乔治接着说，"兔子便会产一窝崽，因此，我们便会有足够多的兔子可供食用和出售了。我们再饲养几只鸽子，它们会在风车的上方飞来飞去，就像我小时候见过的那样。"他出神地看着伦尼脑袋上方的墙壁。"那个地方是属于我们的，任何人都无法赶我们走。假如我们不喜欢某个人，我们便可以说'滚出去'，天哪，他就必须得滚蛋了。假如某个朋友来了，嘿，我们有了空床铺，便可以说：'何不在这儿过夜呢？'天哪，他就会留下来过夜。我们还要饲养一只塞特犬，两只带条纹的猫，但你得当心猫，别让它们逮着小兔子。"

伦尼的气息重了起来。"你让它们逮兔子试一试，

Of Mice and Men

their God damn necks. I'll . . . I'll **smash**① 'em with a stick." He **subsided**②, **grumbling**③ to himself, threatening the future cats which might dare to disturb the future rabbits.

George sat **entranced**④ with his own picture.

When Candy spoke they both jumped as though they had been caught doing something **reprehensible**⑤. Candy said, "You know where's a place like that?"

George was on guard immediately. "S'pose I do," he said. "What's that to you?"

"You don't need to tell me where it's at. Might be any place."

"Sure," said George. "That's right. You couldn't find it in a hundred years."

Candy went on excitedly, "How much they want for a place like that?"

George watched him suspiciously. "Well—I could get it for six hundred bucks. The ol' people that owns it is **flat**⑥ **bust**⑦ an' the **ol'**⑧ lady needs an operation. Say—what's it to you? You got nothing to do with us."

Candy said, "I ain't much good with on'y one hand. I lost my hand right here on this ranch. That's why they give me a job swampin'. An' they give me two hunderd an' fifty dollars 'cause I los' my hand. An' I got fifty more saved up right in the bank, right now. Tha's three hunderd, and I got fifty more comin' the end a the month. Tell you what—" He leaned forward eagerly. "S'pose I **went in with**⑨ you guys. **Tha's**⑩ three hunderd an' fifty bucks I'd put in. I ain't much good, but I could cook and tend the chickens and **hoe**⑪ the garden some. How'd that be?"

George half-closed his eyes. "I gotta think about that. We was always gonna do it by ourselves."

Candy interrupted him, "I'd make a **will**⑫ an' leave my **share**⑬ to you guys in case I **kick off**⑭, 'cause I ain't got no relatives nor nothing. You guys got any money? Maybe we could **do**⑮ **her**⑯ right now?"

George **spat**⑰ on the floor disgustedly. "We got ten bucks between us." Then he said thoughtfully, "Look, if me an' Lennie work a month an' don't spen'

人鼠之间

① smash [smæʃ] v.（哗啦一声）打碎，打破，摧毁
② subside [səb'saɪd] v. 平静，平息
③ grumble ['grʌmb(ə)l] v. 咕哝
④ entrance [in'trɑ:ns] v. 使着迷
⑤ reprehensible [ˌrepri'hensib(ə)l] a. 应受斥责的，应受指摘的

⑥ flat [flæt] ad.〈口〉完全地，彻底地
⑦ bust [bʌst] a. 破产了的
⑧ ol'=old

⑨ go in with 和……联合起来，与……合作，与……合伙（went [went] v. go 的过去式）
⑩ tha's = that's
⑪ hoe [həu] v. 用锄为（庄稼等）除草松土，用锄为（作物）间苗，用锄除（草），用锄整（地）
⑫ will [wil] n. 遗嘱
⑬ share [ʃεə] n. 一份，份（儿）
⑭ kick off〈口〉死亡
⑮ do [du:] v. 处理
⑯ her 指前文提到的土地
⑰ spat [spæt] v. 吐唾沫，吐痰（spit 的过去式和过去分词）

看我不拧断它们该死的脖子。我会……我会用棍子敲死它们。"他情绪平静了下来，咕哝着喃喃自语，对胆敢触碰未来兔子的那些未来的猫儿说着威胁的话。

乔治坐在那儿，沉浸在自己想象的场景中。

坎迪开口说话后，他们两个人跳了起来，仿佛他们在做什么应该受到指责的事情被人给逮住了。坎迪说："你知道哪儿有这样一片地方吗？"

乔治立刻警觉起来。"就算我知道吧，"他说，"与你又有什么关系呢？"

"你不必告诉我具体在什么地方，什么地方都有可能。"

"可以啊，"乔治说，"这就对啦。你一百年都无法找到那个地方。"

坎迪激动地问："那样一片土地要卖多少钱呢？"

乔治注视着他，满腹狐疑。"这么说吧——我可以用六百块钱买到它。拥有那片土地的那对老夫妻已经完全破产了。老太太还需要做手术。嘿——这与你有什么关系呢？你与我们没有任何关系。"

坎迪说："我行动很不方便，因为我只有一只手。我就是在这座农场上失去另外一只手的，因此，他们派给了我一份清扫的差事。我失去了一只手，他们赔偿了我两百五十块钱。我现在在银行里还有五十多块钱存款呢。这样总共加起来有三百块钱，到了月底时还有五十多块进账。这么对你说吧——"他热切地倾身向前，"假如我和你们两个合作，那就算我出三百五十块吧。我干活儿不是很方便，但我能够做饭，喂鸡，给菜园子锄锄草什么的。这样如何呢？"

乔治半闭上眼。"这事我得考虑一下。我们一直都打算自己干的。"

坎迪打断他的话说："我会立个遗嘱，万一我翘辫子了，我会把自己的份额留给你们两个人，因为我无亲无故。你们有些钱了吗？我们或许可以立刻付诸实施呢。"

乔治对着地板啐了一口唾沫，表露出厌恶的神情。"我们两个人合在一起共有十块钱。"他随即思索着说，

· 103 ·

nothing, we'll have a hunderd bucks. That'd be four fifty. I bet we could **swing**① her for that. Then you an' Lennie could go get her started an' I'd get a job an' make up the **res'**②, an' you could sell eggs an' stuff like that."

They fell into a silence. They looked at one another, amazed. This thing they had never really believed in was coming true. George said **reverently**③, "Jesus Christ! I bet we could swing her." His eyes were full of wonder. "I bet we could swing her," he repeated softly.

Candy sat on the edge of his bunk. He scratched the **stump**④ of his wrist nervously. "I got hurt four year ago," he said. "They'll can me **purty soon**⑤. Jus' as soon as I can't swamp out no bunk houses they'll **put me on**⑥ the county. Maybe if I give you guys my money, you'll let me hoe in the garden even after I ain't no good at it. An' I'll wash dishes an' little chicken stuff like that. But I'll be on our own place, an' I'll be let to work on our own place." He said miserably, "You seen what they done to my dog tonight? They says he wasn't no good to himself nor nobody else. When they can me here I wisht somebody'd shoot me. But they won't do nothing like that. I won't have no place to go, an' I can't get no more jobs. I'll have thirty dollars more comin', time you guys is ready to quit."

George stood up. "We'll do her," he said. "We'll fix up that little old place an' we'll go live there." He sat down again. They all sat still, all **bemused**⑦ by the beauty of the thing, each mind was **popped**⑧ into the future when this lovely thing should come about.

George said wonderingly, "S'pose **they was**⑨ a **carnival**⑩ or a **circus**⑪ come to town, or a ball game, or any damn thing." Old Candy nodded in appreciation of the idea. "We'd just go to her," George said. "We wouldn't ask nobody if we could. Jus' say, 'We'll go to her,' an' we would. Jus' **milk**⑫ the cow and **sling**⑬ some grain to the chickens an' go to her."

① swing [swiŋ] v. 成功地处置
② res' = rest

③ reverently ['revərəntli] ad. 恭敬地，虔诚地

④ stump [stʌmp] n. 残肢
⑤ purty soon = pretty soon
⑥ put on 加负担于

⑦ bemused [bi'mju:zd] a. 出神的，痴想的，沉思的
⑧ pop [pɔp] v. 冷不防地出现（或发生），（突然）冒出
⑨ they〈非规范〉[与动词 to be 连用，表示"有"的意思]=there
⑩ carnival ['kɑ:niv(ə)l] n. 〈美〉（流动）游艺团
⑪ circus ['sə:kəs] n. 马戏团，马戏演出
⑫ milk [milk] v. 挤……的奶
⑬ sling [sliŋ] v. 抛，投，掷，扔

"听我说，假如我和伦尼干一个月活儿，不花销什么，我们便可以积攒一百块。那样合起来就有四百五十块了。我敢说，有了这笔钱，我们便可以先抵押过来。然后，你和伦尼先过去，我再找一份差事，弥补剩余的欠款。你们还可以卖些鸡蛋什么的。"

他们不再说话了，而是面面相觑，心中诧异。这种从来都没有真正相信的事情竟然会梦想成真。乔治毕恭毕敬地说："天哪！我敢打赌，我们能够获得那片土地的。"他的目光中洋溢着惊叹的神情，"我敢打赌，我们可以获得那片土地的。"他柔声重复着说。

坎迪坐到床沿，神情紧张，不停地挠着断手的腕部。"我是四年前受伤的，"他说，"他们过了不多久就会要我走人的，一旦我不能清扫宿舍了，他们就会让我进救济院去。说不定，我要是把钱给你们两个人，即便不中用了，你们还会让我给菜园子锄锄草什么的。我还可以洗洗碗碟，喂喂鸡什么的。但我总归是待在属于自己的地盘上，是在属于自己的地盘上干活儿。"他悲痛地说，"你今晚看见他们是怎样对待我的牧羊犬的吧？他们说，我的牧羊犬不中用了，对其他人也没有任何用处。等到他们撵我离开这儿时，我巴不得什么人一枪毙了我。但是，他们绝不会这样做的。到时候我无处可去，也不可能找得到差事干。等到你们两个人辞职离开时，我还有三十块钱的进账。"

乔治站起来。"我们会获得那片土地的，"他说，"我们可以搞定那一小片地方，到那片土地上生活。"他重新坐下来。他们全部平静地坐着，沉浸在这件美好的事情当中，每个人的心里都在憧憬着获得那片土地后的前景。

乔治用充满了惊叹的口气说："假如城里有狂欢节，或者来了马戏团，或者球赛，或者任何好玩的事情。"老坎迪听得连连点头，"我们便只管去，"乔治说，"我们不需要问任何人能不能去。只需要说：'我们去吧。'就可以去了。只要给牛挤了奶，给鸡喂过谷子，我们就可以出发了。"

Of Mice and Men

"An' put some grass to the rabbits," Lennie broke in. "I wouldn't never forget to feed them. When we gon'ta do it, George?"

"In one month. Right squack in one month. Know what I'm **gon'ta**① do? I'm gon'ta write to them old people that owns the place that we'll take it. An' Candy'll send a hunderd dollars to **bind**② her."

"Sure will," said Candy. "They got a good stove there?"

"Sure, got a nice stove, burns coal or wood."

"I'm gonna take my pup," said Lennie. "I bet by Christ he likes it there, by Jesus."

Voices were approaching from outside. George said quickly, "Don't tell nobody about it. Jus' us three an' nobody else. They **li'ble**③ to can us so we can't make no stake. Jus' go on like we was gonna buck barley the rest of our lives, then all of a sudden some day we'll go get our pay an' scram outa here."

Lennie and Candy nodded, and they were grinning with delight. "Don't tell nobody," Lennie said to himself.

Candy said, "George."

"Huh?"

"I ought to of shot that dog myself, George. I shouldn't ought to of let no stranger shoot my dog."

The door opened. Slim came in, followed by Curley and Carlson and Whit. Slim's hands were black with tar and he was scowling. Curley **hung**④ close to his elbow.

Curley said, "Well, I didn't mean nothing, Slim. I just ast you."

Slim said, "Well, you been askin' me too often. I'm gettin' God damn sick of it. If you can't look after your own God damn wife, what you expect me to do about it? You lay offa me."

"I'm jus' tryin' to tell you I didn't mean nothing," said Curley. "I jus' thought you might of saw her."

"Why'n't you tell her to stay the hell home where she belongs?" said Carlson. "You let her hang around bunk houses and pretty soon you're gonna

① gon'ta = gonna

② bind [baind] v. 使（交易、契约等）定局

③ li'ble = liable ['laiəb(ə)l] a. 会……的，有……倾向的

④ hung [hʌŋ] v.（hang 的过去式和过去分词）逗留，徘徊

"还要割些草给兔子吃，"伦尼冷不防冒出一句，"我决不会忘记喂兔子的。我们什么时候才能去做这件事情呢，乔治？"

"过一个月吧。一个月就够了。知道我准备怎么做吗？我打算给那对拥有那片土地的老夫妻写封信，说我们要买下那片土地。坎迪可以寄去一百块钱当定金。"

"没有问题，"坎迪说，"那儿的炉子好用吗？"

"当然啦，那炉子好用着呢，煤炭和木柴都可以烧。"

"我要带上我那条小狗崽，"伦尼说，"我对天发誓，小狗狗会喜欢那儿的，天哪。"

室外有说话的声音临近。乔治急忙说："这件事情不要告诉任何人，就我们三个人知道，任何其他人都别说。他们会解雇我们的，那样的话，我们便积攒不了那笔钱了。"

坎迪和伦尼点了点头，两人都咧开嘴，高兴地笑了。"不要告诉任何人。"伦尼自言自语说。

坎迪说："乔治。"

"嗯？"

"我应该自己开枪打死那条牧羊犬的，乔治。我不应该让一个陌生人开枪打死自己的狗。"

宿舍的房门开了。斯利姆走了进来，后面跟着柯利、卡尔森和惠特。斯利姆的双手沾满了黑色的沥青。他沉着脸，柯利紧跟在他身后。

柯利说："好啦，我没有别的意思，斯利姆，只是问问你而已。"

斯利姆说："哼，你问的次数也太多了。我他妈的都被问烦了。要是你都看不住你该死的老婆，你还指望我干点儿什么呢？你离我远点儿。"

"我只是想告诉你，我并没有别的什么意思。"柯利说，"我只是觉得，你可能看见过她呢。"

"你干吗不告诉她，她应该待在家里，那才是她该待的地方呢？"卡尔森说，"你让她成天跑到宿舍区来

· 107 ·

have **som'pin**[1] on your hands and you won't be able to do nothing about it."

Curley **whirled**[2] on Carlson. "You keep outa this **les'**[3] you wanta step outside."

Carlson laughed. "You God damn punk," he said. "You tried to **throw a scare into**[4] Slim, an' you couldn't make it **stick**[5]. Slim threw a scare inta you. You're **yella**[6] as a frog belly. I don't care if you're the best **welter**[7] in the country. You come for me, an' I'll kick your God damn head off."

Candy joined the attack with joy. "Glove fulla vaseline," he said disgustedly. Curley glared at him. His eyes slipped on past and lighted on Lennie; and Lennie was still smiling with delight at the memory of the ranch.

Curley stepped over to Lennie like a terrier. "What the hell you laughin' at?"

Lennie looked **blankly**[8] at him. "Huh?"

Then Curley's **rage**[9] exploded. "Come on, ya big bastard. Get up on your feet. No big son-of-a-bitch is gonna laugh at me. I'll show ya who's yella."

Lennie looked helplessly at George, and then he got up and tried to **retreat**[10]. Curley was **balanced**[11] and **poised**[12]. He **slashed**[13] at Lennie with his **left**[14], and then smashed down his nose with a **right**[15]. Lennie gave a cry of terror. Blood **welled**[16] from his nose. "George," he cried. "Make 'um let me alone, George." He backed until he was against the wall, and Curley followed, **slugging**[17] him in the face. Lennie's hands remained at his sides; he was too frightened to defend himself.

George was on his feet yelling, "Get him, Lennie. Don't let him do it."

Lennie covered his face with his huge **paws**[18] and **bleated**[19] with terror. He cried, "Make 'um stop, George." Then Curley attacked his stomach and **cut off**[20] his **wind**[21].

Slim jumped up. "The dirty little **rat**[22]," he cried, "I'll get 'um myself."

① som'pin = something
② whirl [wə:l] v.（突然）转向
③ les' = unless
④ throw a scare into sb. 使某人吓一跳
⑤ stick [stik] v. 被认为有效，继续有效
⑥ yella = yellow ['jeləu] a.〈口〉胆小的，卑怯的，卑鄙的
⑦ welter ['weltə] n. 大人物，大东西，大家伙
⑧ blankly ['blæŋkli] ad. 茫然地，无表情地，惶惑地
⑨ rage [reidʒ] n.（一阵）盛怒
⑩ retreat [ri'tri:t] v. 后退，退避，躲避
⑪ balance ['bæləns] v.（在重量、力量、效果等方面）使相等，和……相等，使相称，和……相称
⑫ poise [pɔiz] v. 使平衡，使平稳
⑬ slash [slæʃ] v. 挥击
⑭ left [left] n.（尤指拳击中的）左手，左手拳
⑮ right [rait] n.（拳击中的）右手，右手拳
⑯ well [wel] v. 流出，涌出，冒出，溢出
⑰ slug [slʌg] v.（用拳头）重击
⑱ paw [pɔ:] n.〈主贬〉（尤指笨拙的）手
⑲ bleat [bli:t] v. 以颤抖的声音说话
⑳ cut off 切断，阻断，截断，停止
㉑ wind [wind] n. 气息，呼吸，呼吸能力
㉒ rat [ræt] n.〈喻〉耗子，鼠辈，獐头鼠目的人，卑鄙小人

瞎转悠，过不了多久，准惹上一身骚，到时候你就束手无策了。"

柯利飞快地朝卡尔森转过身。"这事用不着你管，除非你想要到外面去较量一番。"

卡尔森哈哈笑了起来。"你这该死的蠢货，"他骂道，"你想要吓唬斯利姆，结果不奏效。斯利姆反过来把你给唬住了。你这软柿子。你是不是全国最优秀的轻量级拳击手，我才不在乎呢。你尽管冲着我来就是，看我不一脚踢掉你该死的脑袋。"

坎迪兴致勃勃地加入了这场攻击行动。"手套上还涂满了凡士林呢。"他带着厌恶的表情说。柯利瞪了他一眼，便移开目光，落到伦尼身上时眼睛一亮。伦尼仍在想象着那座农场，心满意足地微笑着。

柯利像一条猂犬似的朝着伦尼走过去。"见鬼，你笑什么笑？"

伦尼一脸茫然地看着他。"嗯？"

这时，柯利的怒火爆发了。"听着，你这笨蛋大个子，还坐着干吗，没有哪个狗娘养的大个子敢嘲笑我。我要让你瞧瞧到底谁软弱。"

伦尼看着乔治，显得很无助，然后站起身，企图向后退。柯利平衡了一下身子，摆好了架势。他朝着伦尼挥了一记左拳，紧接着又给伦尼的鼻子来了一记右拳。伦尼惊恐万状地叫喊起来，鼻子血流如注。"乔治，"他喊叫着，"让他放过我吧，乔治。"他一路后退，最后顶着墙壁了，柯利步步紧逼，不住地往他脸上揍。伦尼的双手一直放在身子两侧。他害怕得要命，连自卫都不会了。

乔治站起来大声吆喝："按住他，伦尼，别让他打你。"

伦尼用自己的大手掌捂住脸，诚惶诚恐，说话的声音都是颤抖的。他大声说着："让他住手吧，乔治。"话一说完，柯利便朝他的腹部给了一拳，让他喘不过气来。

斯利姆一跃身子跳了起来。"你这卑鄙小人，"他大喊起来，"我亲自来对付他吧。"

· 109 ·

Of Mice and Men

George **put out**① his hand and **grabbed**② Slim. "Wait a minute," he shouted. He **cupped**③ his hands around his mouth and yelled, "Get 'im, Lennie!"

Lennie took his hands away from his face and looked about for George, and Curley slashed at his eyes. The big face was covered with blood. George yelled again, "I said get him."

Curley's fist was swinging when Lennie reached for it. The next minute Curley was **flopping**④ like a fish on a line, and his closed fist was lost in Lennie's big hand. George ran down the room. "Leggo of him, Lennie. Let go."

But Lennie watched in terror the flopping little man whom he held. Blood ran down Lennie's face, one of his eyes was cut and closed. George **slapped**⑤ him in the face again and again, and still Lennie held on to the closed fist. Curley was white and **shrunken**⑥ by now, and his struggling had become weak. He stood crying, his fist lost in Lennie's paw.

George shouted over and over. "Leggo his hand, Lennie. Leggo. Slim, come help me while the guy got any hand left."

Suddenly Lennie let go his hold. He crouched **cowering**⑦ against the wall. "You tol' me to, George," he said miserably.

Curley sat down on the floor, looking in wonder at his **crushed**⑧ hand. Slim and Carlson bent over him. Then Slim straightened up and regarded Lennie with horror. "We got to get him in to a doctor," he said. "Looks to me like ever' bone in his han' is bust."

"I didn't wanta," Lennie cried. "I didn't wanta hurt him."

Slim said, "Carlson, you get the **candy wagon**⑨ **hitched up**⑩. We'll take 'um into Soledad an' get 'um **fixed up**⑪." Carlson hurried out. Slim turned to the whimpering Lennie. "It ain't your fault," he said. "This punk sure had it comin' to him. But—Jesus! He ain't hardly got no han' left." Slim hurried out, and in a moment returned with a tin cup of water. He held it to Curley's lips.

George said, "Slim, will we get canned now? We need the stake. Will

① put out 伸出
② grab [græb] v. 抓取
③ cup [kʌp] v. 使（手等）窝成杯状

④ flop [flɔp] v.（啪啪作响地）扑动，摇荡

⑤ slap [slæp] v.（用手掌或扁平物）掴，拍

⑥ shrunken ['ʃrʌŋkən] a. 皱缩的，缩小的

⑦ cower ['kauə] v. 蜷缩，抖缩

⑧ crush [krʌʃ] v. 压碎，压坏，压伤
⑨ candy wagon 这里指马车
⑩ hitch up 把挽畜套到车上（或工具上）
⑪ fix up 治愈

乔治一把抓住斯利姆。"稍等片刻。"他大声吼道。他双手在嘴巴周围窝成杯子状，大声吆喝道："按住他，伦尼！"

伦尼拿开捂住脸庞的双手，正扭头找乔治的工夫，柯利挥拳朝他的眼睛打了过来，打得一张大脸上满是鲜血。乔治又大声吆喝起来："我说了按住他。"

伦尼伸出手，正巧抓住了柯利挥出的拳头。下一刻，柯利便如上了钩的鱼似的扑腾起来，紧握着拳头没入了伦尼的大手里。乔治跑过去。"放开他，伦尼，快放开。"

但是，伦尼只是满眼恐惧地盯着手下来回扑腾的小个子看。伦尼的脸上流淌着鲜血，他的一只眼眶被打裂了，肿得只能闭起来。乔治不停地在他脸上扇耳掴子，但伦尼还是牢牢地抓住那个紧握着的拳头不放。柯利脸色煞白，蜷起了身子，渐渐放弃了挣扎。他站在那儿哭了起来，拳头被伦尼的大手掌紧握着。

乔治一遍又一遍大声吼着："放开他的手，伦尼，快放开。斯利姆，趁着这家伙的手还没被捏碎掉，过来帮我一把。"

伦尼突然松开了手，蹲下身子，蜷缩着靠在墙壁上。"是你叫我抓住的，乔治。"他痛苦地说。

柯利坐在地板上，难以置信地看着自己那只被捏碎的手。斯利姆和卡尔森在他旁边俯下身。斯利姆随即直起身子，惊恐地看了伦尼一眼。"我们得领他去看医生，"他说，"我瞧着，他手上的每一根骨头都碎了。"

"我不想的，"伦尼大声说，"我并不想伤害他的。"

斯利姆说："卡尔森，你去把运货马车套好。我们得送他到索莱达去治伤。"卡尔森急忙出了门。斯利姆转身面对呜咽着的伦尼。"这不是你的错，"他说，"这个蠢货自作自受。但是——天哪！他的手差不多被捏碎了。"斯利姆快步走出了门，片刻过后端回了一个锡杯，里面盛着水，他把杯子凑近柯利的嘴边。

乔治说："斯利姆，我们现在会被开除吗？我们需

· 111 ·

Curley's **old man**① can us now?"

Slim smiled **wryly**②. He knelt down beside Curley. "You got your senses **in hand**③ enough to listen?" he asked. Curley nodded. "Well, then listen," Slim went on. "I think you got your han' caught in a machine. If you don't tell nobody what happened, we ain't going to. But you jus' tell an' try to get this guy canned and we'll tell ever'body, an' then will you get the **laugh**④."

"I won't tell," said Curley. He avoided looking at Lennie.

Buggy⑤ wheels sounded outside. Slim helped Curley up. "Come on now. Carlson's gonna take you to a doctor." He helped Curley out the door. The sound of wheels **drew away**⑥. In a moment Slim came back into the bunk house. He looked at Lennie, still crouched fearfully against the wall. "Le's see your hands," he asked.

Lennie stuck out his hands.

"Christ awmighty, I hate to have you mad at me," Slim said.

George broke in, "Lennie was jus' scairt," he explained. "He didn't know what to do. I told you nobody ought never to fight him. No, I guess it was Candy I told."

Candy nodded **solemnly**⑦. "That's jus' what you done," he said. "Right this morning when Curley first **lit intil**⑧ your **fren'**⑨, you says, 'He better not **fool with**⑩ Lennie if he knows what's good for 'um.' That's jus' what you says to me."

George turned to Lennie. "It ain't your fault," he said. "You don't need to be scairt no more. You done jus' what I tol' you to. Maybe you better go in the wash room an' clean up your face. You look like hell."

Lennie smiled with his **bruised**⑪ mouth. "I didn't want no trouble," he said. He walked toward the door, but just before he came to it, he turned back. "George?"

"What you want?"

"I can still tend the rabbits, George?"

"Sure. You ain't done nothing wrong."

"I di'n't mean no harm, George."

"Well, get the hell out and wash your face."

① old man〈口〉父亲
② wryly ['raili] ad.（表示厌恶、乐趣等时的面部表情）面部扭曲地，露出怪相地
③ in hand 在掌握中，在控制下
④ laugh [lɑ:f] n. 嘲笑

⑤ buggy ['bʌgi] n.〈美〉四轮单马轻便马车
⑥ draw away（迅速）移开

⑦ solemnly ['sɔləmli] ad. 严肃地，庄重地，认真地，一本正经地
⑧ light into〈美口〉猛烈攻击，痛击（lit [lit] v. light 的过去式和过去分词，intil = into）
⑨ fren'= friend
⑩ fool with〈口〉瞎弄，乱弄，戏弄
⑪ bruise [bru:z] v. 打青，使受瘀伤

要那笔钱啊。柯利的老爸现在会开除我们吗？"

斯利姆露出一个怪笑，跪到柯利身边。"你有足够的知觉听人说话吗？"他问了一声。柯利点了点头。"那就听好了，"斯利姆接着说，"我认为，你的手被机器伤着了。如果你不把发生的情况告诉任何人，我们也不会。不过，你只要说出实情，设法让这个家伙走人，我们也会告诉所有人，到头来，你便成为笑料啦。"

"我不会说出去的。"柯利说。他回避着，不看伦尼。

室外响起了马车轮子转动的声音。斯利姆搀扶着柯利站起来。"出发吧，卡尔森会送你去看医生的。"他搀扶着柯利出了门。马车轮子转动的声音远去了。片刻过后，斯利姆回到了宿舍。他看着伦尼，后者仍然蹲着靠在墙壁上，诚惶诚恐。"让我看看你的手。"他要求道。

伦尼伸出了双手。

"天哪，我可不愿惹你对我生气啊。"斯利姆说。

乔治突然插话道："伦尼只是被吓着了，"他解释说，"他不知所措。我对你说过的，任何人都不该和他打架。不对，我想起来了，我是对坎迪说的。"

坎迪郑重其事地点了点头。"你是这样说来着，"他说，"就在今天上午，柯利头回找你朋友的茬时，你说：'假如他知道什么才是对自己好，就最好别去惹伦尼。'你就是这样对我说的。"

乔治朝伦尼转过身。"这事不是你的错，"他说，"你用不着再害怕了。你只是按我说的做了而已。你最好还是去洗把脸吧。你看上去糟透了。"

伦尼咧开受伤的嘴笑了一下。"我并不想惹麻烦的。"他说，随即朝着门边走去，但快要到门口时，又转过了身。"乔治？"

"干什么？"

"我还能照料那些兔子吗，乔治？"

"当然，你又没有做错什么事情。"

"我并不是存心要伤害人的，乔治。"

"好啦，赶紧出去洗洗你的脸吧。"

Crooks, the Negro stable buck, had his bunk in the harness room; a little shed that leaned off the wall of the barn. On one side of the little room there was a square four-**paned**① window, and on the other, a narrow **plank**② door leading into the barn. Crooks' bunk was a long box filled with straw, on which his blankets were **flung**③. On the wall by the window there were pegs on which hung broken harness in process of being mended; strips of new leather; and under the window itself a little bench for leather-working tools, curved knives and needles and balls of linen thread, and a small hand **riveter**④. On pegs were also pieces of harness, a split **collar**⑤ with the horsehair **stuffing**⑥ sticking out, a broken **hame**⑦, and a trace chain with its leather covering split. Crooks had his apple box over his bunk, and in it a range of medicine bottles, both for himself and for the horses. There were cans of **saddle**⑧ soap and a **drippy**⑨ can of tar with its paint brush sticking over the edge. And scattered about the floor were a number of personal possessions; for, being alone, Crooks could leave his things about, and being a stable buck and a cripple, he was more permanent than the other men, and he had accumulated more possessions than he could carry on his back.

Crooks possessed several pairs of shoes, a pair of rubber boots, a big alarm clock and a single-barreled shotgun. And he had books, too; a **tattered**⑩ dictionary and a **mauled**⑪ copy of the California **civil**⑫ **code**⑬ for 1905. There were battered magazines and a few **dirty**⑭ books on a special shelf over his bunk. A pair of large gold-rimmed **spectacles**⑮ hung from a **nail**⑯ on the wall

① pane [pein] v. 镶玻璃于，镶嵌板于
② plank [plæŋk] n.（5.1 厘米至 10 厘米厚、20 厘米宽的）厚（木）板
③ flung [flʌŋ] v.（fling 的过去分词）（用力地）扔，掷，抛，丢
④ riveter ['rivitə(r)] n. 铆钉枪
⑤ collar ['kɒlə] n. 马轭，（马具）颈圈
⑥ stuffing ['stʌfiŋ] n. 填充物，填料
⑦ hame [heim] n.（马）颈轭（驾车时加在马颈上的两块曲木之一）
⑧ saddle ['sæd(ə)l] n. 鞍，马鞍，鞍具
⑨ drippy ['dripi] a. 滴水的，湿淋淋的
⑩ tattered ['tætəd] a.（衣服等）破烂的，破旧的
⑪ maul [mɔːl] v. 粗手粗脚地摆弄（或使用）
⑫ civil ['siv(ə)l; -il] a.【律】民事的（与刑事相对）
⑬ code [kəud] n. 法典，法规
⑭ dirty ['dəːti] a. 下流的，色情的，黄色的
⑮ spectacles ['spektək(ə)lz] n.【复】〈英〉眼镜
⑯ nail [neil] n. 钉子

　　负责马厩的黑鬼叫克鲁克斯，他的床铺安顿在马具间里，那是一间靠着牲口棚搭建起来的简易小房子。简易房的一侧开着一扇四格的方形窗户，另一侧开了一扇狭窄的木门，通往牲口棚。克鲁克斯的床铺是一个填满了稻草的长方形箱子，上面铺了几张毯子。窗户边的墙壁上钉了一些木钉子，上面依次挂着一排需要修复的破损马具，还挂了几条新的皮带。窗户下方摆放着一张小长凳，上面摆着加工皮革的工具，有弯刀、针、线团，还有一把手工操作的小铆钉枪。木钉上还挂了一些零零散散的马具，有一个开裂的马匹颈圈，里面填充的马鬃都露出来了，有一块断裂的马轭[1]，还有一根缰绳链，包在表面的皮革已经开裂了。克鲁克斯的床铺上方也有苹果箱，搁板上摆放着各种药瓶子，药品中既有供自己服用的，也有供骡马服用的。上面还摆放着几罐洗革皂[2]和一罐滴滴答答的沥青，刷子从罐子开口处探出了头。地板上散落着诸多个人物品。因为克鲁克斯独自一人居住，可以四处摆放物品。他负责马厩的差事，腿脚不便，相对于其他人，他的差事更加稳定持久。他已经积累了不少个人物品，数量之多，他都无法随身带走。

　　克鲁克斯有几双鞋子、一双橡胶靴子、一座很大的闹钟和一支单管猎枪。他还有几本书，一部是破旧的词典，一部是翻烂了的 1905 年版《加利福尼亚民法典》。他床铺上方还有一个很特别的架子，上面摆满了破旧的杂志和一些淫秽书籍。床铺上方的一个钉子上还挂着一

1 指驾车时加在马颈上的两块曲木之一。
2 洗革皂用来清洗、保护鞍具或皮革制品。

· 115 ·

Of Mice and Men

above his bed.

This room was swept and fairly neat, for Crooks was a proud, **aloof**① man. He kept his distance and demanded that other people keep theirs. His body was bent over to the left by his crooked spine, and his eyes lay deep in his head, and because of their depth seemed to glitter with intensity. His lean face was lined with deep black wrinkles, and he had thin, pain-tightened lips which were lighter than his face.

It was Saturday night. Through the open door that led into the barn came the sound of moving horses, of feet **stirring**②, of teeth **champing**③ on **hay**④, of the **rattle**⑤ of **halter**⑥ chains. In the stable buck's room a small electric globe threw a meager yellow light.

Crooks sat on his bunk. His shirt was out of his jeans in back. In one hand he held a bottle of liniment, and with the other he rubbed his spine. Now and then he poured a few drops of the liniment into his pink-palmed hand and reached up under his shirt to rub again. He **flexed**⑦ his muscles against his back and shivered.

Noiselessly Lennie appeared in the open doorway and stood there looking in, his big shoulders nearly filling the opening. For a moment Crooks did not see him, but on raising his eyes he stiffened and a scowl came on his face. His hand came out from under his shirt.

Lennie smiled helplessly in an attempt to make friends.

Crooks said sharply, "You got no right to come in my room. This here's my room. Nobody got any right in here but me."

Lennie **gulped**⑧ and his smile grew more **fawning**⑨. "I ain't doing nothing," he said. "Just come to look at my puppy. And I seen your light," he explained.

"Well, I got a right to have a light. You go on get outa my room. I ain't wanted in the bunk house, and you ain't wanted in my room."

"Why ain't you wanted?" Lennie asked.

"'Cause I'm black. They play cards in there, but I can't play because I'm

① aloof [ə'lu:f] *a.* 冷漠的，超然离群的

② stir [stə:] *v.* 微动，移动
③ champ [tʃæmp] *v.* 大声地咀嚼（草料等）
④ hay [hei] *n.*（作饲料用的）干草
⑤ rattle ['ræt(ə)l] *n.* 碰撞声，格格声
⑥ halter ['hɔ:ltə] *n.*（马等的）笼头，缰绳，牲口套
⑦ flex [fleks] *v.* 使（肌肉）收缩

⑧ gulp [gʌlp] *v.* 喘不过气来，哽住
⑨ fawning ['fɔ:niŋ] *a.* 摇尾乞怜的，奉承的，谄媚的

副硕大的金边眼镜。

　　房间经过了打扫，显得挺清洁卫生的，因为克鲁克斯是个孤傲而清高的人。他离群索居，与他人保持距离，而且要求他人也与他保持距离。他脊椎骨歪掉了，身子倾向左侧。他眼睛深陷，因此，目光中似乎透出强烈的光芒。他脸部瘦削，布满了深深的黑色皱纹。他嘴唇很薄，因为疼痛而紧抿着，相对于面部的肤色，嘴唇处的色泽显得更淡。

　　这是星期六晚上，透过通向牲口棚敞开着的门，传来了骡马的动静，有蹄子踩踏地面的声音，有骡马的牙齿咀嚼干草的声音，有缰绳链子抖动时发出的叮当声。马厩黑鬼的房间里，一盏很小的球状电灯投下微弱的黄色光线。

　　克鲁克斯坐在床上，衬衫的后摆从牛仔工装裤里扯了出来。他一只手上拿着一瓶搽剂，另一只手搓揉着自己的脊椎。他时不时地用搽剂瓶往粉红色的手掌心里倒上几滴，然后把手伸到后背的衬衫下面搓揉起来。他收缩着背部的肌肉，身子颤抖着。

　　伦尼悄无声息地出现在敞开着的门口，伫立在那儿朝着室内看，宽阔的肩膀几乎把整个门口给挡得严严实实。一开始，克鲁克斯并没有发现，但抬起头来时，他身子一僵，蹙起了眉。他把手从衬衫下面抽了出来。

　　伦尼无措地笑着，企图示好。

　　克鲁克斯厉声说："你无权进入我的房间，这儿是我的房间。除了我自己，任何人都没有权利进来。"

　　伦尼大口吸着气，笑容越发显得讨好了。"我没干什么呀，"他说，"只是过来看看我的小狗崽，正好看见你房间里的灯亮着。"他解释着。

　　"得了吧，我有权利亮着灯呢。你得离开我的房间。那边的宿舍不要我，我的房间也不要你。"

　　"那边宿舍为什么不要你呀？"伦尼问。

　　"因为我是黑人。他们在那边玩扑克牌，但我因为是黑人就不能玩。他们说我身上有臭味。哼，我告诉你，

· 117 ·

Of Mice and Men

black. They say I stink. Well, I tell you, you all of you stink to me."

Lennie **flapped**① his big hands helplessly. "Ever'body went into town," he said. "Slim an' George an' ever'body. George says I gotta stay here an' not get in no trouble. I seen your light."

"Well, what do you want?"

"Nothing—I seen your light. I thought I could jus' come in an' set."

Crooks stared at Lennie, and he reached behind him and took down the spectacles and adjusted them over his pink ears and stared again. "I don't know what you're doin' in the barn anyway," he complained. "You ain't no skinner. **They's**② no **call**③ for a bucker to come into the barn at all. You ain't no skinner. You ain't got nothing to do with the horses."

"The pup," Lennie repeated. "I come to see my pup."

"Well, go see your pup, then. Don't come in a place where you're not wanted."

Lennie lost his smile. He **advanced**④ a step into the room, then remembered and backed to the door again. "I looked at 'em a little. Slim says I ain't to pet 'em very much."

Crooks said, "Well, you been takin' 'em out of the nest all the time. I wonder the **old lady**⑤ don't move 'em someplace else."

"Oh, she don't care. She lets me." Lennie had moved into the room again.

Crooks scowled, but Lennie's **disarming**⑥ smile defeated him. "Come on in and set a while," Crooks said. "'Long as you won't get out and leave me alone, you might as well set down." His tone was a little more friendly. "All the boys gone into town, huh?"

"All but old Candy. He just sets in the bunk house sharpening his pencil and sharpening and figuring."

Crooks adjusted his glasses. "Figuring? What's Candy figuring about?"

Lennie almost shouted, "'Bout the rabbits."

"You're nuts," said Crooks. "You're crazy as a **wedge**⑦. What rabbits you talkin' about?"

① flap [flæp] v. 使拍动，使摆动

② they〈非规范〉[与动词 to be 连用，表示"有"的意思，=there]

③ call [kɔ:l] n. [主要用于否定或疑问句] 必要，需要，理由

④ advance [əd'vɑ:ns] v. 前进，向前移动

⑤ old lady〈口〉母亲

⑥ disarming [dis'ɑ:miŋ] a. 使人消气的，解人疑虑的，消除敌意的

⑦ wedge [wedʒ] n.（木、橡胶、金属等制成的）楔子，三角木

我觉得你们所有人身上都有臭味。"

伦尼无助地挥动着那双大手。"大家都进城去了，"他说，"斯利姆和乔治，还有其他人。乔治说，我得待在这儿，不要惹麻烦。我看见你这儿亮着灯。"

"得了吧，你想要干什么？"

"什么都不干——我就是看见你房间里亮着灯，于是觉得可以过来待一会儿。"

克鲁克斯盯着伦尼看了一会儿，然后伸手到身后取下那副眼镜，戴在粉红色的双耳上调整了一下，又盯着对方看起来。"反正我不知道你在牲口棚里干什么，"他抱怨道，"你不是赶牲口的。扛大麦包的没有理由进牲口棚。你不是赶牲口的，你与骡马毫无关系。"

"小狗崽，"伦尼重复着说，"我是来看我的小狗崽的。"

"哼，那就看你的小狗崽去吧。不需要你的地方不要随便进入好吧。"

伦尼不笑了，他朝前走一步进入了房间，随即意识到了自己的行为，又退回到了门口。"我看了一会儿小狗崽。斯利姆说，我不能总去抚摸小狗崽。"

克鲁克斯说："哼，你总是把小狗崽抱出狗窝。我就纳闷了，那狗娘怎么不把小狗崽挪到别的地方去。"

"噢，它不在乎的，它由着我来呢。"伦尼再次踏入了房间。

克鲁克斯沉下脸，但想到伦尼令人消气的微笑，便缴械投降了。"那就进来坐一会儿吧，"克鲁克斯说，"你这么长时间赖着不出去，不让我消停，还不如干脆坐下来算了。"他的语气听起来稍稍友好了一些，"那些家伙全部都进城去了，是吗？"

"除了老坎迪之外，全部都去了。老坎迪坐在宿舍里削铅笔，又是削铅笔又是算数的。"

克鲁克斯整了整眼镜。"算数？坎迪在算什么数啊？"

伦尼几乎喊了出来："算着兔子的数呢。"

"你疯了，"克鲁克斯说，"你简直就是个疯子。你说什么兔子呢？"

"The rabbits we're gonna get, and I get to tend 'em, cut grass an' give 'em water, an' like that."

"Jus' nuts," said Crooks. "I don't blame the guy you travel with for keepin' you outa sight."

Lennie said quietly, "It ain't no lie. We're gonna do it. Gonna get a little place an' live on the fatta the lan'."

Crooks settled himself more comfortably on his bunk. "Set down," he invited. "Set down on the nail **keg**①."

Lennie hunched down on the little barrel. "You think it's a lie," Lennie said. "But it ain't no lie. Ever' word's the truth, an' you can ast George."

Crooks put his dark **chin**② into his pink palm. "You travel aroun' with George, don't ya?"

"Sure. Me an' him goes ever' place together."

Crooks continued. "Sometimes he talks, and you don't know what the hell he's talkin' about. Ain't that so?" He leaned forward, **boring**③ Lennie with his deep eyes. "Ain't that so?"

"Yeah . . . sometimes."

"Jus' talks on, an' you don't know what the hell it's all about?"

"Yeah . . . sometimes. But . . . not always."

Crooks leaned forward over the edge of the bunk. "I ain't a southern Negro," he said. "I was born right here in California. My old man had a chicken ranch, 'bout ten acres. The white kids come to play at our place, an' sometimes I went to play with them, and some of them was pretty nice. My ol' man didn't like that. I never knew till long later why he didn't like that. But I know now." He hesitated, and when he spoke again his voice was softer. "There wasn't another colored family for miles around. And now there ain't a colored man on this ranch an' there's jus' one family in Soledad." He laughed. "If I say something, why it's just a nigger sayin' it."

Lennie asked, "How long you think it'll be before them pups will be old enough to pet?"

① keg [keg] n. 小桶，桶（容量从 5 加仑至 30 加仑不等）

② chin [tʃin] n. 颏，下巴

③ bore [bɔː] v. 盯住看

"我们将要饲养的兔子。我得照料那些兔子，给它们割草喂水，诸如此类的事情。"

"真是说胡话，"克鲁克斯说，"那个和你待在一起的家伙把你丢在这儿，我可不怪他。"

伦尼语气平静地说："我说的不是假话。我们确实想要这么干来着。我们准备购买一小片地，依靠那片土地过日子。"

克鲁克斯坐在床上变换了一下姿势，坐得更加舒适一些。"坐下吧，"他邀请着说，"就坐那只钉子桶上吧。"

伦尼弓身坐到那只小桶上。"你认为我说的是假话，"伦尼说，"但这不是假话。我说的句句是真的，你可以去问乔治。"

克鲁克斯用一只粉红色的手掌托着自己黝黑的下巴颏。"你是与乔治一块儿来的吧？"

"当然。我和他去哪儿都在一块儿。"

克鲁克斯接着说："他有时候说话时，你都不知道他在说些什么鬼东西呢。是这么回事吗？"他把身子向前倾，深陷的眼睛盯着伦尼看，"是这么回事吗？"

"是啊……有时候是。"

"只管说个不停，你都不知道他在说些什么鬼东西对吧？"

克鲁克斯把身子探出了床沿。"我不是南方的黑人，"他说，"我就出生在加利福尼亚这儿。我老爸有一座养鸡场，大概十英亩的样子。白人家的孩子会去我们那儿玩耍。我有时候也会和他们一块儿玩，他们中有些人挺好的。我老爸不喜欢那样。很久以后我才知道，他为什么不喜欢那样。我现在知道了。"他迟疑起来。等到他再次开口说话时，语气听起来柔和了一些。"那时方圆数英里范围内没有另外的黑人家庭。现在这座农场上也没有另外的黑人。整个索莱达也只有一个黑人家庭。"他哈哈笑了起来，"假如我说了什么话，嘿，那只是一个黑鬼说的话罢了。"

伦尼问道："等小狗崽长大，可以抚摸了，你觉得要多久呢？"

· 121 ·

Of Mice and Men

Crooks laughed again. "A guy can talk to you an' be sure you won't go **blabbin'**①. Couple of weeks an' them pups'll be all right. George knows what he's about. Jus' talks, an' you don't understand nothing." He leaned forward excitedly. "This is just a nigger talkin', an' a busted-back nigger. So it don't mean nothing, see? You couldn't remember it anyways. I seen it over an' over— a guy talkin' to another guy and it don't make no difference if he don't hear or understand. The thing is, they're talkin', or they're settin' still not talkin'. It don't make no difference, no difference." His excitement had increased until he pounded his knee with this hand. "George can tell you **screwy**② things, and it don't matter. It's just the talking. It's just bein' with another guy. That's all." He paused.

His voice grew soft and persuasive. "S'pose George don't come back no more. S'pose he **took a powder**③ and just ain't coming back. What'll you do then?"

Lennie's attention came gradually to what had been said. "What?" he demanded.

"I said s'pose George went into town tonight and you never heard of him no more." Crooks **pressed forward**④ some kind of private victory. "Just s'pose that," he repeated.

"He won't do it," Lennie cried. "George wouldn't do nothing like that. I been with George a long a time. He'll come back tonight—" But the doubt was too much for him. "Don't you think he will?"

Crooks' face lighted with pleasure in his **torture**⑤. "Nobody can't tell what a guy'll do," he observed calmly. "Le's say he wants to come back and can't. S'pose he gets killed or hurt so he can't come back."

Lennie struggled to understand. "George won't do nothing like that," he repeated. "George is careful. He won't get hurt. He ain't never been hurt, 'cause he's careful."

"Well, s'pose, jus' s'pose he don't come back. What'll you do then?"

① blab [blæb] v. 乱说，胡扯

② screwy ['skru:i] a.〈俚〉〈主美〉古怪的，怪诞的，异常的

③ take a (runout) powder〈美口〉匆忙离去，逃跑，离去

④ press forward 继续进行

⑤ torture ['tɔ:tʃə] n. 折磨，痛苦，苦恼

克鲁克斯再次哈哈笑了起来。"跟你说话的人大可放心，回头你肯定不会到处乱说的。等上两个星期，小狗崽就没有问题了。乔治干什么事情，他自己心里清楚，尽管说就是，你反正听不明白。"他激动地向前倾身，"这只是个黑鬼说的话，一个驼背黑鬼。因此，他说的话一点儿都不算数的，明白吗？你反正也记不住。这样的事情我见得多了——一个人对着另外一个人说话，至于对方有没有听见或者有没有听明白，那无关紧要。重要的是，他们或者不停地说着，或者干坐着什么也不说，随便怎样都行，反正没有区别，没有区别。"他越说越带劲，说到最后用一只手击打着自己的膝盖，"乔治可以对你说些稀奇古怪的事情，反正也没有什么关系，只是说说而已。只是与另外一个人待在一起，没有更多意思。"他说着停顿了下来。

他放轻了声音，语气里带上了劝诱之意。"假如乔治不回来了，假如他逃跑了，不回来了，那你怎么办呢？"

伦尼慢慢回过神来，开始注意对方说的话了。"什么？"他问。

"我说啊，假如乔治今晚进城去了，从此再也没消息了。"克鲁克斯带着某种私密的得意神情继续道。"你想想看。"他重复了一声。

"他不会这样的，"伦尼大声说，"乔治绝不会做这样的事情。我和乔治在一块儿很长时间了。他今晚会回来的——"但他接受不了这样的怀疑，"你难道认为他不会回来吗？"

克鲁克斯脸上因伦尼所受的折磨露出了喜色。"一个人会干出什么事情来，谁也说不准。"他态度平静地说，"我们不妨假设他想要回来，但是没办法回来。假设他被人杀害了，或受伤了，结果回不来了。"

伦尼铆足了劲儿想要理解对方的意思。"乔治不会这样的，"他重复说着，"乔治很小心，不会受伤的。他从来都没有受过伤，因为他很小心的。"

"好啦，假如，只是假如他回不来了，你到时候怎么办呢？"

· 123 ·

Lennie's face wrinkled with apprehension. "I don' know. Say, what you doin' anyways?" he cried. "This ain't true. George ain't got hurt."

Crooks bored in on him. "Want me ta tell ya what'll happen? They'll take ya to the **booby hatch**①. They'll tie ya up with a **collar**②, like a dog."

Suddenly Lennie's eyes centered and grew quiet, and mad. He stood up and walked dangerously toward Crooks. "Who hurt George?" he demanded.

Crooks saw the danger as it approached him. He edged back on his bunk to get out of the way. "I was just supposin'," he said. "George ain't hurt. He's all right. He'll be back all right."

Lennie stood over him. "What you supposin' for? Ain't nobody goin' to suppose no hurt to George."

Crooks removed his glasses and wiped his eyes with his fingers. "Jus' set down," he said. "George ain't hurt."

Lennie growled back to his seat on the nail keg. "Ain't nobody goin' to talk no hurt to George," he grumbled.

Crooks said gently, "Maybe you can see now. You got George. You *know* he's goin' to come back. S'pose you didn't have nobody. S'pose you couldn't go into the bunk house and play **rummy**③ 'cause you was black. How'd you like that? S'pose you had to sit out here an' read books. Sure you could play horseshoes till it got dark, but then you got to read books. Books ain't no good. A guy needs somebody—to be near him." He whined, "A guy goes nuts if he ain't got nobody. Don't make no difference who the guy is, long's he's with you. I tell ya," he cried, "I tell ya a guy gets too lonely an' he gets sick."

"George gonna come back," Lennie **reassured**④ himself in a frightened voice. "Maybe George come back already. Maybe I better go see."

① booby hatch〈美俚〉精神病院，疯人院
② collar ['kɔlə] n.（狗等的）颈圈

③ rummy ['rʌmi] n. 拉米纸牌戏

④ reassure [ˌriːə'ʃɔː(r)] v. 向……再保证，安慰，使放心，使消除疑虑

伦尼担心得五官紧蹙。"我不知道呢，嘿，你这是要干什么呀？"他大声说，"这种事情不会是真的。乔治不会受伤的。"

克鲁克斯紧盯着伦尼。"要我告诉你会发生什么事情吗？他们会把你带到疯人院去，给你脖子上套上项圈，像对待狗一样。"

伦尼的目光突然聚焦到了一起，神态冷静而疯狂。他站起身，神色凶狠地朝着克鲁克斯走去。"谁伤害了乔治？"他质问道。

克鲁克斯看出，危险正向自己逼近，于是把身子往后缩了缩，避开危险。"我只是假设，"他说，"乔治没有受伤，他好好的，一定会平安回来的。"

伦尼俯身站立在他跟前。"你为什么要这样假设呢？谁都不能假设乔治会受伤。"

克鲁克斯取下眼镜，用手指揉了揉眼睛。"坐下来吧，"他说，"乔治没有受伤。"

伦尼低吼着坐回到钉子桶上。"谁都不可能伤害到乔治。"他咕哝着说。

克鲁克斯语气温和地说："你现在可能已经明白了。你身边有乔治，知道他一定会回来的。假如你身边没有任何人，假如你不能去宿舍里玩拉米纸牌戏[1]，就因为你是黑人，你觉得那会是什么滋味呢？假如你不能进宿舍，只能坐在这儿看看书，当然，你可以去玩掷马蹄铁游戏，一直玩到天黑，但随后又只能去看书了。书能有什么用，人是需要有伴儿的——有个伴儿待在他身边。"他咕哝着说，"人要是身边没有个伴儿，他会发疯的。只要有个人在你身边，无论什么人都可以，我跟你说，"他大声说，"我跟你说，一个人孤单寂寞时间长了会生病的。"

"乔治会回来的，"伦尼自我安慰着，声音里透着恐惧，"乔治或许已经回来了呢，我或许最好还是去看看。"

---

1 拉米纸牌戏的基本玩法是形成三四张同点的套牌或不少于三张的同花顺。

Of Mice and Men

Crooks said, "I didn't mean to scare you. He'll come back. I was talkin' about myself. A guy sets alone out here at night, maybe readin' books or thinkin' or stuff like that. Sometimes he gets thinkin', an' he got nothing to tell him what's so an' what ain't so. Maybe if he sees somethin', he don't know whether it's right or not. He can't turn to some other guy and ast him if he sees it too. He can't tell. He got nothing to measure by. I seen things out here. I wasn't drunk. I don't know if I was asleep. If some guy was with me, he could tell me I was asleep, an' then it would be all right. But I jus' don't know." Crooks was looking across the room now, looking toward the window.

Lennie said miserably, "George **wun't**[①] go away and leave me. I know George wun't do that."

The stable buck went on dreamily, "I remember when I was a little kid on my old man's chicken ranch. Had two brothers. They was always near me, always there. Used to sleep right in the same room, right in the same bed—all three. Had a strawberry patch. Had an alfalfa patch. Used to turn the chickens out in the alfalfa on a sunny morning. My brothers'd set on a fence **rail**[②] an' watch 'em—white chickens they was."

Gradually Lennie's interest **came around**[③] to what was being said. "George says we're gonna have alfalfa for the rabbits."

"What rabbits?"

"We're gonna have rabbits an' a berry patch."

"You're nuts."

"We are too. You ast George."

"You're nuts." Crooks was **scornful**[④]. "I seen hunderds of men **come by**[⑤] on the road an' on the ranches, with their bindles on their back an' that same damn thing in their heads. Hunderds of them. They come, an' they quit an' go on; an' every damn one of 'em's got a little piece of land in his head. An' never a God damn one of 'em ever gets it. Just like heaven. Ever'body wants a little

① wun't = won't

② rail [reil] *n.* 横条，横杆，横档，栏杆

③ come around 达到

④ scornful ['skɔːnful; -f(ə)l] *a.* 轻蔑的，嘲笑的

⑤ come by（从……旁）经过

克鲁克斯说："我并不是存心想要吓唬你的。他会回来的。我刚才是在说我自己呢。一个人晚上孤孤单单地坐在这儿，可能看看书，想想心事，或者干点儿诸如此类的事情。有时候，他有了什么想法，却没人告诉他是与不是。或许假如他看见了什么情况，也没法判断真假。他无法去找其他人，问那个人他是否也看见了。他辨不出，他没有任何情况可供参照的。我在这儿看到过东西。我没有喝醉酒。我不知道自己是否在睡梦中。假如有某个人与我待在一起，他便能够告诉我，我是否处在睡梦中，那么，事情就结了。但是，我就是不知道。"此时此刻，克鲁克斯朝着房间另一端看去，朝着窗户看去。

伦尼痛苦地说："乔治不会撇下我自己跑掉的。我知道，乔治不会这样做的。"

马厩黑鬼神情恍惚，接着说："我还记得小时候在我老爸养鸡场的情形。我有两个哥哥，他们一直待在我旁边，一直都在。我们睡在同一个房间，而且是同一张床上——我们三个孩子一块儿。那儿有一片草莓地，还有一片苜蓿地。阳光灿烂的早晨，我们把鸡赶到那片苜蓿地里去。我两个哥哥会坐在围栏上看着——那是些白色的鸡。"

伦尼的兴趣慢慢转到了对方所说的事情上。"乔治说了，我们将拥有一片苜蓿地，喂兔子用的。"

"什么兔子？"

"我们会饲养兔子，而且拥有一片草莓地。"

"你疯了。"

"我们都疯了。你去问问乔治吧。"

"你疯了。"克鲁克斯露出蔑视的神情，"我看见过几百人来来去去，或在路上，或在农场上，他们背上背着铺盖卷，脑袋里想的全是同样该死的事情。那几百人全都是。他们来了，又离开了，继续踏上行程。他们没有哪个人获得过一片土地，就像进天堂似的。每个人都奢望着有小片土地来着。我在这儿看过很多书。没有任何人进入过天堂，没有任何人获得过土地。那只是他们

piece of lan'. I read plenty of books out here. Nobody never gets to heaven, and nobody gets no land. It's just in their head. They're all the time talkin' about it, but it's jus' in their head." He paused and looked toward the open door, for the horses were moving **restlessly**① and the halter chains **clinked**②. A horse **whinnied**③. "I guess somebody's out there," Crooks said. "Maybe Slim. Slim comes in sometimes two, three times a night. Slim's a real skinner. He **looks out for**④ his team." He pulled himself painfully **upright**⑤ and moved toward the door. "That you, Slim?" he called.

Candy's voice answered. "Slim went in town. Say, you seen Lennie?"

"Ya mean the big guy?"

"Yeah. Seen him around any place?"

"He's in here," Crooks said shortly. He went back to his bunk and lay down.

Candy stood in the doorway scratching his bald wrist and looking blindly into the lighted room. He made no attempt to enter. "Tell ya what, Lennie. I been figuring out about them rabbits."

Crooks said **irritably**⑥, "You can come in if you want."

Candy seemed embarrassed. "I do' know. 'Course, if ya want me to."

"Come on in. If ever'body's comin' in, you might just as well." It was difficult for Crooks to conceal his pleasure with anger.

Candy came in, but he was still embarrassed, "You got a nice cozy little place in here," he said to Crooks. "Must be nice to have a room all to yourself this way."

"Sure," said Crooks. "And a **manure**⑦ pile under the window. Sure, it's swell."

Lennie broke in, "You said about them rabbits."

Candy leaned against the wall beside the broken collar while he scratched the wrist stump. "I been here a long time," he said. "An' Crooks been here a long time. This's the first time I ever been in his room."

① restlessly ['restlisli] *ad.* 焦躁不安地，显示焦躁不安地

② clink [kliŋk] *v.* 发出叮当声

③ whinny ['wini] *v.* 嘶叫，欢嘶

④ look out for 留心守候，注意防备

⑤ upright ['ʌprait] *ad.* 挺直着，竖立着，垂直地

⑥ irritably ['irətəbli] *ad.* 易怒地，急躁地

⑦ manure [mə'njuə] *n.* 肥料，粪肥

脑袋里想象的东西。他们总是在谈论着这样的事情，但终究只是脑袋里的想象而已。"说到这儿他停顿下来，朝着敞开的门口看过去，因为骡马躁动不安起来，缰绳的链子叮当响着。有匹马发出了嘶鸣声。"我估计外面有人，"克鲁克斯说，"可能是斯利姆。斯利姆有时候一个晚上会来个两三趟。斯利姆是个真正的赶牲口人。他时刻留心自己的队伍。"他费劲儿地站起来，朝着门口走去。"是你吗，斯利姆？"他喊了一声。

坎迪的应答声传来，"斯利姆进城了。嘿，你看见伦尼了吗？"

"你是指那个大个子吗？"

"对啊，看见他在附近了吗？"

"他在这儿呢。"克鲁克斯简短地回答说。他返回自己床边躺下了。

坎迪站立在门口，一边挠着裸露的断手腕，一边朝房间里看，双眼被灯光晃得一时难以视物。他没有打算进房间。"告诉你怎么回事吧，伦尼。我一直在计算那些兔子的数量呢。"

克鲁克斯不耐烦地说："你想进来就进来吧。"

坎迪面露窘色。"我不知道呢，当然，假如你想让我进来的话。"

"进来吧。别人都进来了，你还站在外面干吗。"克鲁克斯假装恼火地说，却没能掩饰住心中的欣喜。

坎迪进了房间，但窘色未曾消减。"你这个小房间很温馨呢，"他对克鲁克斯说，"像这样有一个属于自己的房间，一定会感到很惬意的。"

"可不是嘛，"克鲁克斯说，"窗户下面还有一个粪堆呢。说得对，感觉好极了。"

伦尼突然插话了："你刚才说到了兔子的事情。"

坎迪把身子倚在墙壁上，靠在开裂的马匹颈圈旁站定，挠起断手腕来。"我在这儿待了很长时间，"他说，"克鲁克斯在这儿也待了很长时间。我这还是第一次进入这个房间呢。"

Crooks said darkly, "Guys don't come into a **colored**① man's room very much. Nobody been here but Slim. Slim an' the boss."

Candy quickly changed the subject. "Slim's as good a skinner as I ever seen."

Lennie leaned toward the old swamper. "About them rabbits," he insisted.

Candy smiled. "I got it figured out. We can make some money on them rabbits if we **go about**② it right."

"But I get to tend 'em," Lennie broke in. "George says I get to tend 'em. He promised."

Crooks interrupted **brutally**③. "You guys is just kiddin' yourself. You'll talk about it a hell of a lot, but you won't get no land. You'll be a swamper here till they take you out in a **box**④. Hell, I seen too many guys. Lennie here'll quit an' be on the road in two, three weeks. Seems like ever' guy got land in his head."

Candy rubbed his cheek angrily. "You God damn right we're gonna do it. George says we are. We got the money right now."

"Yeah?" said Crooks. "An' where's George now? In town in a whorehouse. That's where your money's goin'. Jesus, I seen it happen too many times. I seen too many guys with land in their head. They never get none under their hand."

Candy cried, "Sure they all want it. Everybody wants a little bit of land, not much. Jus' som'thin' that was his. Someth' he could live on and there couldn't nobody **throw** him **off**⑤ of it. I never had none. I planted crops for damn near ever'body in this state, but they wasn't my crops, and when I **harvested**⑥ 'em, it wasn't none of my **harvest**⑦. But we gonna do it now, and don't you make no mistake about that. George ain't got the money in town. That money's in the bank. Me an' Lennie an' George. We gonna have a room to ourself. We're gonna

① colored ['kʌləd]〈美〉= coloured a.（属）有色人种（尤指黑种）的

② go about 着手干，做

③ brutally ['bruːtəli] ad. 冷酷地，无理性地，蛮横地，粗暴地
④ box [bɔks] n.〈口〉棺材

⑤ throw off 摆脱掉
⑥ harvest ['hɑːvist] v. 收割，收获
⑦ harvest ['hɑːvist] n. 收成，收获量，产物

克鲁克斯沉着脸说："大家都不怎么进入黑人的房间。除了斯利姆，除了斯利姆和场主，没有谁进过这个房间。"

坎迪急忙变换了话题。"斯利姆是我见过最能干的赶牲口人了。"

伦尼把身子朝着老清扫工倾过去。"说说兔子的事情吧。"他锲而不舍地说。

坎迪笑了。"我算出兔子的数来了。我们要把兔子给饲养好了，那就可以挣些钱。"

"但我必须得照料兔子来着，"伦尼突然插话说，"乔治说我可以照料兔子的。他承诺了的。"

克鲁克斯粗鲁地打断了他的话。"你们这些人只是在欺骗自己罢了。你们絮絮叨叨说个没完，但你们不可能获得土地的。你会一直在这儿当个清扫工，最后被他们装在棺材里运出去。哼，我见过的人可多啦。这个伦尼两三个星期后便会辞职上路。看起来，人人脑袋里都想着有那么一片土地呢。"

坎迪愤怒地搓揉着自己的一侧脸颊。"你他妈的等着瞧，我们一定会获得土地的。乔治说了，我们一定会获得土地的。我们现在筹到钱了。"

"真的吗？"克鲁克斯说，"乔治此刻在哪儿呢？在城里的一家窑子里呢。你们的钱就是用到那儿去了。脑袋里面想着要购买一片土地的人，我可是见多啦。但他们从来都没有弄到手过。"

坎迪喊起来："毫无疑问，他们都想要获得土地。每个人都想要获得一小片土地，用不着太多，仅仅是一点儿属于他们自己的东西。那是一片他们可以在上面生活的土地，任何人都不能把他们从那片土地上驱逐。我从来不曾拥有属于自己的东西。我几乎给这个地区里所有的人种植过庄稼，但那不是我的庄稼。当我收获庄稼时，收获的东西不属于我。但是，我们现在要拥有自己的土地，这一点你可不要搞错了。乔治没有拿着钱进城，钱都存在银行里了。我、伦尼和乔治，我们将拥有属于我们自己的房间。我们将养一条狗，还有兔子，还有鸡。

have a dog an' rabbits an' chickens. We're gonna have green **corn**① an' maybe a cow or a goat." He stopped, **overwhelmed**② with his picture.

Crooks asked, "You say you got the money?"

"Damn right. We got most of it. Just a little bit more to get. Have it all in one month. George got the land all picked out, too."

Crooks reached around and **explored**③ his **spine**④ with his hand. "I never seen a guy really do it," he said. "I seen guys nearly crazy with loneliness for land, but ever' time a whore house or a **blackjack**⑤ game took what it takes." He hesitated. " . . . If you . . . guys would want a hand to work for nothing—just his **keep**⑥, why I'd come an' lend a hand. I ain't so crippled I can't work like a son-of-a-bitch if I want to."

"Any you boys seen Curley?"

They **swung**⑦ their heads toward the door. Looking in was Curley's wife. Her face was heavily made up. Her lips were slightly **parted**⑧. She breathed strongly, as though she had been running.

"Curley ain't been here," Candy said **sourly**⑨.

She stood still in the doorway, smiling a little at them, rubbing the nails of one hand with the thumb and forefinger of the other. And her eyes **traveled**⑩ from one face to another. "They left all the weak ones here," she said finally. "Think I don't know where they all went? Even Curley. I know where they all went."

Lennie watched her, fascinated; but Candy and Crooks were scowling down away from her eyes. Candy said, "Then if you know, why you want to ast us where Curley is at?"

She regarded them amusedly. "Funny thing," she said. "If I catch any one man, and he's alone, I get along fine with him. But just let two of the guys get together an' you won't talk. Jus' nothing but mad." She dropped her fingers and

① corn [kɔ:n] n. 〈美〉玉米
② overwhelm [ˌəuvə'welm] v.（感情、影响等）使受不了，使不知所措
③ explore [ik'splɔ:] v.【医】仔细检查，探察（伤处等）
④ spine [spain] n.【解】脊柱，脊椎
⑤ blackjack ['blækdʒæk] n. 〈主美〉【牌】二十一点（一种坐庄牌戏）
⑥ keep [ki:p] n. 生计，生活所需
⑦ swung [swʌŋ] v.（swing 的过去式和过去分词）使转向
⑧ part [pɑ:t] v. 分开
⑨ sourly ['sauəli] ad. 敌对地，敌意地
⑩ travel ['træv(ə)l] v.（眼睛等）转动，扫视

我们将种植绿油油的玉米，或许还会饲养一头母牛和一只山羊。"他打住没有说下去，沉浸在自己想象的美景之中，不能自拔。

克鲁克斯问道："你说，你们已经有钱了？"

"说得没错。我们已经积攒得差不多了，只需要再挣一点点，也就是一个月的工夫吧。乔治都已经选好地方了。"

克鲁克斯把一只手反到背后，触摸着自己的脊椎。"我从来都没有看见过哪个人成功的，"他说，"我看到过很多寂寞得发狂的人，他们都梦想着要土地，但每次到头来都把钱花费在窑子里或二十一点牌戏[1]上。"说到这儿，他犹豫起来，"……假如你们……这些人需要免费的劳动力——只需要管吃住就行，嘿，我倒是愿意过去帮忙呢。我残得不是很严重呢，只要我乐意，干起活儿来不会是熊样子。"

"你们有谁看见柯利了吗？"

他们扭过头看向门口。探着脑袋朝室内看的是柯利的老婆。她脸上浓妆艳抹，嘴唇微微张开着。她喘着粗气，好像是跑着过来的。

"柯利没有到过这儿。"坎迪沉着脸说。

她安安静静地站立在门口，对着他们笑了笑，一只手的拇指和食指摩擦着另一只手的指甲。她逐个打量着三个人的面孔。"他们把几个老弱病残留在了这儿，"她最后开口说，"你们以为我不知道他们都到哪儿去了吗？甚至包括柯利在内，他们去了哪儿我都知道。"

伦尼注视着她，一副着迷的样子，但坎迪和克鲁克斯却阴沉着脸，回避了她的目光。坎迪说："这么说来，既然你都知道了，为什么还来问我们柯利到哪儿去了呢？"

她兴致勃勃地看着他们。"真是有意思的事情呢，"她说，"只要我发现了某个男人，看见他独自一人待着，我便能够与他融洽相处。但只要让两个男人待在一块儿，你们便就不说话了，什么都不干，就是生气。"她停下

1　一种坐庄牌戏，玩者力争取得二十一点总牌点，或比发牌人更加接近二十一点，但不能超过。

Of Mice and Men

put her hands on her hips. "You're all scared of each other, that's what. Ever' one of you's scared the rest is goin' to **get**① something **on**② you."

After a pause Crooks said, "Maybe you better go along to your own house now. We don't want no trouble."

"Well, I ain't giving you no trouble. Think I don't like to talk to somebody ever' once in a while? Think I like to **stick**③ in that house alla time?"

Candy laid the stump of his wrist on his knee and rubbed it gently with his hand. He said **accusingly**④, "You gotta **husban'**⑤. You got no call foolin' aroun' with other guys, causin' trouble."

The girl **flared up**⑥. "Sure I gotta husban'. You all seen him. Swell guy, ain't he? Spends all his time sayin' what he's gonna do to guy he don't like, and he don't like nobody. Think I'm gonna stay in that two-by-four house and listen how Curley's gonna **lead**⑦ with his left **twicet**⑧, and then bring in the ol' right **cross**⑨? 'One-two,' he says. 'Jus' the ol' one-two an' he'll go down.'" She paused and her face lost its **sullenness**⑩ and grew interested. "Say—what happened to Curley's **han'**⑪?"

There was an embarrassed silence. Candy stole a look at Lennie. Then he coughed. "Why . . . Curley . . . he got his han' caught in a machine, ma'am. Bust his han'."

She watched for a moment, and then she laughed. "**Baloney**⑫! What you think you're sellin' me? Curley started som'pin' he didn' finish. Caught in a machine—baloney! Why, he ain't give nobody the good ol' one-two since he got his han' bust. Who bust him?"

Candy repeated sullenly, "Got it caught in a machine."

"Awright," she said **contemptuously**⑬. "Awright, **cover** 'im **up**⑭ if ya wanta. Whatta I care? You bindle **bums**⑮ think you're so damn good. Whatta ya think I am, a kid? I tell ya I could of went with shows. Not jus' one, neither. An' a guy tol' me he could put me in **pitchers**⑯ . . ." She was breathless with **indignation**⑰. "—**Sat'iday**⑱ night. Ever'body out doin' som'pin'. Ever'body!

① get [get] v. 抓住
② on [ɔn] prep. 〔表示反对、碰撞等的目标〕针对，对着
③ stick [stik] v. 停留，留下
④ accusingly [əˈkjuziŋli] ad.（表情、声调等）指责地，谴责地
⑤ husban' = husband
⑥ flare up 突然（或激动）
⑦ lead [li:d] v.（拳击中）打出第一拳，（为试探对手的防卫而）出击
⑧ twicet [ˈtwaiset] n. =jab（拳击中的）刺拳（指伸直手臂的一击）
⑨ cross [krɔs] n.（拳击中用勾拳的）迎击
⑩ sullenness [ˈsʌlnnis] n. 愠怒
⑪ han' = hand
⑫ baloney [bəˈləuni] n.〈美俚〉（尤指唬人的）胡扯，鬼话
⑬ contemptuously [kənˈtemptjuəsli] ad. 表示轻蔑地，鄙视地
⑭ cover up 掩盖，掩饰
⑮ bum [bʌm] n.〈主美口〉流浪汉，懒汉，游手好闲的醉鬼
⑯ pitchers = pictures，picture [ˈpiktʃə] n. 影片，电影
⑰ indignation [indigˈneiʃ(ə)n] n. 愤怒，愤慨，义愤
⑱ Sat'iday = Saturday

了手指的动作，双手搭在臀上。"你们彼此害怕对方，就是这么回事。你们每个人都害怕别人算计自己。"

停顿了一会儿后，克鲁克斯说："你现在最好还回你自己的房子去吧。我们不想惹麻烦。"

"好吧，我不会给你们惹麻烦的。你认为我不想时不时和人家聊聊天吗？你认为我愿意一直都待在那房子里吗？"

坎迪把断腕搁在膝上，用另一只手轻柔地抚摸着。他带着责备的语气说："你有丈夫了，不能与别的男人在一起瞎混，惹麻烦。"

眼前的女人突然情绪激动起来。"我当然有丈夫了。你们全部都看见过他。很棒的一个人，对吧？他成日里说，要对自己不喜欢的人怎么怎么样。他谁都看不上眼。你们以为我喜欢待在那幢狭窄的房子里，听柯利讲述如何用左拳挥动两下，然后用右拳击打吗？'一、二，'他说，'只需要一、二，他便趴下了。'"她说着停顿了下来，怒色从她脸上褪去，取而代之的是一脸兴味，"嘿——柯利的手怎么啦？"

屋里出现了一阵尴尬的沉默。坎迪悄然瞥了一眼伦尼，随即咳嗽了一声。"呃……柯利……他的一只手给绞到机器里面了，太太。他的手断掉了。"

她注视了片刻，然后哈哈大笑起来。"胡说八道！你认为自己是在对我说什么呢？柯利挑衅人家，结果没有打赢。还说什么绞到机器里面了——胡说八道！哈，既然他的手断掉了，就再也不可能用一、二这种老套路揍人了。谁打断了他的手？"

坎迪阴沉着脸重复说："他的手绞到机器里面了。"

"好吧，"她语气轻蔑地说，"好吧，你想替他掩饰那就掩饰好啦。我在乎什么呢？你们这一帮流浪汉自以为聪明绝顶。你们当我是什么人，小孩子吗？我可告诉你们，我本来有机会去演戏的，而且还不止一次呢。有个家伙告诉过我说，他能够介绍我去拍电影呢……"她说着愤愤不平起来，激动得呼吸都急促了，"周六晚上，

135

Of Mice and Men

An' what am I doin'? Standin' here talkin' to a bunch of bindle **stiffs**①—a nigger an' a **dum-dum**② and a **lousy**③ ol' **sheep**④—an' likin' it because they ain't nobody else."

Lennie watched her, his mouth half open. Crooks had **retired**⑤ into the terrible protective dignity of the Negro. But a change came over old Candy. He stood up suddenly and knocked his nail keg over backward. "I had enough," he said angrily. "You ain't wanted here. We told you you ain't. An' I tell ya, you got **floozy**⑥ idears about what us guys **amounts to**⑦. You ain't got sense enough in that **chicken head**⑧ to even see that we ain't stiffs. S'pose you get us canned. S'pose you do. You think we'll hit the highway an' look for another lousy two-bit job like this. You don't know that we got our own ranch to go to, an' our own house. We ain't got to stay here. We gotta house and chickens an' fruit trees an' a place a hunderd time prettier than this. An' we got fren's, that's what we got. Maybe there was a time when we was scared of gettin' canned, but we ain't no more. We got our own lan', and it's ours, an' we **c'n**⑨ go to it."

Curley's wife laughed at him. "Baloney," she said. "I seen too many you guys. If you had two bits in the **worl'**⑩, why you'd be in gettin' two shots of **corn**⑪ with it and **suckin'**⑫ the bottom of the glass. I know you guys."

Candy's face had grown redder and redder, but before she was done speaking, he had control of himself. He was the master of the situation. "I might of knew," he said gently. "Maybe you just better go along an' **roll your hoop**⑬. We ain't got nothing to say to you at all. We know what we got, and we don't care whether you know it or not. So maybe you better jus' **scatter along**⑭ now, 'cause Curley maybe ain't gonna like his wife out in the barn with us 'bindle stiffs.'"

She looked from one face to another, and they were all closed against her. And she looked longest at Lennie, until he dropped his eyes in embarrassment. Suddenly she said, "Where'd you get them **bruises**⑮ on your face?"

① stiff [stif] n. 流浪汉，游民
② dum-dum〈美俚〉笨蛋，傻瓜
③ lousy ['lauzi] a.〈口〉有病的，身体差的
④ sheep [ʃi:p] n. 胆小鬼，懦弱的人，蠢人
⑤ retire [ri'taiə] v. 退出，退下，引退，退隐
⑥ floozy ['fluzi] a.〈俚〉放荡女子（的），荡妇（的），妓女（的）
⑦ amount to（在意义、效果、价值等方面）等同，接近
⑧ chicken head 笨蛋，蠢人

⑨ c'n = can
⑩ worl' = world
⑪ corn [kɔ:n] n.〈口〉=corn whisky〈美〉（玉米）威士忌酒
⑫ suck [sʌk] v. 吸食，吮吸

⑬ roll one's hoop〈美俚〉只管自己的事
⑭ scatter along 消散

⑮ bruise [bru:z] n.（人体跌、碰后产生的）青肿，挫伤

人人都出去玩了，人人都去了！而我在干什么呢？站在这儿对着一伙扛铺盖卷的流浪汉说话呢——一个是黑鬼，一个是傻蛋，还有一个是病怏怏的胆小鬼——就这样我还乐在其中呢，因为反正没有别人了。"

伦尼注视着她，嘴巴半张开着。克鲁克斯恢复到了那种要极度保护黑人尊严的姿态。但是，老坎迪的态度有了变化。他突然站起来，身下的钉子桶被他撞得向后倒了下去。"我受够了，"他愤怒地说，"这儿不需要你。我们已经跟你说过了。我现在告诉你，我们这些人能够成就什么大事，你这骚娘儿们是不会明白的。你那笨脑瓜里空空荡荡，根本看不出我们不是流浪汉。假如你们开除了我们，假如真这样做了，你以为我们只能走上大路，再找一份卑微而又一钱不值的差事。你不知道，我们有属于自己的农场可去呢，而且有属于我们自己的房子可住。我们才不必待在这儿呢。我们建了房子，养了鸡，种了果树，有一个比这儿漂亮上百倍的地方。我们还结交了朋友，这才是我们拥有的东西。或许曾几何时，我们诚惶诚恐，担心被开除，但我们不再害怕了。我们有了自己的土地，那是属于我们的土地，我们可以上那儿去。"

柯利的老婆冲着他哈哈大笑。"胡说八道，"她说，"你们这样的人我可是见得太多了。你们身上只要有二角五分钱，哼，你们便会跑去喝上两杯，临了连杯子底都要舔一舔。我太了解你们这些人了。"

坎迪的脸庞涨得越来越红，但她尚未把话说完，他便已经控制住了自己的情绪。他是现场局面的控制者。"这我都清楚。"他语气和蔼地说，"你或许最好还是回去管好你自己的事情吧。我们和你没有什么好说的了。我们知道我们拥有什么就行了，你知不知道我们不在乎。因此，你还是现在开溜的好，因为柯利或许不乐意看见自己的老婆与我们这样一伙扛铺盖卷的流浪汉待在牲口棚里。"

她挨个地打量着在场每个人的面孔，而他们全都不理睬她。她打量伦尼的时间最长，直盯得他窘迫地低下了头。她突然开口说："你脸上的伤痕是怎么来的？"

Lennie looked up guiltily. "Who—me?"

"Yeah, you."

Lennie looked to Candy for help, and then he looked at his lap again. "He got his han' caught in a machine," he said.

Curley's wife laughed. "O.K., Machine. I'll talk to you later. I like machines."

Candy broke in. "You let this guy alone. Don't you do no messing aroun' with him. I'm gonna tell George what you says. George won't have you messin' with Lennie."

"Who's George?" she asked. "The little guy you come with?"

Lennie smiled happily. "That's him," he said. "That's the guy, an' he's gonna let me tend the rabbits."

"Well, if that's all you want, I might get a couple rabbits myself."

Crooks stood up from his bunk and faced her. "I had enough," he said coldly. "You got no rights comin' in a colored man's room. You got no rights messing around in here at all. Now you jus' get out, an' get out quick. If you don't, I'm gonna ast the boss not to ever let you come in the barn no more."

She turned on him in scorn. "Listen, Nigger," she said. "You know what I can do to you if you open your **trap**①?"

Crooks stared hopelessly at her, and then he sat down on his bunk and **drew**② into himself.

She **closed**③ **on**④ him. "You know what I could do?"

Crooks seemed to grow smaller, and he pressed himself against the wall. "Yes, ma'am."

"Well, you **keep your place**⑤ then, Nigger. I could get you **strung**⑥ upon a tree so easy it ain't even funny."

Crooks had **reduced**⑦ himself to nothing. There was no personality, no **ego**⑧—nothing to **arouse**⑨ either like or dislike. He said, "Yes, ma'am," and his voice was **toneless**⑩.

For a moment she stood over him as though waiting for him to move so

伦尼心虚地抬起头。"谁——我吗？"

"是啊，就是你。"

伦尼向坎迪投以求助的目光，然后又低头看着自己的膝部。"他的手给绞到机器了。"他说。

柯利的老婆哈哈大笑起来。"好吧，就算是机器吧。我回头再和你说。我喜欢机器。"

坎迪突然插话了。"你放过这个小伙子，不要再纠缠他了。我会把你说过的话告诉乔治的。乔治是不会允许你纠缠伦尼的。"

"谁是乔治？"她问了一声，"与你一块儿来的那个小个子吗？"

伦尼露出了开心的微笑。"正是他呢，"他说，"正是那位，他会让我照料兔子的。"

"好啦，假如你只想要这个，我可以亲自给你弄两只兔子来。"

克鲁克斯从坐着的床上站起来面对着她。"我受够了，"他语气冷漠地说，"你没有权利进入一个黑人住的房间。你没有任何权利在这儿胡搅蛮缠。你现在要做的就是出去，赶紧出去。假如你不出去，我就去找场主，让他再也不允许你到牲口棚来。"

她蔑视地冲他道："听着，你这黑鬼，"她说，"你知道，假如你再不闭嘴，我能够对你采取什么行动吧？"

克鲁克斯一脸无助，眼睛盯着她看，然后坐回床上，缩起了身子。

她朝他逼近。"你知道我能够采取什么行动吗？"

克鲁克斯的身子似乎变得更小了，他用力靠在墙壁上。"知道，太太。"

"行了，那你就乖乖地待着，黑鬼。我可以轻而易举地把你吊在一棵树上，那可不是什么好玩的。"

克鲁克斯整个人缩减到无形了。他没有了个性，没有了自我——没有了任何唤醒别人喜爱或厌恶的东西。他说："知道了，太太。"他声音里没有了声调。

她在他身前站了一会儿，仿佛只待他身子一动，便

---

① trap [træp] n.〈口〉嘴

② draw [dru:] v.（draw 的过去式）缩拢，皱缩

③ close [kləuz] v. 接触，接近

④ on [ɔn] prep.［表示方向］向，朝

⑤ keep one's place 知道自己（低微）的地位而安分守己，守本分，知趣，识相

⑥ strung [strʌŋ] v.（string 的过去式和过去分词）（用绳、线等）缚，扎

⑦ reduce [ri'dju:s] v. 缩小

⑧ ego ['i:gəu; 'e-] n. 自我，自己；自尊心

⑨ arouse [ə'rauz] v. 引起，唤起，激起；唤醒

⑩ toneless ['təunlis] a. 缺乏声调（或色调）的，单调的，平板的，沉闷的

that she could **whip**① at him again; but Crooks sat perfectly still, his eyes **averted**②, everything that might be hurt **drawn in**③. She turned at last to the other two.

Old Candy was watching her, fascinated. "If you was to do that, we'd tell," he said quietly. "We'd tell about you **framin'**④ Crooks."

"Tell an' be **damned**⑤," she cried. "Nobody'd listen to you, an' you know it. Nobody'd listen to you."

Candy subsided. "No . . ." he agreed. "Nobody'd listen to us."

Lennie **whined**⑥, "I wisht George was here. I wisht George was here."

Candy stepped over to him. "Don't you worry none," he said. "I jus' heard the guys comin' in. George'll be in the bunk house right now, I bet." He turned to Curley's wife. "You better go home now," he said quietly. "If you go right now, we won't tell Curley you was here."

She **appraised**⑦ him coolly. "I ain't sure you heard nothing."

"Better not **take no chances**⑧," he said. "If you ain't sure, you better take the safe way."

She turned to Lennie. "I'm glad you bust up Curley a little bit. He got it comin' to him. Sometimes I'd like to bust him myself." She slipped out the door and disappeared into the dark barn. And while she went through the barn, the halter chains rattled, and some horses snorted and some **stamped**⑨ their feet.

Crooks seemed to come slowly out of the layers of protection he had put on. "Was that the truth what you said about the guys come back?" he asked.

"Sure. I heard 'em."

"Well, I didn't hear nothing."

"The gate banged," Candy said, and he went on, "Jesus Christ, Curley's wife can move quiet. I guess she had a lot of practice, though."

① whip [wip] *v.* 严厉批评，痛斥
② avert [ə'və:t] *v.* 转移（目光、注意力等）
③ draw in 缩小，收缩
④ frame [freim] *v.*〈口〉诬陷，捏造（罪名等）
⑤ damn [dæm] *v.* 使失败，注定……要失败

⑥ whine [wain] *v.* 发哀叫（或哀诉、哀鸣）声

⑦ appraise [ə'preiz] *v.* 评价
⑧ take one's chance(s) 碰运气，准备冒险

⑨ stamp [stæmp] *v.* 跺（脚），踩踏

再劈头盖脸骂他一顿。但克鲁克斯纹丝不动，他挪开了目光，收起了一切可能受到伤害的东西。她最后转向另外两个人。

老坎迪注视着她，仿佛被震慑住了。"假如你那样做，我们就会说出去，"他小声说，"我们会说出去的，说你诬陷克鲁克斯。"

"说出去好啦，怕个屁，"她大声说，"没有人会听你们的，这一点你们清楚。没有人会听你们的。"

坎迪的气势减弱了。"对……"他表示同意，"没有人会听我们的。"

伦尼哀哀地说："要是乔治在这儿就好啦。要是乔治在这儿就好啦。"

坎迪朝着他走了过去。"不用担心，"他说，"我刚刚听见那些人回来了。乔治此时应该到宿舍里了，我敢打赌。"他转身对着柯利的老婆，"你还是现在回家去吧，"他小声说，"假如你现在就回去，我们不会对柯利说你到过这儿的。"

她神情冷漠地打量着他。"我不确定你听见了什么动静。"

"那就最好还是不要冒险，"他说，"假如你不确定，你最好还是采取稳妥的办法。"

她转身对着伦尼。"我很高兴你让柯利吃了点儿苦头。他这是自找的。有时候，我自己也想让他吃点儿苦头。"她说完溜出了门口，消失在黑暗的牲口棚里。她走过牲口棚时，骡马抖了抖缰绳链子发出了叮当声，有几匹马喷起了鼻息，有的跺了跺蹄子。

克鲁克斯似乎从自己披上的重重保护层中缓慢走了出来。"你说那些人回来了，这是真的吗？"他问了一声。

"当然，我听见他们回来了。"

"这样啊，我什么都没有听见呢。"

"大门砰地响了一声。"坎迪说，"天哪，柯利的老婆离开时不声不响，没有动静呢。不过，我估计，她是熟能生巧了。"

· 141 ·

Of Mice and Men

Crooks avoided the whole subject now. "Maybe you guys better go," he said. "I ain't sure I want you in here no more. A colored man got to have some rights even if he don't like 'em."

Candy said, "That bitch didn't ought to of said that to you."

"It wasn't nothing," Crooks said **dully**①. "You guys comin' in an' settin' made me forget. What she says is true."

The horses snorted out in the barn and the chains rang and a voice called, "Lennie. Oh, Lennie. You in the barn?"

"It's George," Lennie cried. And he answered, "Here, George. I'm right in here."

In a second George stood **framed**② in the door, and he looked **disapprovingly**③ about. "What you doin' in Crooks' room? You hadn't ought to be here."

Crooks nodded. "I tol' 'em, but they come in anyways."

"Well, why'n't you kick 'em out?"

"I di'n't care much," said Crooks. "Lennie's a nice fella."

Now Candy **aroused**④ himself. "Oh, George! I been figurin' and figurin'. I got it **doped out**⑤ how we can even make some money on them rabbits."

George scowled. "I thought I tol' you not to tell nobody about that."

Candy was **crestfallen**⑥. "Didn't tell nobody but Crooks."

George said, "Well you guys get outa here. Jesus, seems like I can't go away for a minute."

Candy and Lennie stood up and went toward the door. Crooks called, "Candy!"

"Huh?"

"'**Member**⑦ what I said about hoein' and doin' **odd**⑧ jobs?"

"Yeah," said Candy. "I remember."

① dully [dʌli] ad. 没精打采地，沮丧地，无生气地

② framed [freim] v. 作为……的背景

③ disapprovingly [ˌdisə'pruviŋli] ad. 不赞成地，不同意地

④ arouse [ə'rauz] v. 使……奋发，使……行动起来

⑤ dope out 〈口〉想出，解出，弄清楚，推断出，发现

⑥ crestfallen ['krestˌfɔːl(ə)n] a. 沮丧的，羞愧的

⑦ 'member = remember

⑧ odd [ɔd] a. 临时的，不固定的，非经常的，各种各样的

克鲁克斯现在彻底回避了这个话题。"你们俩现在最好回去吧，"他说，"我不想让你们再待在这儿了。黑人也该有些权利的，哪怕这权利他们并不喜欢。"

坎迪说："那条母狗不该对你说那样的话。"

"那没有什么，"克鲁克斯没精打采地说，"你们进来坐着，我一时间忘记了自己的处境。她说的话没有错。"

牲口棚那边的马匹喷了喷鼻息，缰绳链子叮当作响，有个声音喊着："伦尼，喂，伦尼。你在牲口棚吗？"

"是乔治呢。"伦尼大声说。他随即应道："在这儿呢，乔治。我在这儿呢。"

没过一会儿，乔治站到了门口，他不赞同地四处打量了一番。"你们在克鲁克斯的房间里干什么？你们不应该到这儿来的。"

克鲁克斯点了点头。"我跟他们说了，但他们还是进来了。"

"那么，你怎么没有一脚把他们踢出去呢？"

"我并不介意他们进来呢，"克鲁克斯说，"伦尼是个很棒的小伙子。"

坎迪现在振作了起来。"噢，乔治！我算了一遍又一遍，终于算好了，我们即便卖兔子也能够挣钱的。"

乔治沉下脸。"我记得我告诉过你们，这件事情不能告诉任何人。"

坎迪面露愧色。"除了克鲁克斯，没别人知道了。"

乔治说："好啦，你们两个离开这儿吧。天哪，看起来我一分钟都不能离开呢。"

坎迪和伦尼站起身，朝着门口走去。克鲁克斯喊道："坎迪！"

"嗯？"

"我说过，我可以锄草和打杂什么的，你还记得吗？"

"嗯，"坎迪说，"我记得呢。"

"嗯，忘了我说过那话吧，"克鲁克斯说，"我不是当真的，只是说着玩儿的。我不会想要去那样的地方的。"

· 143 ·

"Well, jus' forget it," said Crooks. "I didn't mean it. Jus' foolin'. I wouldn' want to go no place like that."

"Well, O.K., if you feel like that. Good night."

The three men went out of the door. As they went through the barn the horses snorted and the halter chains rattled.

Crooks sat on his bunk and looked at the door for a moment, and then he reached for the liniment bottle. He pulled out his shirt in back, poured a little liniment in his pink palm and, reaching around, he fell slowly to rubbing his back.

"嗯，好吧，你要这样想也行。那晚安吧。"

三个人出了门。他们走过牲口棚时，骡马喷了喷鼻息，晃得缰绳链子叮当作响。

克鲁克斯坐在床上，朝着门口看了片刻，然后伸手去拿搽剂瓶子。他扯起衬衫后摆，往粉红色的手掌心里倒出几滴搽剂，然后把手伸到后面，慢慢地搓揉起背部来。

One end of the great barn was piled high with new hay and over the pile hung the four-**taloned**[①] **Jackson fork**[②] **suspended**[③] from its **pulley**[④]. The hay came down like a mountain **slope**[⑤] to the other end of the barn, and there was a **level**[⑥] place as yet unfilled with the new crop. At the sides the feeding racks were visible, and between the **slats**[⑦] the heads of horses could be seen.

It was Sunday afternoon. The resting horses nibbled the remaining **wisps**[⑧] of hay, and they stamped their feet and they bit the wood of the **mangers**[⑨] and rattled the halter chains. The afternoon sun **sliced**[⑩] in through the **cracks**[⑪] of the barn walls and lay in bright lines on the hay. There was the **buzz**[⑫] of flies in the air, the lazy afternoon **humming**[⑬].

From outside came the clang of horseshoes on the playing peg and the shouts of men, playing, encouraging, **jeering**[⑭]. But in the barn it was quiet and humming and lazy and warm.

Only Lennie was in the barn, and Lennie sat in the hay beside a **packing case**[⑮] under a manger in the end of the barn that had not been filled with hay. Lennie sat in the hay and looked at a little dead puppy that lay in front of him. Lennie looked at it for a long time, and then he put out his huge hand and stroked it, stroked it **clear**[⑯] from one end to the other.

And Lennie said softly to the puppy, "Why do you got to get killed? You ain't so little as mice. I didn't **bounce**[⑰] you hard." He bent the pup's head up and looked in its face, and he said to it, "Now maybe George ain't gonna let me tend no rabbits, if he **fin's**[⑱] out you got killed."

He **scooped**[⑲] a little **hollow**[⑳] and laid the puppy in it and covered it over

① talon ['tælən] n. 爪状物，爪状部分
② Jackson fork 一种有四个叉子的干草叉
③ suspend [sə'spend] v. 悬，挂，吊
④ pulley ['puli] n. 滑轮，滑车，滑轮组，皮带轮
⑤ slope [sləup] n. 斜坡，坡地
⑥ level ['lev(ə)l] a. 平的，平坦的
⑦ slat [slæt] n. 板条
⑧ wisp [wisp] n. 小把，束
⑨ manger ['mein(d)ʒə] n.（马、牛等的）食槽
⑩ slice [slais] v. 把……分成若干部分（或份）
⑪ crack [kræk] n. 裂缝，裂口，缝隙
⑫ buzz [bʌz] n.（蜂、蚊等的）嗡嗡声
⑬ hum [hʌm] v. 发连续低沉的声音（如蜜蜂、马达等的嗡嗡声）
⑭ jeer [dʒiə] v. 嘲笑，嘲弄
⑮ packing case（尤指木制的）装货箱
⑯ clear [kliə] ad. 完全，整整，〈美〉一直
⑰ bounce [bauns] v. 使弹起，使反弹，使颠跳
⑱ fin's = finds
⑲ scoop [sku:p] v. 挖出
⑳ hollow ['hɔləu] n. 坑，洞，穴

大牲口棚一端高高地堆起了新收的干草。干草堆上方悬挂着从滑轮上垂下的四爪干草叉。越往牲口棚的另一端，干草堆得越矮，仿佛绵延而下的山坡，只剩下一块平地还没有堆上。干草堆的两侧是饲料槽，饲料槽板条的缝隙之间隐约露出马匹的头部。

星期天下午，歇息的马匹一口口嚼着剩下的几束干草。马匹时而跺跺蹄子，时而咬咬饲料槽的木头，晃得缰绳链子叮当作响。午后的阳光透过牲口棚墙壁的空隙照射进来，形成一束束光线，在干草上投下一道道闪亮的线条。苍蝇在空中嗡嗡飞舞着，这是令人倦怠的午后声响。

室外传来马蹄铁击中铁柱发出的当当声，还有男人们的叫喊声。他们玩着游戏，相互鼓劲，相互打趣。但是，牲口棚里了无人声，只有苍蝇嗡嗡飞着，令人倦怠和温暖。

牲口棚里只有伦尼一个人。伦尼坐在没有堆上干草的那一头一个饲料槽下方的干草里，身旁是一只木质装货箱。伦尼坐在干草里，看着面前那只已经死亡的小狗崽。伦尼久久看着它，然后伸出一只大手抚摸起来，从头摸到尾。

伦尼声音柔和地对小狗崽说："你怎么就死了呢？你并不像老鼠那样瘦小呢。我并没有使劲儿颠你啊。"他把小狗崽的头向上一抬，看着它的脸说道："现在，假如乔治发现你死掉了，他可能不会让我照料那些兔子了。"

他在干草堆里挖出一个坑，把小狗崽放了进去，再

Of Mice and Men

with hay, out of sight; but he continued to stare at the **mound**① he had made. He said, "This ain't no bad thing like I got to go hide in the brush. Oh! No. This ain't. I'll tell George I foun' it dead."

He unburied the puppy and inspected it, and he stroked it from ears to tail. He went on sorrowfully, "But he'll know. George always knows. He'll say, 'You done it. Don't try to put nothing over on me.' An' he'll say, 'Now jus' for that you don't get to tend no rabbits!'"

Suddenly his anger arose. "God damn you," he cried. "Why do you got to get killed? You ain't so little as mice." He picked up the pup and **hurled**② it from him. He turned his back on it. He sat bent over his knees and he whispered, "Now I won't get to tend the rabbits. Now he won't let me." He **rocked**③ himself back and forth in his sorrow.

From outside came the clang of horseshoes on the iron stake, and then a little **chorus**④ of cries. Lennie got up and brought the puppy back and laid it on the hay and sat down. He stroked the pup again. "You wasn't big enough," he said. "They tol' me and tol' me you wasn't. I di'n't know you'd get killed so easy." He worked his fingers on the pup's **limp**⑤ ear. "Maybe George won't care," he said. "This here God damn little son-of-a-bitch wasn't nothing to George."

Curley's wife came around the end of the last **stall**⑥. She came very quietly, so that Lennie didn't see her. She wore her bright cotton dress and the mules with the red ostrich feathers. Her face was made-up and the little sausage curls were all in place. She was quite near to him before Lennie looked up and saw her.

In a panic he **shoveled**⑦ hay over the puppy with his fingers. He looked **sullenly**⑧ up at her.

She said, "What you got there, **sonny**⑨ boy?"

Lennie glared at her. "George says I ain't to have nothing to do with you—talk to you or nothing."

She laughed. "George giving you orders about everything?"

① mound [maund] n. 土堆，沙石堆

② hurl [hə:l] v. 猛投，力掷

③ rock [rɔk] v. 使轻轻摇摆，轻轻摇动，使摇晃

④ chorus ['kɔ:rəs] n. 齐声，异口同声，齐声说的话（或发出的喊声）

⑤ limp [limp] a. 软的，松沓的

⑥ stall [stɔ:l] n. 马厩，牲口棚

⑦ shovel ['ʃʌv(ə)l] v.〈口〉把……大量（或胡乱）投入

⑧ sullenly ['sʌlənli] ad. 郁郁寡欢地

⑨ sonny ['sʌni] n.〈口〉〈昵〉小弟弟，小家伙，宝宝，乖儿

盖上干草，不让人看见。但是，他还是不断地盯着自己刚才隆起的草堆看。他说："这并不是我一定要藏到灌木丛里去的坏事情吧。噢！不是呢。这才不是呢。我就跟乔治说我发现小狗崽死了吧。"

他又把小狗崽翻了出来，仔细查看着，用手从耳朵一直抚摸到尾巴上。他悲伤地接着说："但是，他会知道的，乔治每次都知道。他会说：'你干的好事，别以为能瞒过我。'他还会说，'这下你就别想照料那些兔子啦！'"

他突然怒火中烧。"你这该死的，"他大喊了一声，"你为什么非要死掉不可呢？你并不像老鼠那样小啊。"他抓起小狗崽，扔了出去。他背过身子，抱着膝盖坐了下来，小声说着话，"我现在不能照料那些兔子了。他现在不会让我照料那些兔子了。"他身子前后摇晃着，悲痛不已。

室外传来马蹄铁打中铁柱发出的当当声，随即一小群人齐声叫好。伦尼站起身，拿回了小狗崽放在干草上，然后坐了下来。他再次抚摸着小狗崽。"你还没长大，"他说，"他们跟我说了很多遍，你还没长大。我不知道你这么容易就死掉了。"他用手指摆弄着小狗崽软绵绵的耳朵。"乔治或许并不在乎呢，"他说，"这个该死的小狗杂种在乔治眼里算不得什么。"

柯利的老婆从最边上一个马厩旁走了过来。她脚步很轻，因此伦尼没有注意到她。她身穿色彩艳丽的棉布衣裙，脚上趿着那双装饰着红色鸵鸟羽毛的拖鞋。她脸上化了妆，小香肠一样的发卷梳理得很到位。她已经距离很近了，伦尼这才抬起头看到她。

惊慌失措之中，他用手指抓起大把大把的干草遮盖住小狗崽。他抬头看着她，一脸闷闷不乐的神情。

她说："你这是干什么呢，小家伙？"

伦尼瞪着眼睛看她。"乔治说了，我不能与你有半点儿瓜葛——不能和你说话什么的。"

她哈哈大笑起来。"任何事情乔治都要给你指令吗？"

Lennie looked down at the hay. "Says I can't tend no rabbits if I talk to you or anything."

She said quietly, "He's scared Curley'll get mad. Well, Curley got his arm in a **sling**①—an' if Curley gets tough, you can break his other han'. You didn't put nothing over on me about gettin' it caught in no machine."

But Lennie was not to be drawn. "No, sir. I ain't gonna talk to you or nothing."

She knelt in the hay beside him. "Listen," she said. "All the guys got a horseshoe **tenement**② goin' on. It's on'y about four o'clock. None of them guys is goin' to leave that tenement. Why can't I talk to you? I never get to talk to nobody. I get **awful**③ lonely."

Lennie said, "Well, I ain't supposed to talk to you or nothing."

"I get lonely," she said. "You can talk to people, but I can't talk to nobody but Curley. Else he gets mad. How'd you like not to talk to anybody?"

Lennie said, "Well, I ain't supposed to. George's scared I'll get in trouble."

She changed the subject. "What you got covered up there?"

Then all of Lennie's **woe**④ came back on him. "Jus' my pup," he said sadly. "Jus' my little pup." And he swept the hay from on top of it.

"Why, he's dead," she cried.

"He was so little," said Lennie. "I was jus' playin' with him . . . an' he **made like**⑤ he's gonna bite me . . . an' I made like I was gonna **smack**⑥ him . . . an' . . . an' I done it. An' then he was dead."

She **consoled**⑦ him. "Don't you worry none. He was jus' a **mutt**⑧. You can get another one easy. The whole country is fulla mutts."

"It ain't that so much," Lennie explained miserably. "George ain't gonna let me tend no rabbits now."

"Why don't he?"

"Well, he said if I done any more bad things he ain't gonna let me tend the rabbits."

① sling [sliŋ] n.【医】悬带，挂带，吊腕带

② tenement ['tenəm(ə)nt] n. = tournament 比赛

③ awful ['ɔ:ful] ad.〈主美口〉十分，极度地

④ woe [wəu] n. 痛苦，苦恼，悲伤，哀伤

⑤ make like〈主美口〉假装，装作，模仿

⑥ smack [smæk] v. 掴，打

⑦ console [kən'səul] v. 安慰，抚慰，慰问

⑧ mutt [mʌt] n.〈口〉〈贬〉狗，杂种狗，野狗

伦尼低头看着干草。"乔治说了，我要是和你说了话什么的，我便不能照料那些兔子了。"

她小声地说："他是害怕柯利会生气。行啦，柯利的手臂吊着绷带呢——柯利要是撒起野来，你就弄断他另外那只手好了。说什么他的手绞到机器里面了，你们瞒不了我。"

但是，伦尼不为所动。"不，太太，我不能和你说话什么的。"

她在他旁边的干草上跪了下来。"听着，"她说，"那些人全都参加掷马蹄铁比赛了。现在才四点左右的样子，他们谁都不会中途退场的。我为什么不能和你说说话呢？我从来没有和谁说过话。我孤单寂寞死啦。"

伦尼说："可是，我是不应该和你说话的。"

"我孤单寂寞着呢，"她说，"你可以和别人说话，但我除了柯利之外不能和任何人说话，否则，他就会生气。不和任何人说话，你乐意呀？"

伦尼说："可是，我不应该那样做。乔治担心我会惹麻烦的。"

她变换了话题。"你这儿遮盖着什么东西啊？"

她话音刚落，伦尼的忧伤一股脑儿地涌上了心头。"只是我的小狗崽而已，"他悲痛地说，"只是我的小狗崽而已。"他拨开了遮盖在小狗崽上面的干草。

"天哪，它死了呢。"她大声说。

"它太小了，"伦尼说，"我只是和它玩了玩……它装作要咬我的样子……我装作要扇它的样子……然后……然后，我真的扇了它。然后，它就死掉了。"

她安慰他，"别伤心了，它只是一条小狗而已。再弄一条也费不了什么事。这地方到处都有狗。"

"不是这么回事呢，"伦尼痛苦地解释说，"乔治现在不会让我照料那些兔子了。"

"他为什么不让呢？"

"是这样的，他说了，假如我做了什么坏事，他就不让我照料那些兔子了。"

Of Mice and Men

She moved closer to him and she spoke **soothingly**[①]. "Don't you worry about talkin' to me. Listen to the guys yell out there. They got four dollars bet in that tenement. None of them ain't gonna leave till it's over."

"If George sees me talkin' to you he'll give me hell," Lennie said cautiously. "He tol' me so."

Her face grew angry. "Wha's the matter with me?" she cried. "Ain't I got a right to talk to nobody? Whatta they think I am, anyways? You're a nice guy. I don't know why I can't talk to you. I ain't doin' no harm to you."

"Well, George says you'll get us in a mess."

"Aw, nuts!" she said. "What kinda harm am I doin' to you? Seems like they ain't none of them cares how I gotta live. I tell you I ain't used to livin' like this. I coulda **made somethin' of myself**[②]." She said darkly, "Maybe I will yet." And then her words **tumbled**[③] out in a passion of communication, as though she hurried before her listener could be taken away. "I lived right in Salinas," she said. "Come there when I was a kid. Well, a show come through, an' I met one of the actors. He says I could go with that show. But my ol' lady wouldn't let me. She says because I was on'y fifteen. But the guy says I coulda. If I'd went, I wouldn't be livin' like this, you bet."

Lennie stroked the pup back and forth. "We gonna have a little place—an' rabbits," he explained.

She went on with her story quickly, before she could be interrupted. "'**Nother**[④] time I met a guy, an' he was in pitchers. Went out to the Riverside Dance Palace with him. He says he was gonna put me in the movies. Says I was a natural. Soon's he got back to Hollywood he was gonna write to me about it." She looked closely at Lennie to see whether she was impressing him. "I never got that letter," she said. "I always thought my ol' lady stole it. Well, I wasn't gonna stay no place where I couldn't get nowhere or make something of myself,

· 152 ·

① soothingly ['suðɪŋli] ad. 安慰地，抚慰性地

② make something of oneself 有所成就，获得成功
③ tumble ['tʌmb(ə)l] v. 滚下

④ 'nother = another

她挪了挪身子，距离他更近了，用安慰的语气说道："不用担心和我说话的事情。你听，那些人正在外面大喊大叫呢。他们用四块钱赌比赛的输赢，不等到比赛结束，没有谁会中途离开的。"

"乔治要是看见我和你说话，一定会骂我的，"伦尼谨慎地说，"他是这样对我的。"

她面露愠色。"我怎么了？"她大声说，"我就没有权利和人说话吗？他们到底把我当成什么啊？你是个很棒的小伙子。我不知道我为什么不能和你说话。我又没伤害你。"

"哦，乔治说你会让我们惹上麻烦的。"

"呵，真是胡扯！"她说，"我怎么伤害你了？我日子过得怎么样，他们好像没有谁会关心的。我告诉你吧，我可过不惯这种日子。我本来是可以有所作为的。"她阴沉着脸说，"或许现在也还可以。"接着，在倾诉欲的驱使下，她把心里话一股脑儿倒了出来。她说得很快，好像是为了赶在听众被人带走之前说完似的。"我以前就住在萨利纳斯，"她说，"我是很小的时候去那儿的。后来呢，有个戏班子来了，我遇上了里面的一个演员。他说，我可以随戏班子走。但是，我老妈不让我走，她说是因为我才十五岁。不过，那个演员说我可以去。你可以打赌，假如我当时去了，我的生活就不会是这个样子的。"

伦尼来回抚摸着小狗崽。"我们将拥有一片小地方——还有兔子呢。"他解释着说。

趁着还没有彻底被对方打断，她赶紧讲下去，"后来又有一次，我遇上了一个人，他是个拍电影的。我跟他去了河畔舞厅。他说他要介绍我去演电影，说我天生是个演电影的料儿，他回到好莱坞之后，很快就会给我写信，跟我说这事。"她紧盯着伦尼，想看看自己是否给伦尼留下了深刻的印象，"我从来没收到过那样一封信，"她说，"我心里一直觉得，我老妈偷了那封信。这么说吧，没有前途，无可事事，连信都有人偷的地方，

· 153 ·

an' where they stole your letters. I ast her if she stole it, too, an' she says no. So I married Curley. Met him out to the Riverside Dance Palace that same night." She demanded, "You listenin'?"

"Me? Sure."

"Well, I ain't told this to nobody before. Maybe I ought'n to. I don' *like* Curley. He ain't a nice fella." And because she had **confided**① in him, she moved closer to Lennie and sat beside him. "Coulda been in the movies, an' had nice clothes—all them nice clothes like they wear. An' I coulda sat in them big hotels, an' had pitchers took of me. When they had them **previews**② I coulda went to them, an' spoke in the radio, an' it wouldn'ta cost me a cent because I was in the pitcher. An' all them nice clothes like they wear. Because this guy says I was a **natural**③." She looked up at Lennie, and she made a small grand gesture with her arm and hand to show that she could act. The fingers **trailed**④ after her leading wrist, and her little finger stuck out grandly from the rest.

Lennie sighed deeply. From outside came the clang of a horseshoe on metal, and then a chorus of cheers. "Somebody made a **ringer**⑤," said Curley's wife.

Now the light was lifting as the sun went down, and the sun streaks climbed up the wall and fell over the feeding racks and over the heads of the horses.

Lennie said, "Maybe if I took this pup out and threw him away George wouldn't never know. An' then I could tend the rabbits without no trouble."

Curley's wife said angrily, "Don't you think of nothing but rabbits?"

"We gonna have a little place," Lennie explained patiently. "We gonna have a house an' a garden and a place for alfalfa, an' that alfalfa is for the rabbits, an' I take a sack and get it all fulla alfalfa and then I take it to the rabbits."

She asked, "What makes you so nuts about rabbits?"

Lennie had to think carefully before he could come to a conclusion. He moved cautiously close to her, until he was right against her. "I like to pet

① confide [kən'faid] v. 吐露秘密（以示信任、求教等）

② preview ['pri:vju:] n.（影片、电视节目等的）预映，试映

③ natural ['nætʃrəl] n.〈口〉生就具有特定才能的人，天生的料子，天才

④ trail [treil] v. 跟随

⑤ ringer ['riŋə] n.（一次）套环投掷

我是不会继续待的。我还问了她，问她是否偷了我的信，她说没有。于是，我便嫁给了柯利。我们是在我去河畔舞厅的那一同晚邂逅的。"她问，"你在听吗？"

"我？当然在听了。"

"嗯，有件事我从来没有告诉过任何人。我或许不应该告诉别人。我不喜欢柯利。他不是个好人。"由于她向他吐露了这样的秘密，她移动着身子，距离伦尼更近了，近到就坐在他身边。"我本来是可以去拍电影的，可以穿上漂亮的衣服——演电影的人穿的都是漂亮衣服。我可以坐在大饭店里，让人给我拍照片。等到电影试映时，我可以去观看，还可以去做广播节目，由于我是演电影的，这些事情都不需要花费我一分钱。还有数不尽的漂亮衣服，因为那个演员说我是个天生演电影的料儿。"她抬头看着伦尼，用手臂和手做了一个细微而庄重的动作，表明她能够表演。她把小指高高翘起，手指跟着手腕转动。

伦尼深深地叹息了一声。室外传来马蹄铁击打在铁柱上发出"当"的一声，然后是一阵喝彩声。"有人得分了。"柯利的老婆说。

随着太阳西下，牲口棚的太阳光线上升了。阳光爬上了墙壁，照射在饲料槽的上方和马匹的头部上方。

伦尼说："我要是把这条小狗崽拿出去扔掉，乔治或许就不会知道了。这样我便省去了麻烦，可以照料那些兔子了。"

柯利的老婆愤怒地说："除了兔子，你就不会想点儿别的什么东西吗？"

"我们将拥有一小片土地，"伦尼耐心地解释说，"我们将拥有一幢房子、一片菜园子、一片苜蓿地，苜蓿是用来喂养兔子的，我会拿上一个口袋，往里面装满苜蓿，然后拿去喂兔子。"

她问道："你怎么会对兔子这么痴迷呢？"

伦尼认真思索了一番，然后才得出了结论。他小心翼翼地一点一点向她靠，直到就在她身旁停了下来。"我

· 155 ·

Of Mice and Men

nice things. Once at a fair I seen some of them long-hair rabbits. An' they was nice, you bet. Sometimes I've even pet mice, but not when I could get nothing better."

Curley's wife moved away from him a little. "I think you're nuts," she said.

"No I ain't," Lennie explained earnestly. "George says I ain't. I like to pet nice things with my fingers, sof' things."

She was a little bit reassured. "Well, who don't?" she said. "Ever'body likes that. I like to feel silk an' **velvet**①. Do you like to feel velvet?"

Lennie chuckled with pleasure. "You bet, by God," he cried happily. "An' I had some, too. A lady give me some, an' that lady was—my own Aunt Clara. She give it right to me—'bout this big a piece. I wisht I had that velvet right now." A frown came over his face. "I lost it," he said. "I ain't seen it for a long time."

Curley's wife laughed at him. "You're nuts," she said. "But you're a kinda nice fella. Jus' like a big baby. But a person can see kinda what you mean. When I'm doin' my hair sometimes I jus' set an' stroke it 'cause it's so soft." To show how she did it, she ran her fingers over the top of her head. "Some people got kinda **coarse**② hair," she said **complacently**③. "Take Curley. His hair is jus' like **wire**④. But mine is soft and fine. 'Course I brush it a lot. That makes it fine. Here—feel right here." She took Lennie's hand and put it on her head. "Feel right aroun' there an' see how soft it is."

Lennie's big fingers fell to stroking her hair.

"Don't you **muss**⑤ it up," she said.

Lennie said, "Oh! That's nice," and he stroked harder. "Oh, that's nice."

"Look out, now, you'll muss it." And then she cried angrily, "You stop it now, you'll mess it all up." She jerked her head sideways, and Lennie's fingers

喜欢抚摸漂亮的东西。有一次在集市上,我看见了一些长毛兔。它们真是漂亮啊。有时候,我甚至会抚摸老鼠,不过,要是有更合适的,那就另说了。"

柯利的老婆从他身边挪开了一点儿。"我觉得你疯了。"她说。

"不,我没有疯,"伦尼态度诚恳地解释说,"乔治说我没有。我喜欢用手指抚摸漂亮的东西、柔软的东西。"

她稍稍安心了一点儿。"是啊,谁不喜欢呢?"她说,"那样的东西人人都喜欢的。我喜欢触摸丝绸和天鹅绒。你喜欢触摸天鹅绒吗?"

伦尼高兴得咯咯笑了起来。"这还用说,天哪,"他快乐地叫了起来,"我还有过一块呢。一位太太给了我一块,那位太太是——我的亲姨妈克拉拉。她直接给了我——大概这么大一块。我要是现在把那块天鹅绒带在身边该有多好啊。"他皱起了眉头,"我把它给弄丢了,"他说,"我很长时间都没有见过了。"

柯利的老婆冲着他哈哈大笑起来。"你疯了,"她说,"不过,你是个善良的好小伙子,跟一个大婴儿似的。但别人大约听得懂你的意思。有时候,我在梳理头发时,也会去摸一摸,因为头发很柔软。"为了展示她是怎样抚摸头发的,她把手指插入头顶上的头发中,"有些人的头发很粗硬,"她扬扬得意地说,"比如柯利吧,他的头发像铁丝一样。但我的头发又细又软。当然,我经常梳理。这样头发才能又细又软。就这儿——你摸一摸看。"她拉起伦尼的一只手,放到她的头上,"摸摸这里,感受感受我的头发有多么柔软。"

伦尼的大手指开始抚摸她的头发。

"你可不要把头发给弄乱了啊。"她说。

伦尼说:"噢!真好哇。"他摸得更用力了,"噢,真好哇。"

"小心点儿,哎呀,你会把头发弄乱的。"接着她生气地大喊起来,"快住手,你这样会把头发全部弄乱

① velvet ['velvit] n. 丝绒,平绒,天鹅绒

② coarse [kɔːs] a. 粗的,粗糙的
③ complacently [kəm'pleisəntli] ad. 自满地,沾沾自喜地
④ wire [waiə] n. 金属丝,金属线
⑤ muss [mʌs] v. 〈美口〉使凌乱,把弄乱(up)

closed on[①] her hair and hung on. "Let go," she cried. "You let go!"

Lennie was in a panic. His face was **contorted**[②]. She screamed then, and Lennie's other hand closed over her mouth and nose. "Please don't," he begged. "Oh! Please don't do that. George'll be mad."

She struggled violently under his hands. Her feet **battered**[③] on the hay and she **writhed**[④] to be free; and from under Lennie's hand came a **muffled**[⑤] screaming. Lennie began to cry with fright. "Oh! Please don't do none of that," he begged. "George gonna say I done a bad thing. He ain't gonna let me tend no rabbits." He moved his hand a little and her hoarse cry came out. Then Lennie grew angry. "Now don't," he said. "I don't want you to yell. You gonna get me in trouble jus' like George says you will. Now don't you do that." And she continued to struggle, and her eyes were wild with terror. He shook her then, and he was angry with her. "Don't you go yellin'," he said, and he shook her; and her body flopped like a fish. And then she was still, for Lennie had broken her neck.

He looked down at her, and carefully he removed his hand from over her mouth, and she lay still. "I don't want to hurt you," he said, "but George'll be mad if you yell." When she didn't answer nor move he bent closely over her. He lifted her arm and let it drop. For a moment he seemed **bewildered**[⑥]. And then he whispered in fright, "I done a bad thing. I done another bad thing."

He **pawed**[⑦] up the hay until it partly covered her.

From outside the barn came a cry of men and the double clang of shoes on metal. For the first time Lennie became conscious of the outside. He crouched down in the hay and listened. "I done a real bad thing," he said. "I shouldn't of did that. George'll be mad. An' . . . he said . . . an' hide in the brush till he come. He's gonna be mad. In the brush till he come. Tha's what he said." Lennie went back and looked at the dead girl. The puppy lay close to her. Lennie picked it up. "I'll throw him away," he said. "It's bad enough like it is." He put the pup under

① close on 抓住
② contort [kən'tɔ:t] v.（剧烈地）扭曲，歪曲

③ batter ['bætə] v. 连续猛击
④ writhe [raið] v.（因痛苦等）扭动身体，蠕动
⑤ muffle ['mʌfl] v. 使（声音）低沉（或轻微），消灭（声音）

⑥ bewildered [bi'wildəd] a. 困惑的，昏乱的，不知所措的
⑦ paw [pɔ:] v. 翻找，笨拙地触摸

的。"她把头用力向一边偏去，但伦尼的手指抓住她的头发不放。"放开，"她大喊着，"你快放开！"

伦尼慌了神，五官都扭曲了。她又尖叫了起来。伦尼用另一只手捂住她的嘴巴和鼻子。"请不要叫，"他恳求着，"噢！请不要这样。乔治会生气的。"

她在他的双手下猛烈地挣扎着。她的双脚不住地蹬着干草，身子来回扭着想要挣脱开去。伦尼那只捂住她的手下，传出了一声闷叫。伦尼害怕地哭了起来。"噢！别叫了，"他恳求着，"乔治会说我做了一件坏事情。他不会让我照料那些兔子的。"他的手移动了一点点，她沙哑的叫声便传了出来。这下，伦尼生气了。"现在不要叫了，"他说，"我不想你大喊大叫的。你这样会给我惹麻烦的，乔治就是这么说的。你现在不要叫了。"她继续挣扎着，眼神狂乱，充满了恐惧。他开始摇晃她的身体，心里生起她的气来。"你不要再大喊大叫了。"他边说边晃。她的身子像鱼一样扑腾起来。接着她就不动了，因为伦尼晃断了她的脖子。

他低头看着她，小心翼翼地把手从她嘴边移开，而她仍一动不动地躺着。"我并不想要伤害你的，"他说，"但假如你大喊大叫，乔治会生气的。"她既没有回应也没有动弹，他便俯下身子靠近她。他拽起她的一条胳膊，一松手，胳膊垂了下去。一时间，他似乎六神无主。然后他惊恐地小声说："我做坏事了。我又做坏事了。"

他随手抓起一些干草，直到够把她身子的一部分遮盖起来。

牲口棚外面传来了男人们的叫喊声，还有马蹄铁两次碰撞铁柱的当当声。伦尼这才第一次意识到了外面的动静。他蹲在干草上，仔细听着。"我做了一件极坏的事，"他说，"我不应该这样做的。乔治会生气的。还有……他说了……藏到灌木丛里，等待他来找。他会生气的。藏到灌木丛里，直到他来找。他就是这样说来着。"伦尼走回去，看着死了的女人。小狗崽就躺在她身边。伦尼拿起小狗崽。"我要把它扔掉，"他说，"这个情况

· 159 ·

his coat, and he crept to the barn wall and **peered**① out between the cracks, toward the horseshoe game. And then he crept around the end of the last manger and disappeared.

The sun streaks were high on the wall by now, and the light was growing soft in the barn. Curley's wife lay on her back, and she was half covered with hay.

It was very quiet in the barn, and the quiet of the afternoon was on the ranch. Even the clang of the pitched shoes, even the voices of the men in the game, seemed to grow more quiet. The air in the barn was **dusky**② **in advance of**③ the outside day. A pigeon flew in through the open hay door and circled and flew out again. Around the last stall came a shepherd bitch, lean and long, with heavy, hanging **dugs**④. Halfway to the packing box where the puppies were she caught the dead scent of Curley's wife, and the hair arose along her spine. She whimpered and **cringed**⑤ to the packing box, and jumped in among the puppies.

Curley's wife lay with a half-covering of yellow hay. And the **meanness**⑥ and the plannings and the discontent and the **ache**⑦ for attention were all gone from her face. She was very pretty and simple, and her face was sweet and young. Now her **rouged**⑧ cheeks and her reddened lips made her seem alive and sleeping very lightly. The curls, tiny little sausages, were spread on the hay behind her head, and her lips were parted.

As happens sometimes, a moment **settled**⑨ and **hovered**⑩ and remained for much more than a moment. And sound stopped and movement stopped for much, much more than a moment.

Then gradually time awakened again and moved **sluggishly**⑪ on. The horses stamped on the other side of the feeding racks and the halterchains clinked. Outside, the men's voices became louder and clearer.

From around the end of the last stall old Candy's voice came. "Lennie," he called. "Oh, Lennie! You in here? I been figuring some more. Tell you what we can do, Lennie." Old Candy appeared around the end of the last stall. "Oh,

人鼠之间

① peer [piə] v. 仔细地看，费力地看，凝视

② dusky ['dʌski] a. 微暗的，暗淡的

③ in advance of 在……的前面，在……之前

④ dug [dʌg] n. 哺乳动物的乳房（或乳头）

⑤ cringe [krin(d)ʒ] v. 畏缩

⑥ meanness [mi:nəs] n. 卑鄙

⑦ ache [eik] n.〈口〉渴望

⑧ rouge [ru:ʒ] v. 在……上搽胭脂

⑨ settle ['set(ə)l] v. 停留

⑩ hover ['hɔvə] v. 徘徊

⑪ sluggishly ['slʌgiʃli] ad. 缓慢地，慢地

已经够糟糕了。"他把小狗崽放在自己的外套下面，悄悄走到牲口棚的墙边，顺着墙壁上的空隙，朝掷马蹄铁游戏的方向看去。然后，他悄悄绕过最旁边的一个饲料槽，不见了踪影。

此时此刻，太阳的光线高高地映照在墙壁上，牲口棚里的光亮变得柔和了。柯利的老婆仰面躺着，身子一半被干草遮盖着。

牲口棚里显得很寂静，整个农场都笼罩在下午的寂静中。就连掷马蹄铁的当当声和游戏中男人们的呼喊声似乎都显得更加安静了。白昼慢慢逝去，牲口棚里显得越发昏暗了起来。一只鸽子顺着敞开的牲口棚门飞了进来，盘旋了一阵，然后又飞出去了。有条牧羊母犬绕过最后一个马厩出现了。牧羊犬身子又瘦又长，沉甸甸的乳房下垂着。母犬朝放狗崽的装货箱走去，走到一半，她嗅到了柯利老婆尸身的气味，背脊上的毛顿时竖了起来。牧羊犬哀吠着，畏缩着身子跑向装货箱，跳到了小狗崽们中间。

柯利的老婆躺着，身上被泛黄的干草半遮着。她脸上没有了那种卑劣、算计、不满和渴望被人关注的表情。她看上去美丽又单纯，面庞甜美，洋溢着青春。现在，她脸上涂着胭脂，嘴唇涂着口红，仿佛还活着，只是浅浅地睡着。她的卷发犹如香肠一般，散开在脑袋后面的干草上。她的嘴唇张开着。

情况有时候就是这样，一个瞬间会停滞不前，久久徘徊，停留的时间大大超过一瞬间。这期间，声音停止了，活动停止了，持续的时间远远超过了一瞬间。

然后，慢慢地，时间又苏醒了，慵懒倦怠地向前移动。骡马在饲料槽的另一侧跺着蹄子，缰绳链子抖动时发出了叮当声。牲口棚外面，男人们的声音越来越高亢，越来越清晰。

最边上的马厩那边传来了老坎迪声音。"伦尼，"他喊着，"喂，伦尼！你在这儿吗？我又算了算。告诉你我们能够干什么吧，伦尼。"老坎迪出现在最边上的马

· 161 ·

Of Mice and Men

Lennie!" he called again; and then he stopped, and his body stiffened. He rubbed his smooth wrist on his white stubble whiskers. "I di'n't know you was here," he said to Curley's wife.

When she didn't answer, he stepped nearer. "You oughten to sleep out here," he said disapprovingly; and then he was beside her and — "Oh, Jesus Christ!" He looked about helplessly, and he rubbed his beard. And then he jumped up and went quickly out of the barn.

But the barn was **alive**① now. The horses stamped and snorted, and they chewed the straw of their **bedding**② and they clashed the chains of their halters. In a moment Candy came back, and George was with him.

George said, "What was it you wanted to see me about?"

Candy pointed at Curley's wife. George stared. "What's the matter with her?" he asked. He stepped closer, and then he **echoed**③ Candy's words. "Oh, Jesus Christ!" He was down on his knees beside her. He put his hand over her heart. And finally, when he stood up, slowly and stiffly, his face was as hard and tight as wood, and his eyes were hard.

Candy said, "What done it?"

George looked coldly at him. "Ain't you got any idear?" he asked. And Candy was silent. "I should of knew," George said hopelessly. "I guess maybe way back in my head I did."

Candy asked, "What we gonna do now, George? What we gonna do now?"

George was a long time in answering. "Guess . . . we gotta tell the . . . guys. I guess we gotta get 'im an' **lock**④ 'im up. We can't let 'im get away. Why, the poor bastard'd **starve**⑤." And he tried to reassure himself. "Maybe they'll lock 'im up an' be nice to 'im."

But Candy said excitedly, "We oughta let 'im **get away**⑥. You don't know that Curley. Curley gon'ta wanta get 'im lynched. Curley'll get 'im killed."

George watched Candy's lips. "Yeah," he said at last, "that's right, Curley will. An' the other guys will." And he looked back at Curley's wife.

· 162 ·

① alive [ə'laiv] a. 有生气的，活跃的，热闹的
② bedding ['bediŋ] n. 给家畜垫在身下作睡铺的草（或木屑等）
③ echo ['ekəu] v. 重复（他人的话、思想等），重复……的话（或观点等）
④ lock [lɔk] v. 把……关起来（up）
⑤ starve [stɑ:v] v. 挨饿，饿死
⑥ get away 逃脱

厩边。"喂，伦尼！"他又喊了一声，随即停住脚步，僵立不动了。他用光秃的手腕摩擦着自己白色的胡茬。"我不知道你在这儿呢。"他冲着柯利的老婆说。

见对方没有反应，他走近了一些。"你不该睡在这儿。"他不满地说，随即到了她身边，接着——"噢，天哪！"他一脸无助，环顾了一番四周，搓揉着自己的胡子。然后他一跃身子跳了起来，快速跑出了牲口棚。

但是，牲口棚现在充满了生气，骡马跺着蹄子，发出呼哧呼哧的喷鼻声，嚼着马厩里的干草，抖动着缰绳链子。过了一会儿，坎迪回来了，乔治陪同着他。

乔治说："你想要领着我过来干什么啊？"

坎迪指了指柯利的老婆。乔治瞪大了眼。"她这是怎么啦？"他问。他走近了一些，然后跟坎迪说了一样的话。"噢，天哪！"他跪倒在她身边，一只手摸了摸她的心脏处。最后，他站立起来，动作缓慢而僵硬，只见他脸庞像木头一样硬实，目光严峻。

坎迪说："怎么会这样呢？"

乔治神情冷漠地看着他。"你不知道吗？"乔治问，但坎迪沉默不语。"我应该知道的，"乔治绝望地说，"我认为，我脑海深处大约已经知道发生什么了。"

坎迪问："我们现在该怎么办，乔治？我们现在该怎么办？"

乔治过了好一阵才回答："估计……我们得告诉……那些人。我估计，我们得找到他，把他关起来。我们不能让他跑了。唉，那个可怜的笨蛋会饿死的。"他试图让自己安定下来，"他们或许会把他关起来，会好好对待他的。"

但是，坎迪情绪激动地说："我们应该让他逃跑。你不了解那个柯利。柯利会对他用私刑的。柯利会杀了他的。"

乔治盯着坎迪的嘴唇看。"是呢，"他最后说，"说得对啊。柯利会这样做的，其他人也会的。"他回过头看了看柯利的老婆。

· 163 ·

Now Candy spoke his greatest fear. "You an' me can get that little place, can't we, George? You an' me can go there an' live nice, can't we, George? Can't we?"

Before George answered, Candy dropped his head and looked down at the hay. He knew.

George said softly, "—I think I knowed from the very first. I think I know'd we'd never do her. He usta like to hear about it so much I got to thinking maybe we would."

"Then—it's all off?" Candy asked **sulkily**①.

George didn't answer his question. George said, "I'll work my month an' I'll take my fifty bucks an' I'll stay all night in some **lousy**② cat house. Or I'll set in some poolroom till ever'body goes home. An' then I'll come back an' work another month an' I'll have fifty bucks more."

Candy said, "He's such a nice fella. I didn' think he'd do nothing like this."

George still stared at Curley's wife. "Lennie never done it in meanness," he said. "All the time he done bad things, but he never done one of 'em mean." He straightened up and looked back at Candy. "Now listen. We gotta tell the guys. They got to **bring** him **in**③, I guess. They ain't no way out. Maybe they won't hurt 'im." He said sharply, "I ain't gonna let 'em hurt Lennie. Now you listen. The guys might think I was **in on it**④. I'm gonna go in the bunk house. Then in a minute you come out and tell the guys about her, and I'll come along and make like I never seen her. Will you do that? So the guys won't think I was in on it?"

Candy said, "Sure, George. Sure I'll do that."

"O.K. Give me a couple minutes then, and you come runnin' out an' tell like you jus' found her. I'm going now." George turned and went quickly out of the barn.

Old Candy watched him go. He looked helplessly back at Curley's wife, and gradually his sorrow and his anger grew into words. "You God damn tramp", he

① sulkily ['sʌlkili] *ad.* 生气地，愠怒地，绷着脸地
② lousy ['lauzi] *a.* 蹩脚的，劣等的

③ bring in 逮捕
④ be in on it〈口〉熟悉内情

　　这时，坎迪说出了他最大的担忧。"你和我还能够获得那片土地对吧，乔治？你和我能够去那儿好好生活的，对吧，乔治？我们能够这样吧？"

　　还没有等乔治回答，坎迪就垂下了脑袋，眼睛看着干草。他知道了答案。

　　乔治轻声说："——我觉得，我从一开始就已经知道了。我觉得，我知道，我们永远不可能获得那块土地的。他以前那么喜欢听人讲这件事情，我不由得开始觉得，我们能够获得那块土地了。"

　　"这么说来——一切都结束啦？"坎迪沉着脸问。

　　乔治没有回答他的问题。乔治说："我要干满一个月，拿到五十块钱，去某家低级窑子待上整整一宿。或者，待在某个台球室里，待到所有人都回家去为止。然后，我再回来干上一个月，再挣五十块钱。"

　　坎迪说："他是个很棒的小伙子啊。我认为他是不会干出这样的事情来的。"

　　乔治仍然盯着柯利的老婆看。"伦尼绝不可能出于卑劣的动机干出这种事情的，"他说，"他一直干坏事来着，但他没有一件坏事是因为动机不纯干出来的。"他挺直了身子，回头看着坎迪，"好了，听着，我们必须把事情告诉那些人。我估计，他们一定会把他抓回来，因为没有别的办法。他们或许不会伤害他。"他厉声说，"我不会允许他们伤害伦尼的。现在你听好了。那些人可能会认为，我参与了这件事情。我这就到宿舍去。然后，过一会儿，你再出去，把她的事告诉那些人，我会跟过来，装作从未见过她的样子。你做得到吗？这样那些人便会认为，我与此事无关，对吧？"

　　坎迪说："当然，乔治。我当然做得到。"

　　"好吧。那就等我几分钟，然后你跑出去报信，就好像你刚刚发现了她一样。我现在就走。"乔治转过身，迅速离开了牲口棚。

　　老坎迪目送他离去，然后一脸无助地回头看着柯利的老婆。他的悲伤和愤怒慢慢化成了千言万语。"你这该

· 165 ·

said viciously. "You done it, di'n't you? I s'pose you're glad. Ever'body knowed you'd mess things up. You wasn't no good. You ain't no good now, you **lousy**① tart." He **sniveled**②, and his voice shook. "I could of hoed in the garden and washed dishes for them guys." He paused, and then went on in a **singsong**③. And he repeated the old words: "If they was a circus or a baseball game . . . we would of went to her . . . jus' said 'ta hell with work,' an' went to her. Never ast nobody's say so. An' they'd of been a pig and chickens . . . an' in the winter . . . the little fat stove . . . an' the rain comin' . . . an' us jes' settin' there." His eyes **blinded**④ with tears and he turned and went weakly out of the barn, and he rubbed his bristly whiskers with his wrist stump.

Outside the noise of the game stopped. There was a rise of voices in question, a **drum**⑤ of running feet and the men burst into the barn. Slim and Carlson and young Whit and Curley, and Crooks keeping back out of attention range. Candy came after them, and last of all came George. George had put on his blue denim coat and **buttoned**⑥ it, and his black hat was pulled down low over his eyes. The men raced around the last stall. Their eyes found Curley's wife in the **gloom**⑦, they stopped and stood still and looked.

Then Slim went quietly over to her, and he felt her wrist. One lean finger touched her cheek, and then his hand went under her slightly twisted neck and his fingers explored her neck. When he stood up the men crowded near and the **spell**⑧ was broken.

Curley **came** suddenly **to life**⑨. "I know who done it," he cried. "That big son-of-a-bitch done it. I know he done it. Why — ever'body else was out there playin' horseshoes." He worked himself into a **fury**⑩. "I'm gonna get him. I'm going for my **shotgun**⑪. I'll kill the big son-of-a-bitch myself. I'll shoot 'im in the guts. Come on, you guys." He ran furiously out of the barn. Carlson said, "I'll get my Luger," and he ran out too.

① lousy ['lauzi] a.〈口〉污秽的，令人作呕的，讨厌的，卑劣的
② snivel ['sniv(ə)l] v. 哭泣，抽噎，哭诉
③ singsong ['siŋsɔŋ] n. 单调的节奏（或韵律、声音）

④ blind [blaind] v. 使看不见

⑤ drum [drʌm] n.（打鼓似的）咚咚声，敲击声
⑥ button ['bʌtən] v. 把……的纽扣扣上，扣上（扣子）
⑦ gloom [glu:m] n. 黑暗，昏暗，阴暗

⑧ spell [spel] n. 着魔状态
⑨ come to life 苏醒

⑩ fury ['fjuəri] n. 狂怒，暴怒
⑪ shotgun ['ʃɔtgʌn] n. 猎枪，滑膛枪

死的婊子，"他恶狠狠地说，"你干的好事，对不对？我猜，你现在该高兴了吧。谁都知道，你会搅局的。你曾经毫无用处，现在也是毫无用处，你这个卑贱的婊子。"他抽噎起来，声音颤抖，"我本来可以替他们给菜园子锄草，洗洗碗碟的。"他说着停顿了一下，然后声音单调地继续，重复着那些老话："假如来了马戏团或者有棒球比赛……我们就可以去看……只要说'让工作见鬼去吧'，然后就去了。用不着请求谁同意。那儿会养上一头猪，一些鸡……冬天的时候……生起一个很小的大肚子火炉……下雨的时候……我们只是坐在那儿。"眼泪蒙上了他的眼睛，他转过身，有气无力地走出牲口棚，边走边用光秃的手腕摩擦着自己粗硬的胡茬子。

室外已经没了游戏的声音，传来的是各种议论的声音和一阵咚咚的脚步声。人们冲进了牲口棚。斯利姆、卡尔森、小惠特和柯利都来了。克鲁克斯跟在后面，不引人注目。坎迪跟在他们后面，跟在最后的是乔治。乔治穿上了蓝色粗斜棉布外套，扣上了纽扣。头上戴着的黑色帽子压得很低，遮过了眼睛。大家飞快绕过末端的那个马厩。他们的目光落在了昏暗中的柯利老婆身上。他们停住了脚步，一动不动站着看。

过了一会儿，斯利姆平静地朝着她走过去，探了探她的脉搏，用一根瘦削的手指触碰了一下她的脸颊，接着一只手伸到她稍稍扭曲的脖颈下面，用手指在她颈部检查着。他直起身子后，其他人都拥了上来。屏息静气的氛围打破了。

柯利突然清醒过来了。"我知道这是谁干的，"他大声说着，"那个狗娘养的大个子干的。我知道这是他干的。嘿——所有其他人都在外面玩掷马蹄铁的游戏呢。"他怒火中烧，"我要去抓住他。我要去取我的猎枪，亲手杀了那个狗娘养的大个子。我要把他的五脏六腑射成筛子。走吧，你们大家。"他怀着满腔怒火，跑出了牲口棚。卡尔森说："我去取我的卢格尔手枪。"说完他跑出去了。

· 167 ·

Slim turned quietly to George. "I guess Lennie done it, all right," he said. "Her neck's bust. Lennie coulda did that."

George didn't answer, but he nodded slowly. His hat was so far down on his forehead that his eyes were covered.

Slim went on, "Maybe like that time in Weed you was tellin' about."

Again George nodded.

Slim sighed. "Well, I guess we got to get him. Where you think he might of went?"

It seemed to take George some time to free his words. "He—would of went south," he said. "We come from north so he would of went south."

"I guess we gotta get 'im," Slim repeated.

George stepped close. "Couldn' we maybe bring him in an' they'll lock him up? He's nuts, Slim. He never done this to be mean."

Slim nodded. "We might," he said. "If we could **keep** Curley **in**①, we might. But Curley's gonna want to shoot 'im. Curley's still mad about his hand. An' s'pose they lock him up an' **strap**② him down and put him in a cage. That ain't no good, George."

"I know," said George, "I know."

Carlson came running in. "The bastard's stole my Luger," he shouted. "It ain't in my bag." Curley followed him, and Curley carried a shotgun in his good hand. Curley was cold now.

"All right, you guys," he said. "The nigger's got a shotgun. You take it, Carlson. When you see 'um, don't give 'im no chance. Shoot for his **guts**③. That'll **double 'im over**④."

Whit said excitedly, "I ain't got a gun."

Curley said, "You go in Soledad an' get a cop. Get Al Wilts, he's **deputy**⑤ sheriff. Le's go now." He turned suspiciously on George. "You're comin' with

斯利姆无声地朝乔治转过身,"我估计这是伦尼干的,错不了的,"他说,"她的脖子被拧断了。伦尼干得出这种事情。"

乔治没有回答,但缓慢地点了点头。他的帽檐在额头上压得很低,把眼睛都给遮盖住了。

斯利姆接着说:"可能和你告诉过我的那次发生在威德的情况一样呢。"

乔治再次点了点头。

斯利姆叹息了一声,"好啦,我觉得,我们得抓住他。你认为他可能会去哪儿呢?"

乔治似乎费了一些时间才恢复了说话的能力。"他——会往南方走,"他说,"我们是从北方来的,因此,他会往南方走。"

"我觉得,我们得去抓住他。"斯利姆重复了一声。

乔治走到他近旁。"我们就不能把他抓回来,让他们把他关起来吗?他脑子不正常,斯利姆。他不可能出于卑劣的动机干出这种事情。"

斯利姆点了点头。"也许可以,"他说,"我们要是能把柯利留下来,也许可以这样。但柯利会想要一枪毙了他的。柯利还在为他那只手耿耿于怀呢。假如他们把他关起来了,五花大绑,投进一个笼子里。那样也好不到哪儿去,乔治。"

"我知道,"乔治说,"我知道。"

卡尔森跑着进来。"那个笨蛋偷走了我的卢格尔手枪,"他大声嚷嚷着,"手枪不在我的袋子里了。"他身后跟着柯利。柯利用他那只没有受伤的手拿着一管猎枪。柯利现在情绪冷静下来了。

"好吧,伙计们,"他说,"那个黑鬼有一管猎枪,你拿着,卡尔森。你一旦看见了他,不要给他机会。打得他肚子开花,把他打成两截。"

惠特激动地说:"可我没有枪啊。"

柯利说:"你去索莱达,叫个警察来。找艾尔·威尔茨,他是副治安官。现在我们出发吧。"他满腹狐疑

① keep in 留在里面,留在屋内,不外出

② strap [stræp] v. 用带扣住,束牢

③ guts [gʌts] n. 【复】内脏

④ double over(使)(因剧痛或大小等而)弯着身子

⑤ deputy ['depjuti] n. 副职,副手

us, fella."

"Yeah," said George. "I'll come. But listen, Curley. The poor bastard's **nuts**①. Don't shoot 'im. He di'n't know what he was doin'."

"Don't shoot 'im?" Curley cried. "He got Carlson's Luger. 'Course we'll shoot 'im."

George said weakly, "Maybe Carlson lost his gun."

"I seen it this morning," said Carlson. "No, it's been took."

Slim stood looking down at Curley's wife. He said, "Curley—maybe you better stay here with your wife."

Curley's face reddened. "I'm goin'," he said. "I'm gonna shoot the guts outa that big bastard myself, even if I only got one hand. I'm gonna get 'im."

Slim turned to Candy. "You stay here with her then, Candy. The rest of us better get goin'."

They moved away. George stopped a moment beside Candy and they both looked down at the dead girl until Curley called, "You George! You stick with us so we don't think you had nothin' to do with this."

George moved slowly after them, and his feet **dragged**② heavily.

And when they were gone, Candy **squatted**③ down in the hay and watched the face of Curley's wife. "Poor bastard," he said softly.

The sound of the men grew fainter. The barn was darkening gradually and, in their stalls, the horses shifted their feet and rattled the halter chains. Old Candy lay down in the hay and covered his eyes with his arm.

① nuts [nʌts] a.〈口〉发疯的，发狂的

② drag [dræg] v.（沉重缓慢地或费力地）拖着脚步走

③ squat [skwɔt] v. 蹲，蹲坐

地朝乔治转过身，"你随我们去吧，伙计。"

"好吧，"乔治说，"我会去的，但是，听着，柯利，那个可怜的笨蛋脑子不正常。不要朝他开枪。他并不明白自己干了什么事情。"

"不要朝他开枪？"柯利大声吼着，"他偷了卡尔森的卢格尔手枪，我们当然要一枪毙了他。"

乔治底气不足地说："也许卡尔森自己弄丢了枪呢。"

"我今天上午还看到的，"卡尔森说，"不，枪是被他偷走的。"

斯利姆站立着，低头看着柯利的老婆。他说："柯利——你最好还是待在这儿守着你老婆。"

柯利涨红了脸。"我要走，"他说，"我要亲手用枪把那个笨蛋的五脏六腑打出来，即便我只有一只手好使也罢。我要去把他抓住。"

斯利姆转身对着坎迪。"那你待在这儿守着她，坎迪。我们其他人最好该出发了。"

他们离开了。乔治在坎迪旁边停留了片刻。他们两个人都低头看着死了的女人，直到听见柯利的喊声，"喂，乔治，你要是不想让我们怀疑你跟这事有什么瓜葛，就跟我们走。"

乔治慢吞吞地跟在他们后面，步履沉重。

他们离开之后，坎迪在干草中蹲了下来，注视着柯利老婆的脸。"可怜的笨蛋。"他柔声说。

那些人的声音越来越弱。牲口棚里慢慢暗了下来。马儿在自己的马厩里跺着蹄子，抖动缰绳链子发出叮当声。老坎迪在干草上躺下，用双臂遮盖住眼睛。

· 171 ·

The deep green pool of the Salinas River was still in the late afternoon. Already the sun had left the valley to go climbing up the slopes of the Gabilan mountains, and the hilltops were rosy in the sun. But by the pool among the mottled sycamores, a pleasant shade had fallen.

A water snake glided smoothly up the pool, twisting its periscope head from side to side; and it swam the length of the pool and came to the legs of a motionless heron that stood in the shallows. A silent head and **beak**① **lanced**② down and **plucked**③ it out by the head, and the beak swallowed the little snake while its tail waved **frantically**④.

A far rush of wind sounded and a **gust**⑤ drove through the tops of the trees like a wave. The sycamore leaves turned up their silver sides, the brown, dry leaves on the ground **scudded**⑥ a few feet. And row on row of tiny wind waves flowed up the pool's green surface.

As quickly as it had come, the wind died, and the clearing was quiet again. The heron stood in the shallows, motionless and waiting. Another little water snake swam up the pool, turning its periscope head from side to side.

Suddenly Lennie appeared out of the brush, and he came as silently as a creeping bear moves. The heron pounded the air with its wings, **jacked**⑦ itself **clear**⑧ of the water and flew off down river. The little snake slid in among the reeds at the pool's side.

Lennie came quietly to the pool's edge. He knelt down and drank, barely touching his lips to the water. When a little bird skittered over the dry leaves behind him, his head jerked up and he **strained**⑨ toward the sound with eyes

① beak [bi:k] *n.*（鹰、鹦鹉等的）喙
② lance [lɑ:ns] *v.* 猛冲，急速前进
③ pluck [plʌk] *v.* 拖，拉，抽，扯，撕
④ frantically ['fræntikəli] *ad.*（因喜悦、愤怒、痛苦、忧虑等）发狂似的
⑤ gust [gʌst] *n.* 一阵强风，一阵狂风
⑥ scud [skʌd] *v.* 疾行，疾飞，掠过

⑦ jack [dʒæk] *v.*（像用千斤顶似的）举起或移动
⑧ clear [kliə] *ad.* 离开着

⑨ strain [strein] *v.* 尽力，努力，使劲

　　黄昏之时，萨利纳斯河那一湾幽深的碧水显得很平静。太阳已经离开河谷，爬上了加比兰山脉的坡地。夕阳把一座座山顶染成了玫瑰色。但是，静水旁那片表皮斑驳的悬铃木树丛中，一片令人舒心的树荫投了下来。

　　一条水蛇自如地向上游过静水，时不时地向左右两侧扭动着自己潜望镜一般的脑袋。水蛇游过了整个一湾静水，游到一只伫立在浅滩处一动不动的长脚鹭脚边。长脚鹭悄无声息，头和喙猛然向下一啄，便衔着蛇头叼出水面。蛇疯狂地甩动着尾巴，鹭喙却已把它的大半身子吞了下去。

　　远处刮来一阵疾风，强劲的风犹如波浪一般掠过树梢。悬铃木树叶翻起了银白色的底面，地面上棕褐色的枯叶被吹远了几英尺。碧水表面涌起一排排细微的浪花。

　　疾风来得突然，消失得也快，树林的空地上又恢复了平静。长脚鹭伫立在浅滩上，一动不动，耐心等待着。又有一条水蛇从水下游了上来，潜望镜一样的脑袋左右摆动着。

　　伦尼突然从灌木丛中冒了出来，如同潜行着的熊一样悄无声息。长脚鹭拍打着翅膀，猛然飞离水面，往河流的下游飞去。那条小水蛇溜进了静水一侧的芦苇丛中。

　　伦尼悄无声息地来到水边，跪下喝水，嘴唇将将触及水面。一只小鸟在他身后的枯叶上轻快地东蹦西跳，他猛然抬起头，睁大眼睛，竖直耳朵，转向发出

· 173 ·

Of Mice and Men

and ears until he saw the bird, and then he dropped his head and drank again.

When he was finished, he sat down on the bank, with his side to the pool, so that he could watch the **trail's**① entrance. He embraced his knees and laid his chin down on his knees.

The light climbed on out of the valley, and as it went, the tops of the mountains seemed to blaze with increasing brightness.

Lennie said softly, "I di'n't forget, you bet, God damn. Hide in the brush an' wait for George." He pulled his hat down low over his eyes. "George gonna give me hell," he said. "George gonna wish he was alone an' not have me botherin' him." He turned his head and looked at the bright mountain tops. "I can go right off there an' find a cave," he said. And he continued sadly, "—an' never have no ketchup — but I won't care. If George don't want me . . . I'll go away. I'll go away."

And then from out of Lennie's head there came a little fat old woman. She wore thick **bull's-eye**② glasses and she wore a huge **gingham**③ **apron**④ with pockets, and she was **starched**⑤ and clean. She stood in front of Lennie and put her hands on her hips, and she frowned disapprovingly at him.

And when she spoke, it was in Lennie's voice. "I tol' you an' tol' you," she said. "I tol' you, '**Min**'⑥ George because he's such a nice fella an' good to you.' But you don't never take no care. You do bad things."

And Lennie answered her, "I tried, Aunt Clara, ma'am. I tried and tried. I couldn't help it."

"You never give a thought to George," she went on in Lennie's voice. "He been doin' nice things for you alla time. When he got a piece of pie you always got half or more'n half. An' if they was any ketchup, why he'd give it all to you."

"I know," said Lennie miserably. "I tried, Aunt Clara, ma'am. I tried and tried."

She interrupted him. "All the time he coulda had such a good time if it wasn't for you. He woulda took his pay an' raised hell in a whore house, and he

① trail [treil] *n.*（荒野中踩出的）小道，小径

② bull's-eye ['bulzai] *n.* 厚圆透镜
③ gingham ['giŋəm] *a.* 用方格（条纹）布缝制的
④ apron ['eiprən] *n.* 围裙
⑤ starched [stɑ:tʃt] *a.* 上过浆的，浆硬的
⑥ min' = mind [maind] *v.* 服从，听从

声音的方向，直到看见了那只鸟，才再次低下头喝起水来。

他喝过水后便坐在岸边，侧身对着面前的一湾静水，以便观察小路的入口。他双手抱膝，下巴颏枕在膝上。

太阳光向上移出了河谷，移动的过程中，一座座山顶上闪烁着落日余晖，越发显得明亮起来。

伦尼轻声说："我并没有忘记呢，你可以打赌，绝对没有。藏在灌木丛里，等乔治来找。"他压下帽檐，遮住眼睛，"乔治会冲着我大发雷霆的，"他说，"乔治巴不得他独自一人行动，不愿意有我在身边打搅他。"他转过脑袋，看着明亮的山顶，"我可以跑到山上去，找个洞穴。"然后他悲伤地接着说道，"——以后就没有番茄酱吃了——不过我不会在乎的。假如乔治不想要我了……我会离开的。我会离开的。"

片刻过后，伦尼的脑海里突然冒出一个又矮又胖的老太太，只见她戴着厚圆透镜片眼镜，系着一条带口袋的条纹大围裙，衣服浆洗得干干净净。她站在伦尼的面前，双手叉腰，对着他皱眉蹙额，流露出不满。

她一开口，却是伦尼的声音。"我跟你说了多少遍，"她说，"我跟你说，一定要听乔治的话，因为他是个大好人，对你也好。但是，你从来就不往心里记。你总是干坏事。"

伦尼回答她说："我记了，克拉拉姨妈，太太。我记了又记。但我控制不住自己。"

"你从来都没有替乔治着想过，"她接着用伦尼的声音说，"他有什么好事都想着你。他要是有一块馅饼，你总是可以分到半块，甚至半块还多。假如有番茄酱，嘿，他总是会全部给你。"

"我知道，"伦尼痛苦地说，"我记了，克拉拉姨妈，太太。我记了又记了。"

她打断了他的话。"要不是有你，他这些日子可以过得多舒心啊。他可以领了薪水，跑到窑子里去快活

175

Of Mice and Men

coulda set in a pool room an' played **snooker**①. But he got to take care of you."

Lennie **moaned**② with grief. "I know, Aunt Clara, ma'am. I'll go right off in the hills an' I'll fin' a cave an' I'll live there so I won't be no more trouble to George."

"You jus' say that," she said sharply. "You're always sayin' that, an' you know sonofabitching well you ain't never gonna do it. You'll jus' stick around an' **stew**③ the **b'Jesus**④ outa George all the time."

Lennie said, "I might jus' as well go away. George ain't gonna let me tend no rabbits now."

Aunt Clara was gone, and from out of Lennie's head there came a gigantic rabbit. It sat on its **haunches**⑤ in front of him, and it **waggled**⑥ its ears and **crinkled**⑦ its nose at him. And it spoke in Lennie's voice too.

"Tend rabbits," it said scornfully. "You crazy bastard. You ain't fit to lick the boots of no rabbit. You'd forget 'em and let 'em go hungry. That's what you'd do. An' then what would George think?"

"I would *not* forget," Lennie said loudly.

"The hell you wouldn'," said the rabbit. "You ain't worth a **greased**⑧ **jackpin**⑨ to **ram**⑩ you into hell. Christ knows George done ever'thing he could to **jack**⑪ you outa the **sewer**⑫, but it don't do no good. If you think George gonna let you tend rabbits, you're even crazier'n usual. He ain't. He's gonna beat hell outa you with a stick, that's what he's gonna do."

Now Lennie **retorted**⑬ **belligerently**⑭, "He ain't neither. George won't do nothing like that. I've knew George since — I forget when — and he ain't never raised his han' to me with a stick. He's nice to me. He ain't gonna be mean."

"Well, he's sick of you," said the rabbit. "He's gonna beat hell outa you an' then go away an' leave you."

"He won't," Lennie cried frantically. "He won't do nothing like that. I know George. Me an' him travels together."

① snooker ['snu:kə] n.= snooker pool 斯诺克

② moan [məun] v. 呻吟，鸣咽

③ stew [stju:] v.（因担忧、激动等）弄得……不安之极

④ b'Jesus n.〈俚〉=bejesus 或 bejeezus，by Jesus 的委婉语，常用于表示强调，该用法尤其常见于 beat (or scare) the bejesus out of 等短语

⑤ haunch [hɔ:n(t)ʃ] n.（动物的）腰腿

⑥ waggle ['wæg(ə)l] v. 使不停地来回（或上下）摇动（或摆动）

⑦ crinkle ['kriŋk(ə)l] v. 使皱

⑧ grease [gris] v. 给……加润滑油

⑨ jack-pin 千斤顶里的一个零件

⑩ ram [ræm] v. 猛压，用力推，硬塞，塞；猛撞，猛击

⑪ jack [dʒæk] v. 用起重器举起，用千斤顶托起

⑫ sewer ['su:ə; 'sju:ə] n. 污水管，下水道，阴沟

⑬ retort [ri'tɔ:t] v. 反驳，回嘴，驳回

⑭ belligerently [bi'lidʒərəntli] ad. 好战地，好斗地

快活。他可以待在某个台球室里，玩彩色台球[1]。但是，他偏偏得照顾你。"

伦尼悲伤地呜咽起来，"我知道，克拉拉姨妈，太太。我这就进山去，找个洞穴住下来，那样我就不会给乔治添麻烦了。"

"你就只会说这话，"她厉声说，"你向来只会这样说，你心里面清楚得很，做你是绝对做不到的。你还是会赖在乔治身边不走，弄得他成天心神不宁。"

伦尼说："我还是离开的好。乔治现在不会再让我照料那些兔子了。"

克拉拉姨妈消失了，伦尼的脑海里又冒出了一只巨型兔子。兔子在他面前蹲坐着，冲着他又是摆耳朵，又是皱鼻子。兔子一开口，也是伦尼的声音。

"还照料兔子呢，"兔子用蔑视的口气说，"你这个笨蛋疯子。你给兔子舔靴子都不配。你只会忘记它们，让它们饿肚子。这才是你会干的事情。到时候，乔治会怎样想呢？"

"我不会忘记的。"伦尼大声说。

"你不会才怪呢，"兔子说，"你就是个毫无价值的窝囊废。天知道乔治费了多大的劲儿才把你从臭水沟里拉出来，结果一点儿用都没有。假如你认为乔治会让你照料兔子，那你可比平时还傻呢。他不会的。他会用棍子给你一顿好打。这才是他会干的事情。"

于是，伦尼恶狠狠地反驳说："他绝不会这样的。乔治不可能干出这样的事情来。我认识乔治，打从——我忘记了什么时候——但他从来没有用棍子打过我。他对我可好啦。他不会对我心怀恶意的。"

"得了吧，他已经厌倦你啦，"兔子说，"他会给你一顿好打，然后丢下你走人的。"

"他不会的，"伦尼情绪激动得大叫起来，"他绝不会干出这样的事情来的。我了解乔治。我和他形影不离的。"

---

1 属于台球中的一种，用白球一只、红球十五只和彩色球六只，以台盘上全部红球和彩色球被击落袋后各方所得分数多少确定胜负。

177

But the rabbit repeated softly over and over, "He gonna leave you, ya crazy bastard. He gonna leave ya all alone. He gonna leave ya, crazy bastard."

Lennie put his hands over his ears. "He ain't, I tell ya he ain't." And he cried, "Oh! George—George—George!"

George came quietly out of the brush and the rabbit scuttled back into Lennie's brain.

George said quietly, "What the hell you yellin' about?"

Lennie got up on his knees. "You ain't gonna leave me, are ya, George? I know you ain't."

George came stiffly near and sat down beside him. "No."

"I knowed it," Lennie cried. "You ain't that kind."

George was silent.

Lennie said, "George."

"Yeah?"

"I done another bad thing."

"It don't make no difference," George said, and he fell silent again.

Only the **topmost**① **ridges**② were in the sun now. The shadow in the valley was blue and soft. From the distance came the sound of men shouting to one another. George turned his head and listened to the shouts.

Lennie said, "George."

"Yeah?"

"Ain't you gonna give me hell?"

"Give ya hell?"

"Sure, like you always done before. Like, 'If I di'n't have you I'd take my fifty bucks—'"

"Jesus Christ, Lennie! You can't remember nothing that happens, but you remember ever' word I say."

"Well, ain't you gonna say it?"

George shook himself. He said **woodenly**③, "If I was alone I could live so easy." His voice was **monotonous**④, had no emphasis. "I could get a job an' not

但是，兔子一遍又一遍地轻声重复着说："他会丢下你的，你这个笨蛋疯子。他会丢下你独自一人的。他会丢下你的，你这个笨蛋疯子。"

伦尼用双手捂住耳朵。"他不会的，我告诉你，他不会的。"他随即又大声喊起来，"噢！乔治——乔治——乔治！"

乔治静悄悄地从灌木丛中走了出来，兔子急忙逃回伦尼的大脑中。

乔治平静地说："见鬼，你大喊大叫什么？"

伦尼站立起来。"你不会丢下我的，对吧，乔治？我知道你不会的。"

乔治动作僵硬地走近，坐在他身边。"不会的。"

"我就知道是这样，"伦尼大声说，"你不是那种人。"

乔治沉默不语。

伦尼说："乔治。"

"嗯？"

"我又干了一件坏事。"

"没有什么关系了。"乔治说，再次沉默不语。

此时此刻，只有最顶峰处在夕阳里。谷地中的阴影显得湛蓝而又柔和。远处传来人们相互呼喊的声音。乔治转过头，倾听着呼喊声。

伦尼说："乔治。"

"嗯？"

"你不会狠狠骂我吧？"

"狠狠骂你？"

"对呀，像你以前那样。比如，'我要是没有你，我就可以拿着我的五十块钱——'"

"天哪，伦尼！发生过的事情你一样记不住，而我说过的话你倒是每一句都记住了。"

"嗯，你不准备骂我了吗？"

乔治调整了一下情绪。他声音低沉地说："我要是独自一人，我可以生活得很轻松。"他说话的声音干巴

① topmost ['tɔpməust] a. 最高的，最上面的
② ridge [ridʒ] n. 山脊，岭，山脉
③ woodenly ['wudnli] ad. （声音）低沉地，不响亮地
④ monotonous [mə'nɔt(ə)nəs] a. （声音）单调的，无抑扬顿挫的

have no mess." He stopped.

"Go on," said Lennie. "An' when the enda the month come—"

"An' when the end of the month came I could take my fifty bucks an' go to a . . . cat house—" He stopped again.

Lennie looked eagerly at him. "Go on, George. Ain't you gonna give me no more hell?"

"No," said George.

"Well, I can go away," said Lennie. "I'll go right off in the hills an' find a cave if you don' want me."

George shook himself again. "No," he said. "I want you to stay with me here."

Lennie said craftily—"Tell me like you done before."

"Tell you what?"

"'Bout the other guys an' about us."

George said, "Guys like us got no family. They make a little stake an' then they blow it in. They ain't got nobody in the worl' that gives a **hoot**① in hell about 'em—"

"*But not us*," Lennie cried happily. "Tell about us now."

George was quiet for a moment. "But not us," he said.

"Because—"

"Because I got you an'—"

"An' I got you. We got each other, that's what, that gives a hoot in hell about us," Lennie cried in triumph.

The little evening breeze blew over the clearing and the leaves rustled and the wind waves flowed up the green pool. And the shouts of men sounded again, this time much closer than before.

George took off his hat. He said shakily, "Take off your hat, Lennie. The air feels fine."

Lennie removed his hat **dutifully**② and laid it on the ground in front of him. The shadow in the valley was bluer, and the evening came fast. On the wind the sound of crashing in the brush came to them.

巴的，没有任何抑扬起伏，"我可以找到活儿干，不会出任何乱子。"他打住了。

"接着说吧，"伦尼说，"到了月底——"

"到了月底，我可以拿着我的五十块钱逛……窑子……"他又打住了。

伦尼热切地看着他。"接着说吧，乔治。你不会再狠狠骂我了吗？"

"不会。"乔治说。

"你知道，我是可以离开的，"伦尼说，"假如你不想要我了，我就跑到山里去，找个洞穴住下。"

乔治再次振作起了精神。"不，"他说，"我想要你和我待在这儿。"

伦尼趁机说——"像从前一样给我讲讲吧。"

"给你讲讲什么？"

"讲讲其他人，讲讲我们。"

乔治说："像我们这样的人没有家庭，只要挣到了一点儿钱，马上就花光了，世界上没有任何人会在乎他们——"

"但我们不是这样的，"伦尼愉快地大声说，"现在说说我们吧。"

乔治平静了片刻。"但我们不是这样的。"他说。

"因为——"

"因为我有你，而且——"

"我也有你呢。我们拥有彼此，事情就是这样的，因此我们在乎彼此。"伦尼扬扬得意地大声说。

傍晚的微风拂过树林间的空地，树叶飒飒作响，风在碧水表面泛起了波浪。人的呼喊声再次响起，和先前的相比，这一次的距离更近了。

乔治摘下自己的帽子。他颤抖着声音说："摘下你的帽子吧，伦尼。微风吹得很舒服呢。"

伦尼听话地取下帽子，放在自己面前的地上。谷地的阴影显得更加湛蓝了，天色暗得越来越快。顺着风，他们听见从灌木丛中传来了沙沙声。

① hoot [hu:t] n.〈口〉[通常用于否定句] 最少量，一丝一毫

② dutifully ['dju:tifəli] ad. 恭顺地，顺从地

Lennie said, "Tell how it's gonna be."

George had been listening to the distant sounds. For a moment he was business-like. "Look acrost the river, Lennie, an' I'll tell you so you can almost see it."

Lennie turned his head and looked off across the pool and up the darkening slopes of the Gabilans. "We gonna get a little place," George began. He reached in his side pocket and brought out Carlson's Luger; he **snapped**① off the **safety**②, and the hand and gun lay on the ground behind Lennie's back. He looked at the back of Lennie's head, at the place where the spine and skull were joined.

A man's voice called from up the river, and another man answered.

"Go on," said Lennie.

George raised the gun and his hand shook, and he dropped his hand to the ground again.

"Go on," said Lennie. "How's it gonna be. We gonna get a little place."

"We'll have a cow," said George. "An' we'll have maybe a pig an' chickens . . . an' down the flat we'll have a . . . little piece alfalfa—"

"For the rabbits," Lennie shouted.

"For the rabbits," George repeated.

"And I get to tend the rabbits."

"An' you get to tend the rabbits."

Lennie giggled with happiness. "An' live on the fatta the lan'."

"Yes."

Lennie turned his head.

"No, Lennie. Look down there acrost the river, like you can almost see the place."

Lennie obeyed him. George looked down at the gun.

There were crashing footsteps in the brush now. George turned and looked toward them.

"Go on, George. When we gonna do it?"

① snap [snæp] v. 使发出吧嗒一声（关上或打开等）
② safety ['seifti] n.〈美〉= safety catch（枪、炮等的）保险

伦尼说："讲一讲以后的情况会怎样吧。"

乔治倾听着远处传来的声音，他郑重其事地听了一会儿。"看着河对面，伦尼，那样我对你讲时，你便能够看见那种情景。"

伦尼转过头，目光越过这湾静水，沿着渐渐暗下来的加比兰山脉的山坡一路往上。"我们将拥有一小片土地。"乔治开始说。他把手伸进衣服侧面的口袋，掏出卡尔森的卢格尔手枪。他咔嗒一声打开了保险。他把握着枪的手放着在伦尼背后的地上。他看着伦尼的后脑勺，看着他脊椎和头骨的连接处。

有个人的喊声从河流上游传来，另外一个人应了一声。

"接着讲吧。"伦尼说。

乔治举起手枪，手一直在抖，于是他又把手放到了地面。

"接着讲吧，"伦尼说，"将来会怎么样，我们会有一小片地。"

"我们会养一头母牛，"乔治说，"我们可能还会养一头猪、一些鸡……那片浅滩的下游，我们还会有……一小片苜蓿地——"

"为了喂养兔子。"伦尼大声说。

"为了喂养兔子。"乔治重复了一声。

"我一定要照料那些兔子。"

伦尼快乐地咯咯笑起来。"我们会依靠那片土地过日子。"

"是这样。"

伦尼转过脑袋。

"不，伦尼。顺着河流的下游看，好像你真的看到了那个地方一样。"

伦尼照做了。乔治低头看着那支手枪。

这时灌木丛中传来了沙沙的脚步声。乔治转过脑袋朝着他们看去。

"接着讲吧，乔治。我们什么时候能够获得那片土地呢？"

183

"Gonna do it soon."

"Me an' you."

"You . . . an' me. Ever'body gonna be nice to you. Ain't gonna be no more trouble. Nobody gonna hurt nobody nor steal from 'em."

Lennie said, "I thought you was mad at me, George."

"No," said George. "No, Lennie. I ain't mad. I never been mad, an' I ain't now. That's a thing I want ya to know."

The voices came close now. George raised the gun and listened to the voices.

Lennie begged, "Le's do it now. Le's get that place now."

"Sure, right now. I gotta. We gotta."

And George raised the gun and **steadied**① it, and he brought the **muzzle**② of it close to the back of Lennie's head. The hand shook violently, but his face set and his hand steadied. He pulled the **trigger**③. The crash of the shot rolled up the hills and rolled down again. Lennie **jarred**④, and then settled slowly forward to the sand, and he lay without quivering.

George shivered and looked at the gun, and then he threw it from him, back up on the bank, near the pile of old ashes.

The brush seemed filled with cries and with the sound of running feet. Slim's voice shouted. "George. Where you at, George?"

But George sat stiffly on the bank and looked at his right hand that had thrown the gun away. The group burst into the clearing, and Curley was ahead. He saw Lennie lying on the sand. "Got him, by God." He went over and looked down at Lennie, and then he looked back at George. "Right in the back of the head," he said softly.

Slim came directly to George and sat down beside him, sat very close to him. "Never you mind," said Slim. "A guy got to sometimes."

But Carlson was standing over George. "How'd you do it?" he asked.

"I just done it," George said tiredly.

"Did he have my gun?"

"Yeah. He had your gun."

"很快就会获得的。"

"我和你。"

"你……和我。所有人都会很好地对待你。不会再有什么麻烦了。谁也不会伤害谁,谁也不会偷东西。"

伦尼说:"我以为你生我的气了呢,乔治。"

"没有,"乔治说,"没有,伦尼。我没有生气。我从来都没有生过气,现在也没有生气。这正是我想要你知道的事情。"

声音现在很近了。乔治举着手枪,听着声音。

伦尼恳求着说:"我们这就干起来吧,现在就把那片土地买下来。"

"当然,就现在。我会去买的。我们会去买的。"

乔治举起手枪,牢牢握着,枪口靠近伦尼的后脑勺。他的手剧烈地抖动着,但表情却毫不动摇,他稳住了手。他扣动了扳机,枪声回荡在群山之间。伦尼猛然晃动了一下,然后慢慢地向前倒在沙地上,躺在那儿不动了。

乔治浑身颤抖,他看了一眼手枪,然后把它远远地扔掉,扔到了岸边,落到那堆灰烬附近。

灌木丛中似乎充斥了叫喊声和人跑动的脚步声。斯利姆的声音在喊着:"乔治,你在哪儿呢,乔治?"

但乔治身子僵直地坐在岸边,看着自己刚才扔掉枪的右手。人群突然闯进了树林中的空地,领头的便是柯利。他看见伦尼躺在沙地上。"终于逮住他了,天哪。"他走过去俯身看着伦尼,然后又转过头看着乔治。"正好打在后脑勺上呢。"他小声说。

斯利姆立刻朝着乔治走过去,在他身边坐下,坐得靠他很近。"别难过,"斯利姆说,"人有时候身不由己。"

但卡尔森俯身站在乔治跟前。"你是怎样办到的?"他问道。

"就是这么办到的。"乔治疲惫地说。

"他拿了我的枪吗?"

"对,他拿了你的枪。"

① steady ['stedi] v. 使稳,使平稳,使不摇晃
② muzzle ['mʌz(ə)l] n. 枪口
③ trigger ['trɪɡə] n. (枪等的)扳机
④ jar [dʒɑ:] v. 震动,摇动

"An' you got it away from him and you took it an' you killed him?"

"Yeah. Tha's how." George's voice was almost a whisper. He looked steadily at his right hand that had held the gun.

Slim twitched George's elbow. "Come on, George. Me an' you'll go in an' get a drink."

George let himself be helped to his feet. "Yeah, a drink."

Slim said, "You hadda, George. I swear you hadda. Come on with me." He led George into the entrance of the trail and up toward the highway.

Curley and Carlson looked after them. And Carlson said, "Now what the hell ya suppose is **eatin'**[①] them two guys?"

"然后你从他手上弄回了枪,把他打死了,对吧?"

　　"对啊,是这么回事呢。"乔治的话几乎成了耳语了。他目不转睛地盯着自己先前握着枪的右手看。

　　斯利姆轻扯了一下乔治的胳膊肘。"走吧,乔治。我和你一块儿回去喝酒去。"

　　乔治任由对方拉着站起身。"好吧,喝酒去。"

　　斯利姆说:"你是万不得已,乔治。我敢打赌,你是万不得已。随我一块儿走吧。"他领着乔治进入小路的入口,然后朝远处走向公路。

　　柯利和卡尔森看着他们的背影。卡尔森说:"见鬼,你觉得他们两个家伙搞什么鬼名堂啊?"

① eat [iːt] v. 〈美口〉烦扰,打扰